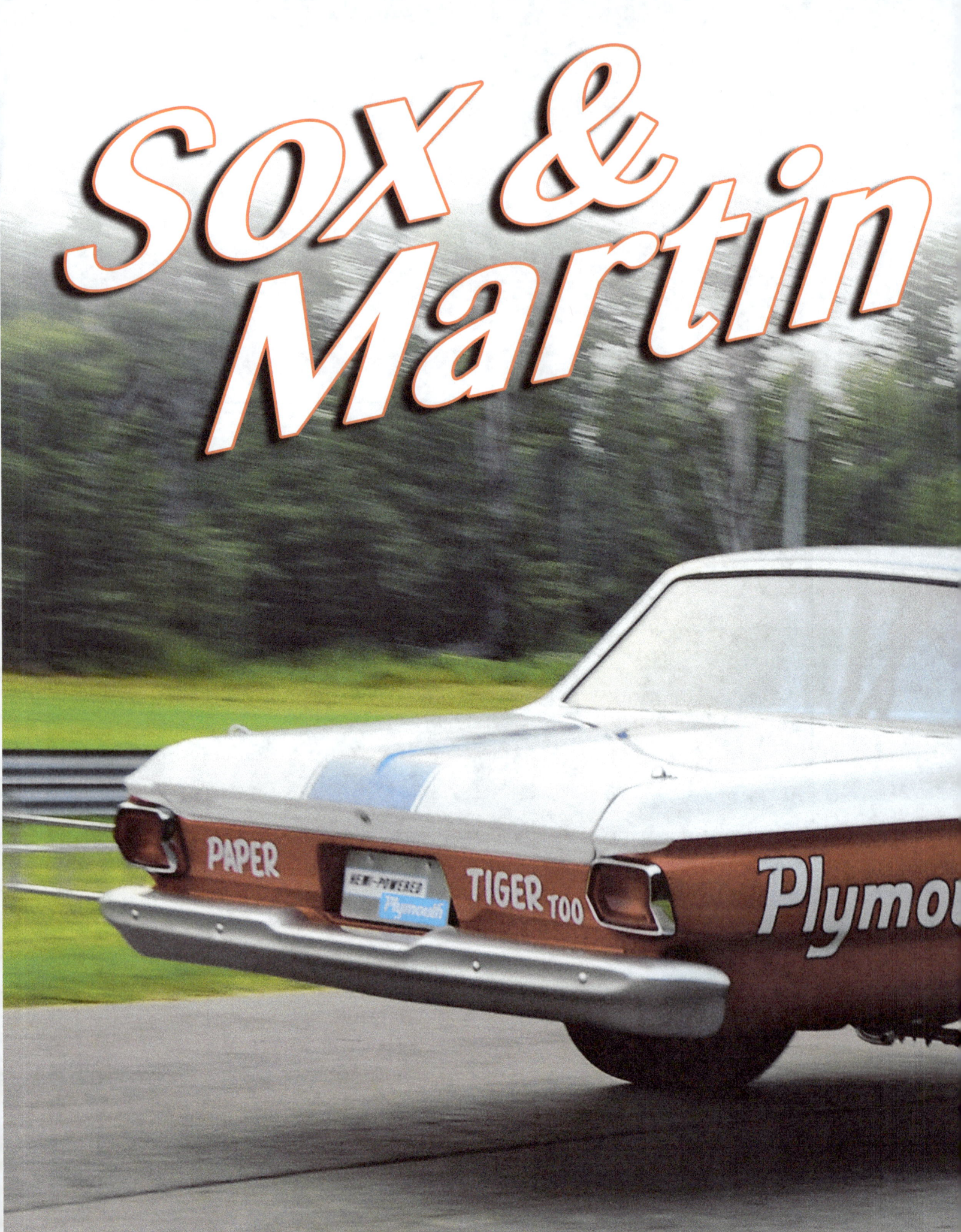

The Most Famous Team in Drag Racing

Jim Schild

CarTech®

CarTech®, Inc.
838 Lake Street South, Forest Lake, MN 55025
Phone: 651-277-1200 or 800-551-4754
Fax: 651-277-1203
www.cartechbooks.com

© 2016 by Jim Schild

All rights reserved. No part of this publication may be reproduced or utilized in any form or by any means, electronic or mechanical, including photocopying, recording, or by any information storage and retrieval system, without prior permission from the Publisher. All text, photographs, and artwork are the property of the Author unless otherwise noted or credited.

The information in this work is true and complete to the best of our knowledge. However, all information is presented without any guarantee on the part of the Author or Publisher, who also disclaim any liability incurred in connection with the use of the information and any implied warranties of merchantability or fitness for a particular purpose. Readers are responsible for taking suitable and appropriate safety measures when performing any of the operations or activities described in this work.

All trademarks, trade names, model names and numbers, and other product designations referred to herein are the property of their respective owners and are used solely for identification purposes. This work is a publication of CarTech, Inc., and has not been licensed, approved, sponsored, or endorsed by any other person or entity. The Publisher is not associated with any product, service, or vendor mentioned in this book, and does not endorse the products or services of any vendor mentioned in this book.

Edit by Wes Eisenschenk
Layout by Monica Seiberlich

ISBN 978-1-61325-478-3
Item No. CT545P

Library of Congress Cataloging-in-Publication Data
Names: Schild, James J., author.
Title: Sox & Martin : the most famous team in drag racing / Jim Schild.
Description: Forest Lake, MN : CarTech, [2016]
Identifiers: LCCN 2015032931 | ISBN 9781613252147
Subjects: LCSH: Sox, Ronnie, 1938-2006 | Martin, Buddy Grey, 1936- | Sox & Martin
  (Drag racing team) | Drag racing--United States. | Drag racers--United States.
Classification: LCC GV1029.3 .S42 2016 | DDC 796.720922--dc23
LC record available at http://lccn.loc.gov/2015032931

Written, edited, and designed in the U.S.A.
Printed in U.S.A.

Front Cover Photos

Large photo: This 1968 Hemi Barracuda is owned by Clark and Colleen Rand and is restored exactly as it looked for the 1969 World Championship race. The Keystone chrome wheels were a Sox & Martin trademark.

Small photo: Ronnie Sox tries to look over the large hood scoop as he steers the 1964 Comet to another wheelstand during a match race in the South. The plain-finish Tyree headers have replaced the red, white, and blue striped set. Buddy can be seen looking over the action behind the car. (Photo Courtesy Randy Hernandez)

Front Flap: Herb McCandless in the 1970 Hemi Duster lines up with Ronnie Sox in the 1970 Hemi 'Cuda for a matchup in pro Stock competition. (Ray Mann photo, quartermilestones.com)

Frontispiece: Buddy Martin, Ronnie Sox, and Jake King pose proudly in front of the huge trophy won at the 1968 AHRA Spring Nationals. This 1968 Hemi Barracuda has blue stripes on the scoop lettered with "Hemi 426." (Photo Courtesy Jake King Collection)

Title Page: The 1965 Plymouth is now equipped with Keystone chrome wheels and wears new door lettering proclaiming Gate City Motor Company as the sponsor. Keystone was a longtime sponsor of Sox & Martin. The location is Dover Drag Strip. (Photo Courtesy Diane Sox)

Back Cover Photos

Top: It was not unusual for Ronnie to pull the front wheels off the ground during the spectacular launches in his 1972 Hemi 'Cuda. The yellow dust is from the resin used to improve traction during these unofficial match races. (John Foster Jr. Photo)

Bottom: Buddy and Ronnie were always dressed in clean, bright, neat uniforms at the racetrack and at all public appearances. Buddy knew from the beginning that a good appearance meant that they would be remembered positively later and it presented a good image for the public. (Photo Courtesy Buddy Martin)

Author note: Some of the vintage photos in this book are of lower quality. They have been included because of their importance to telling the story.

Table of Contents

Acknowledgments 6
Introduction 7

8 — Chapter 1: The Beginning

Ronnie Sox 9	Move to Mercury 18
Buddy Martin 15	Racing in 1964 22
Sox & Martin Racing 16	Move to Chrysler 25

26 — Chapter 2: 1965–1967 Chrysler Super Stock and Funny Cars

1965 A/FX Program 27	New Super Stock Package 39
The Rush to Compete 29	Back to Stock 42
The First Super Stock Nationals 34	1967 Racing Events 44
Match Racer to Funny Car 36	

48 — Chapter 3: 1968–1969 Super Stock Domination

The Importance of Team Image 49	The A-Body Terror 57
Clinic Popularity 51	1968 Drag Racing Season 59
The Winternationals 54	1969 Drag Racing Season 65
Two Road Runners and a Barracuda 55	The Birth of Pro Stock 70

72 — Chapter 4: 1970–1972 Pro Stock 4-Speed Era

Sox & Martin, Inc. 73	1971 Pro Stock Domination 85
Changes for 1970 74	Rules Changes for 1972 92
The E-Body Hemi Pro Stock 75	1972 Meets from Coast to Coast 94
1970 Pro Stock Competition 78	Hemi Duster Number Two 99
New Power For 1971 83	Buddy Martin Steps Up 103

104 — Chapter 5: 1973–1975 Pro Stock Evolution

Chrysler Engineering Innovation 105	The Dodge Hemi Colt 115
1973 Racing Results 106	The Split 120
Hemi Duster Number Three 108	To Race Again? 121
Big Changes for 1974 113	1975 Racing Highlights 123

124 — Chapter 6: 1976–1998 Changes in Relationships

Ronnie Goes It Alone 125	Nostalgia Takes Over 138
Together Again in Dodges 127	Racing the Comet Replica 139
1979 Racing Highlights 130	Another Reunion in 1995 145
1980 Results 132	The Crash 148
1981 Season in a Mustang 133	The Team Goes Truckin' 150
Forced Retirement in 1982 135	Ronnie on His Own Again 155
Jump to a Camaro 135	

158 — Chapter 7: The Continuing Legacy

A Devastating Diagnosis 159	The Race Cars that Keep on Racing 167
The Ronnie Sox Foundation 162	Model Cars and Commemoratives 170
Appreciation of the Legacy 164	The Digital Universe 172

Index 174

Acknowledgments

As with any book of this type, the work could not have been completed without the help, advice, and cooperation of a lot of people. Although I spent a year of direct research and probably 50 years of interest and indirect research, it is the efforts of others and their generous contributions that made this work as complete as possible. I consider myself a serious historian and automotive archeologist, but it is difficult for any one person to know all about every car, race, and experience described in this book. In addition to the drivers, builders, and car owners who offered their knowledge and insights to this story, I have to thank other historians and enthusiasts.

First and foremost is Mark Janaky, of Racine, Wisconsin. Mark is well known as a historian and registrar of the great 1968 Hemi Darts and Barracudas, but I was surprised when a 7-pound box of hundreds of copies of magazine and racing newspaper articles and photos directly relating to Sox & Martin arrived that would have been almost impossible to identify and locate on my own. Without Mark's generous contributions and continuing advice and information, this book could not have been completed accurately.

Mark's collection was added to my own reference collection of *Super Stock & Drag Illustrated, Car Craft, Popular Hot Rodding,* and *Hot Rod* magazines acquired some years ago on my own and from magazine collector and dealer Norman Hechtoff.

As he has for more than 11 years and 9 books, my friend and former Super Stock and Pro Stock driver and builder Larry Griffith of Port Byron, Illinois, contributed rare photos, insight, and personal knowledge into the workings of the Chrysler drag racing programs and cars from the 1960s and 1970s that directly connected to the careers and cars of Ronnie Sox and Buddy Martin. At one point around 1993, Larry even tuned, drove, and competed in UDRA in the 1970/1971 *Lil Boss* Hemi Barracuda that Ronnie drove, then owned by the late Ron Slobe of R&R Salvage in Missouri. Larry and his Hemi Dart also competed in Pro Stock against Ronnie Sox at the *Super Stock* Magazine Nationals at York, Pennsylvania, in 1970.

As with my previous two books on Chrysler racing programs, the help, contributions, and advice of my friend John Mahoney of Overland Park, Kansas, played a great part in the research for this book. John owns one of the 1967 Plymouth Hemi Belvederes raced by Sox & Martin and has been continuously researching those cars since acquiring his in 1986. John personally met with Ronnie and Buddy along with Dave Christie, Carl Clayton, Herb McCandless, and others while restoring his Plymouth. John loaned rare Chrysler and Plymouth promotional items, magazines, and photographs in addition to photos and history of his car that added immensely to the quality of this book.

One of my most important sources of information came out of my March 2015 trip to Fayetteville, North Carolina, to meet with the last surviving members of the Sox & Martin racing team. This exciting meeting was suggested and arranged by veteran Super Stock and Pro Stock champion Herb McCandless. Through Herb's gracious efforts, I was allowed the unique and memorable opportunity to spend an entire day with Buddy Martin, Herb McCandless, Dave Christie, and Chick DeNinno, along with Herb McCandless Jr. and Buddy's son, Chris Martin. The meeting was held in Buddy's impressive EZ Auto Sales operation and, of course, his office was filled with photos, trophies, awards, and memorabilia from the history of Sox & Martin racing. Everyone generously shared their stories and knowledge about their business and racing experiences and brought out a lot of details that would otherwise be lost.

Buddy, Chick, and Dave were especially helpful and loaned me their personal collections of hundreds of photos and other documents so I could scan them for my work. All three generously reviewed and corrected my work and answered questions along the way to be sure it is as accurate as possible, but Dave Christie contributed exceptional details in his final review that only an insider would know.

Of course, Ronnie's wife, Diane, contributed a great deal of personal details about her time with Ronnie and shared her collection of photos and other information. Diane also contributed valuable information about the Ronnie Sox Foundation and its charity work.

I am fortunate to have other friends who own significant and genuine Sox & Martin race cars and they allowed me to photograph them for this book. First were Clark and Colleen Rand of Fair Grove, Missouri, who made available the 1968 BO29 Hemi Barracuda and the 1967 Plymouth Belvedere RO23 Hemi hardtop driven by Ronnie. Thanks to the gracious efforts of Clark and his wife, I have some great color images of these cars in their current correctly restored condition. Clark also related stories of his personal time spent with Ronnie Sox when his cars were displayed at shows around the country.

Second on that list were Greg and Kathy Mosley in Coal Valley, Illinois, who once again opened their fabulous collection of high-performance and maximum performance Mopars so I could photograph the Don Hardy–built 1973 Hemi Duster and the Don Hardy–built Hemi Colt in front of their beautiful private museum facility. Thanks to Greg and Kathy, who have helped and encouraged me in my work for the past 11 years.

Another car owner who offered important information and advice was Fred Ristagno of Sewell, New Jersey. Fred owns the only Pro Stock Hemi Duster built by the Sox & Martin team in the Sox & Martin shop. Fred has owned this car for a number of years and continues to run and display it in exhibition and competition events on the East Coast.

No work about Sox & Martin could be accomplished without the wealth of knowledge and advice from historian, collector, and car builder Reed Koeppe of Reed's Performance in Kearney, Nebraska. Reed owns the restored Omni Pro Stock and the Logghe-built Dodge Hemi Colt. Reed generously took the time to review this work and pay special attention to the history and technical details of the small match race and Pro Stock cars of 1973–1980.

Thanks to veteran automobile journalist, author, and Mopar historian Geoff Stunkard for providing a generous contribution of his own great photos and those from his extensive library of Sox & Martin cars and events. This work could not have been completed without his generous help and advice.

I received a great deal of help, advice, photos, and information from racers, builders, collectors, photographers, and fans, including Doug Boyce, Jack Ashley, Dave Koffel, Ed Miller, Don Grotheer, Don Moats Jr. (owner of the Sox & Martin 1970 F/Stock 340 Duster), Gary Duckworth, Butch Leal, Dick Oldfield, Joe Pappas, Randy Hernandez, Marie McCandless, Virginia (Mrs. Jake) King, Richard Maskin of DART Machinery, J. C. Childress, Mike Galewski, Alan Currans and Acceleration Archives, Roger Phillips, Bob McClurg, Laverne Zachary, Charles Milikin Jr., Joseph Marsingill, Tom Kasch, Tommy Irwin, Hank Gabbert, Carl Rubercht, Bob Rice, Stewart Pomeroy, Steve Reyes, Dan Williams, Robert Duclos, Bill Kuhlmann, Tom Richardson, Mark and Laura Bruederle, John Foster Jr., Bill Truby, David McGee, Mike Sopko, Alan Lewis, and Jerry Haas. I also talked with Ronnie Sox's first wife, Pat, who still lives in North Carolina.

As always, thanks to my wife, Myrna, who assisted with proofreading, editing, and advice.

Last, but most certainly not least, I must thank my CarTech editor, Wes Eisenschenk, who put forth a great deal of effort and time assisting me by locating and coordinating sources of pictures and information. I would have never known about many of these sources if it were not for his personal interest in the project.

Introduction

Top Fuel legend Don Garlits said in an interview on Speed Channel's American Muscle Car, "Looking back, [the super stock era] was the turning point for drag racing that really made it professional. Because, when factories took notice and were producing vehicles just for drag racing, it gave other sponsors the incentive to get involved in drag racing." To carry that a step further, professional drag racing would not exist today if not for Chrysler Corporation's sponsorship and participation in Super Stock and Factory Experimental drag racing. Chrysler's drivers were the sport's first paid professional racers.

Of course, Chrysler's great success in drag racing, especially in the Super Stock and Pro Stock classes, would not have been as successful if it were not for the team of Ronnie Sox and Buddy Martin plus Jake King, Dave Christie, and Chick DeNinno. No other drag racing organization of the time was known not only for the driver, who in this case was the best, but also for the team manager and mechanics, who were all known by name to everyone.

This recognition by fans and the public did not come by mere chance. The professionalism in appearance, business, sportsmanship, and winning accomplishment created and managed by Buddy Martin produced the image and legacy that was Sox & Martin. When Sox & Martin showed up at any race with their professionally finished haulers, uniforms, and spotlessly clean equipment, the fans, promoters, and sponsors knew that they were going to be treated to the most professional show possible.

The story of Ronnie Sox and Buddy Martin and how they became the most famous team in drag racing is clearly one of how this unique combination of people, each with his own unique responsibilities and talents came together to create something far greater than the sum total. They began with simple goals but evolved with the sport over 30 years to leave a lasting excellent impression on everyone interested in the sport.

The Beginning

The Sox & Martin Z11 Impala paid homage to Sox Sinclair Service, Friendly Chevrolet, and Butlers of Burlington. Note the matching trailer wheels. (Dennis Cox Photo)

The roots of drag racing clearly began in the 1930s (and even before that) anytime two cars were lined up at a stop light; someone had to know whose was quicker. After World War II, the enthusiasm for drag racing grew and it wasn't long before the quarter–mile track and racing two cars side-by-side was standardized.

CHAPTER 1

This quest for the best developed most fervently in the early 1950s and almost simultaneously across the country from the California hot rods and dragsters to the stock-bodied cars in the Midwestern and Eastern states.

Each region soon developed its own character and group of avid racers but East Coast drag racing had a strong and unique culture from the beginning. This culture was no more evident than in the Piedmont region of the Carolinas. The area gave birth to one of the most important drag racing teams of all time.

Ronnie Sox

Ronnie Sox was born December 17, 1938, in Greensboro, North Carolina. He had two younger brothers, David and Tommy, as well as a younger sister, Sandra. The family later moved to Burlington, the home of Burlington Industries, one of the most important textile operations in the world. But young Willard Ronald Sox was always more interested in automotive and mechanical things than textiles and that interest was encouraged by working at his father's Sox Sinclair Service (originally Esso), a gas station and repair garage in Burlington. Ronnie's dad, Willard M. "Nub" Sox, owned the station at 805 South Church Street in Burlington and over time it became known as the area's center for performance tuning and engine building.

Early Street Racing

Ronnie started dreaming about racing as early as 1950. His first real car was a 1932 Plymouth coupe that his father bought for him when he was 14. It was black and had a rumble seat and a rear-mounted spare tire. Ronnie and his dad worked together and restored the car, making it available for young Ronnie to practice driving behind the service station. Soon, after hours of practicing shifting and operating the clutch, Ronnie was successful and felt as good as any racer.

One day, after just turning 15, Ronnie got up the nerve to take his practice routine a little too far. His parents were in Greensboro for the day so he

Young Willard Ronald Sox was apparently dreaming of being a junior airmen when this photos was taken. His life in Burlington gave little indication that he would become a hero to thousands of American drag racing enthusiasts a few years later. (Photo Courtesy Diane Sox)

In December 1949 Ronnie got a taste of things to come in the Bell's Bicycle Contest held in downtown Burlington, North Carolina. It wasn't always trophies and beauty queens though; he took home the ninth-place prize. (Photo Courtesy Burlington Times-News)

SOX & MARTIN   9

Chapter 1

Ronnie grew up in the family home much the same as many other American boys. This picture shows a young man enjoying a happy life and a positive future. Ronnie shared his home with his mother, father, two younger brothers, Tommy and David, and a sister, Sandra. (Photo Courtesy Diane Sox)

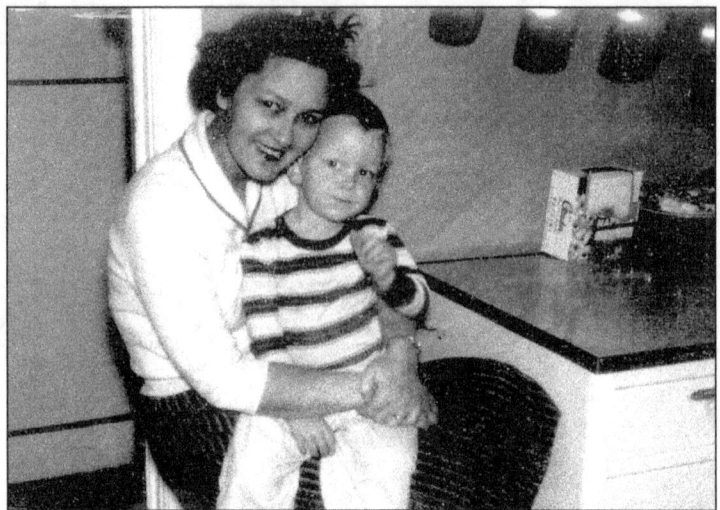

Ronnie's character was shaped not only by his mother and father but also by the new spirit of racing and automobiles that was very strong in the Piedmont Region of North Carolina where they lived. Ronnie was named after his father Willard M. Sox, who owned a gas station and repair shop in Burlington. (Photo Courtesy Diane Sox)

thought it was a good time to make his debut as a race car driver. He brought some friends home from school to show off his skills. He loaded them in the Plymouth and took it out on a back road to Chapel Hill. He backed the car up a few hundred yards, stopped, and pulled the long shift lever into first gear. He revved up the little engine, let out the clutch, and with the rear tires digging into the road, the Plymouth took off with a scream.

Young Ronnie with his mother (right) and his brother, David, and sister, Sandra, posed for a snapshot with one of his relatives in Burlington. Ronnie later shared the home with another brother, Tommy. (Photo Courtesy Diane Sox)

Unfortunately, Ronnie missed second gear and as the gears jammed into reverse, he pretty much destroyed the transmission. The car had to be towed home and Ronnie had no choice other than to wait for his parents to return and face the consequences. That little trip marked the end of the Plymouth and Ronnie's dad sold it the next day.

By the time Ronnie turned 16, his dad had bought him a 1947 Ford coupe and set him to the task of restoring it. His dad rebuilt the Ford's flathead V-8 engine and added some performance parts including Offenhauser heads and twin Stromberg 97 carburetors.

As early as 1956, young Ronnie was already racing his father's gray 1949 four-door Oldsmobile Rocket 88 at the local airport strip and, most of the time, beating his local competition. The Olds had a 1952 engine and transmission from a friend's wrecked car that gave it a bit of an advantage. Later, Ronnie's dad bought a new 1955 Oldsmobile and sold Ronnie the 1949 model.

That car was later modified with milled heads and higher-lift rocker arms. It was fed by a Cadillac carburetor and the automatic transmission was modified for higher-RPM shifts. It was not uncommon for young Ronnie Sox to challenge his friends as a demonstration of his car's acceleration abilities. He stuck a $20 bill on the top of the instrument panel and offered it to anyone who could lean forward and grab it as he was accelerating the Oldsmobile.

Ronnie prepared early and raced this car before school every morning. This street racing came to an end one morning when two local drivers ran an old lady up into a yard and she called the police. They moved their street racing exploits to back roads around Alamance, but that was soon halted. A crash involving one of the boys caused one death and another serious injury. The local police told the boys, "Your street racing days are over." This actually brought about a better situation; the local cops mustered up help and opened a dragstrip at the nearby old airport. The boys now had a legal and safer place to race and were there every weekend. Ronnie soon acquired quite a few trophies from this competition.

Drag Racing Exploits

After a year of racing the Oldsmobile, Ronnie, age 16, saved up enough money to buy his first new car, a 1957 Ford convertible. It was black with a black top and interior, had a 3-speed manual transmission, and a 270-hp 312-ci Y-block V-8 engine with dual 4-barrel carburetors. He continued to win races. This success kept a fire burning in his spirit and he knew that drag racing was what he needed to be doing. In addition, Ronnie married his Williams High School sweetheart, Patricia Perry, in 1957.

The following year found Ronnie racing a new 1958 Chevrolet convertible. He seemed to have a fondness for convertibles. With this one, he won 37 races in a row at Piedmont and other regional tracks. The 1958 Chevy was powered by a 348 W-series V-8 developing 315 hp at 5,600 rpm. It was equipped with solid valve lifters, 11:1 compression ratio, three 2-barrel Carter carburetors, and of course the important Duntov camshaft. A friend of Ronnie's acquired a 4.56:1 rear end with Posi-Traction to increase his performance and the wins kept coming. This was the hottest package available that year.

Ronnie Sox did not confine his racing exploits to the dragstrips in 1958. His enthusiasm for speed and competition sometimes overflowed onto the streets of Burlington. On a number of occasions, this need for speed attracted the attention of the local law enforcement officers. On February 10, 1958, Ronnie was arrested for speeding 85 mph and careless and reckless driving on South Church Street while driving his black 1958 Chevrolet. Ronnie was later released on a $100 bond. He was given a suspended sentence after paying a fine and promising he would not violate motor vehicle laws for 12 months. Ronnie traded that Chevy for a 1959 at the end of the season but ended up taking a break from racing during 1959 to do some relaxation and boating but the lure of the track was too strong.

Ronnie Sox and car owner Jack Ashley pose proudly with Jack's winning 1960 Pontiac. In front of the car are just a few of the numerous drag racing trophies the pair won across the Southeast. Behind the pair is the Hughes Motor Company's Pontiac showroom. (Jack Ashley Photo)

Chapter 1

Jack Ashley's original blue 1961 Pontiac with its 421 Super Duty engine sold at auction in early 2014. The information published with this car was most people's first indication that Ronnie Sox drove a Pontiac at one time. The car sold for more than $151,000. (Jack Ashley Photo)

Driving for Jack Ashley

Ronnie's talent and his string of wins in 1958 were not lost on the crowd. After seeing the success and skills of Sox, local Burlington Pontiac owner Jack Ashley (also known as Jack Strader) asked Ronnie to drive his 1960 Pontiac 389 V-8 aptly named *Untouchable*. Jack had known Ronnie, who he called "Wild Bear," for a number of years so he was very familiar with what Ronnie could do. This nickname was one of a number of such similar names he

> **For the first time, Ronnie Sox's name was in the eyes of the public and the competition.**

gave to the members of the young group Ronnie hung out with in his hometown. Ronnie first drove for Jack in 1956 at Piedmont Dragstrip in a 1956 Corvette.

Jack was an experienced racer himself, and began his drag racing career with a 1932 Ford coupe right after being discharged from the Navy in 1954. Jack later raced a 1956 Chevrolet and won his first sanctioned event at Elizabeth, North Carolina. He stuck with Chevrolets through 1959 and then decided to switch to Pontiac.

Jack was inducted into the East Coast Drag Racing Hall of Fame in 2011 and received the Ronnie Sox Memorial Award for his accomplishments.

Ronnie and Jack did well with *Untouchable*, beginning with the Daytona Speedweeks drag races in Florida organized by Illinoisan Bob Bartel. For some reason, while waiting in the staging lanes of this 50-car field, Sox was asked if he wanted to race the national champion. Ronnie promptly put the champ away. However, when the final eliminations came, the technical inspectors noticed that the Pontiac had an extra rod on the carburetor linkage and he was disqualified, missing an opportunity to race "Farmer" Arnie Beswick. He didn't win this event; but, for the first time, Ronnie Sox's name was in the eyes of the public and the competition. It wasn't long before Ronnie and Jack were receiving appearance money for racing, something previously unknown.

The Pontiac did well during the rest of the season, winning 39 out of 40 races, but it was not enough for Ronnie or for Jack Ashley. Late in the 1960 season, the new Pontiacs were announced and along with them, a new high-performance Super Duty package. No 1961 Super Duty Pontiacs were delivered from the factory but the special parts package could be ordered and installed by the owner or dealer.

Jack saw the advantages of this new setup immediately, so he arranged for the October 1960–built car to be shipped from Pontiac directly to Ray Nichels Engineering

The Beginning

Ronnie's first real race car was this red 1962 Chevrolet Impala bubble-top coupe called Thunder in Carolina. *Sox Sinclair Service sponsored the Chevy, which was equipped with a 409-ci V-8 with two 4-barrel carburetors. (Laverne Zachary Photo)*

in Indianapolis, Indiana, and have it converted to drag racing application. The car was then forwarded to Hughes Pontiac in Burlington for delivery. Ashley's Pontiac was the first of only 11 specially built for the 1961 model year.

Nichels' shop removed the original equipment heater. The car was shipped with the exhaust system deleted behind the headers, but the exhaust hangers were still in place. The Pontiac was equipped with a 389-ci V-8 but the Super Duty package changed the block to a stronger four-bolt main bearing configuration with a forged steel crankshaft and rods. The engine was assembled with 10.75:1 pistons and special cylinder heads with a 540306 casting number (PN 540304). The camshaft was a Mckellar no. 8 (referring to Pontiac high-performance engineer Malcolm "Mac" McKellar), opening and closing 1.92-inch intake valves and 1.66-inch exhaust valves. The intake manifold was a cast-aluminum setup with three 2-barrel Rochester carburetors and the exhaust exited through special free-flowing cast-aluminum manifolds. The engine was rated at 363 hp and 430 ft-lbs of torque.

Ronnie and Jack wasted no time in getting this new car prepared and ready to compete for the 1961 drag racing season. The team continued with their successes of the past year, beating the competition at almost every meeting. The only setbacks were related to transmission breakage. The Borg Warner T-10 4-speed was simply not up to the power of these high-torque engines.

Partnering with Dave Holyfield

Even though the combination of Ronnie and Jack Ashley was a good one for both of them, Ronnie wanted his own car. He soon satisfied his urge with a new 1961 Chevy. Later in the 1961 season, he teamed with another partner, Dave Holyfield, and ordered a 1962 Chevrolet with the W-Series based 409.

The new Chevrolet was a Roman Red Bel Air Sport Coupe; enthusiasts commonly refer to it as a "bubble top." It was equipped with the 409-hp 409-ci W-Series V-8. The 409 had an 11:1 compression ratio and was topped with two AFB 4-barrel carburetors. Of course, like most Sox-driven cars, it was equipped with a 4-speed manual transmission, in this case, a Borg Warner T-10. This was what the Beach Boys were singing about at the time with their "4-speed Dual Quad Posi-Traction 409." The car was lettered with the name *Mr. 409 1*, which was Ronnie Sox's moniker for the rest of the 1962 season. The car itself was appropriately called *Thunder in Carolina*.

Ronnie was not happy with the Chevy's performance and could not figure out why it did not rev as high as it should. He was so frustrated that he called "Dyno Don" Nicholson on the West Coast to ask him to diagnose the trouble. He finally determined that Ronnie's car must have the wrong camshaft. He checked it and apparently, the engine was built and delivered with a cam for

Chapter 1

The Z11 Chevy

The Z11 package was based on the Impala Sport Coupe because Chevrolet Division marketing knew that it would benefit more from promoting its more expensive Impala than the cheaper Bel Air hardtop or two-door sedan, even though these cars were lighter and stronger. The Z11 engine had 430 hp at 6,000 rpm and was based on the same W-Series platform as the 409, but the stroke was increased to 3.65 inches. The cast-iron cylinder block had a casting number of 3830814 with a QM code. The special cylinder heads (PN 3837731) had 2.19-inch intake valves and 1.72-inch exhaust valves opened by a camshaft (PN 3837736) with .556-inch lift and 325 degrees of duration. The intake manifold was unique and made in two pieces, mounting two Carter AFB 4-barrel carburetors. The compression ratio of the Z11 was 13.5:1 and the engine was lightened with an aluminum water pump. The package was finished with 4.11:1 rear axle gears and a Borg Warner aluminum case T-10 4-speed transmission.

The special high-performance package was very limited in production with only 57 Z11-equipped 1963 Impalas. However, 18 extra sets of aluminum front ends were built, allowing owners of standard 1963 Impalas to replace the steel body components of their 409 cars for racing. The base price of a 1963 Chevrolet Impala was $2,774. The RPO Z11 package cost an additional $1,240, so the total price of the new car was about $4,000. With the delivery of the new Chevy, the team of Sox & Martin racing was born.

Buddy Martin's new Z11 Chevy was ordered and acquired through a direct factory connection when Buddy called and, fortunately, spoke with Semon Emil "Bunkie" Knudsen, general manager of Chevrolet Division since 1961. Knudsen had always been performance minded so his interest in the Z11

Ronnie Sox and Buddy Martin followed the common practice of the time, raising the front end of their 1963 Z11 Chevrolet. Most racers believed that this allowed for better weight transfer to the rear and improved acceleration. As they raced more, they learned that this was not the best way to get the job done. (Photo Courtesy Diane Sox)

Team Sox & Martin cut their teeth on the dragstrips of North Carolina and its surrounding states. As such, they were frequent visitors to Louisa Dragway in 1963 with their 427 Chevy. (Dennis Cox Photo)

Buddy talking with Ronnie in the driver's seat of their white 1963 Chevy Z11 hardtop. Sox Sinclair Service was emblazoned on the door and the sponsor's name, Friendly Chevrolet, was on the rear quarter panels. The colorful checkered flags on the door were part of Chevrolet's performance image at the time. (Photo Courtesy Diane Sox)

package was personal and he wanted to see the cars on tracks around the country.

Buddy was able to acquire one of the cars and it was delivered through Alamance Chevrolet at 1222 South Church Street in Burlington. Although Alamance delivered the car, Buddy arranged the team's sponsorship deal with nearby Friendly Chevrolet in Reidsville, North Carolina, just northwest of Burlington. Friendly's advertising was soon painted on the rear quarters of the white Chevrolet. Of course, the name of Sox Sinclair Service was still prominent on the doors. Buddy had a special air scoop installed, like the one on his 1962. "Mr. 427" was lettered just behind the front wheel openings.

One of the unique dragstrips in the Piedmont area of North Carolina was this one with the starting line backed up to a vertical cliff. It was not unusual for spectators to accidentally fall from the top of the wall onto the line during a race. Here, Ronnie Sox faces off against Larry Wilson's Chevy. (Photo Courtesy Diane Sox)

a Powerglide-equipped car. Ronnie changed it and that took care of the problem.

This happened at just about the time that big-time racers, including the Ramchargers and the Golden Commandos, were beginning to show up in the area and the tracks started paying as much as $1,000 for first place. Ronnie began making some good income racing his Chevy against the best. Soon, Ronnie was learning from such luminaries as Hayden Proffitt and Bill Jenkins and continued to advance his successes. He also began to learn to use his own strong points of a good left foot, a strong right arm, and having the best car.

Buddy Martin

Buddy Grey Martin was born April 10, 1936, in Madison, North Carolina, about 25 miles north of Greensboro. Unlike his future partner Ronnie Sox, Buddy Martin did not come from an automobile-related background. He lived in the countryside, not a city, but his interest in automobiles and performance was as strong as anyone from that era. Buddy never had a car in high school because that idea was not as common as it is today. His first car was a 1938 Ford coupe that he purchased for $285; that flathead V-8–powered Ford set him on a path toward destiny. Buddy had a number of jobs after graduating from school, including working at some local retail stores near his hometown but his first "real" job was working

Bird Shoffner drove the black 1962 Chevy Impala owned by Junior Clark and tuned by Larry Brown. Because Ronnie's car was Mr. 409 I, this car was Mr. 409 II. It was also known as the Sox Sinclair Special II. (Dave Christie Photo)

Chapter 1

as an agent for Norfolk and Western Railroad, thanks to a friend's reference. He eventually worked the route from Winston Salem, North Carolina, to Hagerstown, Maryland. Buddy's job was important, but his real interest was drag racing and that is where he spent his weekends. A number of dragstrips were around that part of North Carolina, South Carolina, and Virginia, and Buddy found his way to most of them.

Ronnie Joins Buddy

By the 1962 drag racing season, Buddy Martin was driving a 1962 Chevrolet 409-hp 409 like Ronnie's. However, Buddy's Chevy was a special Impala two-door bubble-top Sport Coupe that was set up by driver and current NASCAR Hall of Fame member Ned Jarrett. Buddy took the initiative when he felt that Ned Jarrett was the man who could connect Buddy with a good engine builder. Buddy had no personal connection to him at that time, so he simply looked up Ned's address in the phonebook, found his home in Lenoir, North Carolina, and knocked on his door. Of course, Ned, being a gracious and generous man, kindly helped out.

Buddy's Chevy was also equipped with the Borg Warner T-10 4-speed transmission but this car was one of only 18 equipped with the lightweight package that included aluminum front fenders, fender liners, brackets, and front bumpers for a 125-pound weight savings. The lightweight package also improved front-to-rear weight transfer for better traction. Like all 1962 409/409 engines, it was equipped with stronger forged connecting rods, revised cylinder heads and a two-4-barrel intake manifold.

The blue Chevy was identified with Buddy Martin's name in large letters on the bottom of the doors. Both Ned Jarrett and Buddy Martin were inducted into the Motorsports Hall of Fame of America.

Buddy did well with his Chevy but it seemed as though every time he came up against Ronnie Sox he came home in second place. After a few months of this disappointment, Buddy decided that the best way to deal with this situation was to have Ronnie drive his car. Buddy described this decision in a later interview stating, "Ronnie's skill as a driver was a gift. He was very coordinated with the hand and foot. In addition to his shifting, his reaction times were outstanding. Although most people drove 4-speed cars at the time, other drivers missed gears left and right, but that never happened with Ronnie. Everybody had an excuse, but Ronnie could get into anyone's car and have no problems whatsoever."

Toward the end of 1962 Buddy approached Ronnie with an offer and told him he was considering purchasing one of the 1963 Chevrolets equipped with the new 427-ci W-Series Z11 engine. He asked Ronnie to drive the car for him. Ronnie agreed and this began the partnership that eventually became Sox & Martin Racing. This took place not long after Ronnie and Patricia's first child and son, Ronald Dean, was born in September 1962, so the timing was perfect. Patricia and Ronnie later had another son, Jeffrey Brandon and a daughter, Rhonda Jo.

Sox & Martin Racing

The team of Ronnie Sox and Buddy Martin soon experienced some of their first serious racing at nearby Piedmont Dragway, conveniently located west of Highway 62 between Burlington and Greensboro. They won that first race and it wasn't long before they got their collective act together and started piling up wins.

They soon spread out farther into other parts of North Carolina, and into South Carolina and Virginia. By mid-1963, Sox & Martin made themselves known as far away as 75-80 Dragway in Monrovia, near Frederick, Maryland. This track, owned by its founder, Bill Wilcom, had just opened and was the site of some important match racing successes for the team and their confidence and notoriety quickly grew.

Ronnie Sox and Buddy Martin quickly became known not only for Ronnie's winning driving but also for their mechanical innovations. One of the first was to investigate what tire pressure and wheel rim width meant to traction and launch. The standard at that time was wide wheels with high air pressure. Because Ronnie and Buddy's

> "Sox & Martin won that first race and it wasn't long before they got their collective act together and started piling up wins."

The Beginning

In addition to their own 1963 Chevrolet Z11, Ronnie teamed with owner Jack May and alternate driver Larry Wilson to campaign another 427 Impala. Sox & Martin kept the original car for legal class racing and used the similar Jack May/Larry Wilson modified car for match races. (Geoff Stunkard Photo)

Chevrolet had a problem with fenderwell clearance, they tried a wider rim to lower the tire's cross-section width. That did not do the job so they tried lowering the tire pressure. Much to their surprise, not only was the clearance problem solved, but the traction and ETs improved considerably, putting the Chevy into mid-11s at 123 mph. They kept quiet about their changes, but soon other drivers took notice. It wasn't long before others realized that the lower air pressure was a factor; everyone soon followed suit.

Soon, Ronnie and Buddy's numerous wins made them heroes in the South. Chevrolet fans especially cheered at their success. They spread out from their home grounds, running at York US 30 in Pennsylvania and 75-80 Raceway in Maryland. Their superiority was noticed, but because no one believed that anyone could be that much better, the outsiders, especially in the North, figured that they must be cheating. Sox & Martin received a lot of close attention and suspicion, even when they made it to the 1963 NHRA Nationals at Indianapolis but that was soon to end.

Match Racing

Meanwhile, Jack May, another racer from Powhatan, Virginia, had just acquired a 1963 Z11 Chevy and was looking for a good driver. He already knew about Ronnie Sox, so, of course, he asked him to drive the car. Ronnie had already agreed to his partnership with Buddy Martin and was very comfortable with that arrangement so he declined May. Ronnie suggested that because he and Buddy were already familiar with running the 427

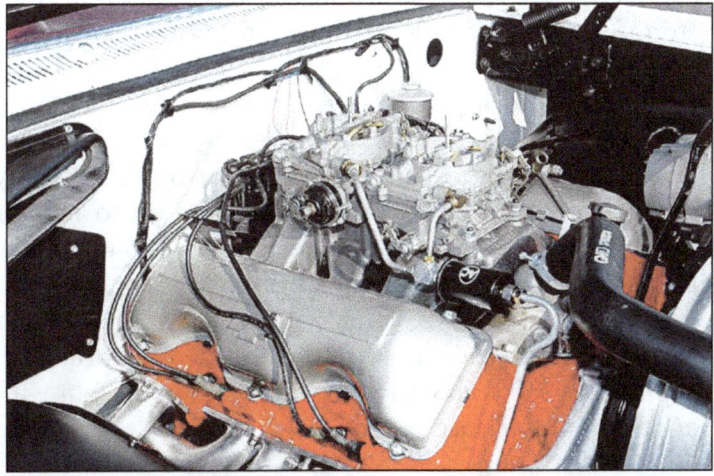

The engine compartment of the May/Wilson Chevy shows the impressive 425-hp 427 W-Series engine. This version is equipped with dual AFB carburetors and special cylinder heads along with a special camshaft. The black opening (left) shows the cold-air intake system. (Geoff Stunkard Photo)

The interior of the May/Wilson Chevy had a red vinyl interior trim; the similar car owned by Buddy Martin had a blue interior. Both were equipped with the aluminum-case BorgWarner T-10 4-speed transmission and floor shifter. Most of Ronnie Sox's race cars were equipped with a 4-speed to take advantage of his unique skills. (Geoff Stunkard Photo)

Chapter 1

The rear quarter panels of the Jack May 1963 Chevy Impala were used as a billboard for Ronnie's dad's Sox Sinclair Service in Burlington. A small note shows that the engine was built by Ronnie Sox. (Geoff Stunkard Photo)

Chevys, perhaps they could participate in May's car by building and tuning it to win. Everyone decided to maintain the original Sox & Martin car as a legal NHRA Super Stock. They modified Jack May's car for match racing, which was not under the strict rules of the Super Stock classes. May's Chevy was just like their original car except for its red rather than blue vinyl interior.

Because the Sox & Martin team was under contract to Chevrolet, the modified match race car was driven primarily by Larry Wilson, with Sox filling in from time to time. With its subtle changes, this car was easily capable of low-11-second runs across the southern match race circuit. The May car's appearance was similar to that of the original car with crossed checkered flags on the doors. But, in place of the familiar Sox Sinclair Service on the Super Stock car, this one had "Good Ole Mr. Wilson" painted prominently below the flags. "Sox Sinclair Service" was lettered on the rear quarters with "Owned by Jack May" called out beneath the sign. The front fenders indicated that the car was "Maintained by Larry and Ronnie" and *Mr. 427 II* was noted on the lower rear of the front wheel opening. This car still exists but the status of the original Z11 car, owned by Buddy Martin, is unknown as of this writing.

Ronnie and Buddy continued through the 1963 racing season, gaining more wins and attention along the way. They struggled for money, but like most drag racers, they were in it for the fun and enjoyment of racing, hoping for and working toward that great sponsorship deal of every racer's dreams. They finally got a big break in the spring of 1963 when they received an offer to run a match race at Frederick, Maryland, for $500 plus their motel expenses. Considering that most sponsorships of the day consisted of spark plugs or oil, that money gave them an incentive to step up.

Although Sox & Martin were already working under a 1962 agreement with Chevrolet, early in 1963 General Motors and Chevrolet banned all racing operations across the board. The previously signed contracts were still supported under the table but Chevrolet otherwise stopped providing any parts, support, and publicity to drag racing in any way.

Ronnie and Buddy knew that money was tight and they would have to find another way to get the support they needed to continue racing at this level. They occasionally had to borrow money just to get to a major event. If an engine was blown in a race, sometimes a bank loan was the only way to get a new engine. Both Ronnie and Buddy knew that with each win they moved a little closer to the attention they needed to attract real support. By late 1963, they found that support, but with another make of race car.

Move to Mercury

In late 1963, Ronnie and Buddy heard that Mercury was getting into racing for the 1964 season. Buddy prepared a proposal package with all of their news clippings and flew to Detroit. When he checked into the Fairlane

The white 1963 Z11 Chevy Impala was equipped with chrome-plated wheels with reversed rims, a standard fad of the times. The centers were removed and welded back into the rims, reversed from their original position. (Geoff Stunkard Photo)

Inn in Dearborn he was surprised to see familiar faces, including Butch Leal, Gas Ronda, Les Richie, Phil Bonner, Dick Brannan, and others, all there for the same reason. Although everyone else was there to talk with Ford, Buddy had already placed a call to Francisco "Fran" Hernandez at Mercury Division.

Connecting with Fran Hernandez

Fran Hernandez was not your average automobile executive and was no stranger to high performance and racing. As a Mexican immigrant and U.S. Navy veteran, he worked at Edelbrock in Southern California. His black 1932 Ford stroked-flathead V-8–powered three-window coupe was featured on the cover of the April 1949 issue of *Hot Rod* magazine after winning a race (at 122.44 mph) against Tom Cobbs' blown 1929 Ford roadster on the dry lakes. Fran had worked for Fred Offenhauser after World War II and later was with Bill Stroppe's race team before landing a job as the director of Autolite's racing division. By 1964, Hernandez was the head of racing for Lincoln-Mercury. He passed away in January 2011.

As Buddy was sitting in a meeting with other drivers and Jacque Passino, Director of Ford Special Products Division, a messenger handed a note to Passino. He saw that the note was for Buddy and asked him what Fran wanted with him. Of course, Buddy acted surprised, even though he knew that Fernandez was merely returning his call. He commented to Passino in front of the crowd that he didn't know why Fran wanted to see him.

When Buddy finally met with Fran, he told him that he had been in the Ford meeting. Fran must have thought that Buddy was playing both ends against the middle; they were both interested.

While waiting to have dinner with Fran that evening, George Hurst (of Hurst-Campbell) came by and asked Buddy what he was doing here. Buddy told him who he was waiting for and Hurst told him to ask Fran to stop by his room and talk to him before they left for dinner. Whatever Hurst said to Hernandez must have been a real sales pitch for Buddy because when he came back down to talk to Buddy he said, "You've got a real fan in George Hurst."

> **" Fran Hernandez was not your average automobile executive and was no stranger to high performance and racing. "**

Later that night Fran put his hand out to Buddy and said, "If you're interested, we've got a deal." Of course Buddy agreed and the deal was closed right then. Although Fran Hernandez arranged the deal, the 427 Comet program was actually handled and directed by Al Turner of Lincoln-Mercury. Al was a competent leader and was known to always be on top of everything that was going on.

Buddy posed the new 427 Comet in the lot after its arrival and lettering at Brinsfield Lincoln-Mercury in Greensboro, then signed and sent this photograph to Fran Hernandez. There is still no indication of Sox & Martin. Just the note that it was maintained by Ronnie and Buddy. (Photo Courtesy Randy Hernandez)

Francisco "Fran" Hernandez was a colorful figure with an important racing and hot rodding history. In the 1960s, he was the High Performance and Evaluation Coordinator for the Lincoln-Mercury Division of Ford Motor Company. He was directly responsible for recruiting and managing the drag racing teams and equipment. (Photo Courtesy Randy Hernandez)

Chapter 1

On November 29, 1963, the actual five-page contract between Buddy Martin and Ford Motor Company was signed. That contract included the direct purchase of the Comet from Ford for $3,000. Of course, like most racing contracts at that time, an initial payment of $50 was made and the balance was due on November 30, 1964. This allowed the team to legally own the Comet, removing any liability from Ford Motor Company and Mercury Division. The team was required to race the car at appropriate events at least once each month and provide information on the performance of the car and results of the race within 72 hours. The contract was witnessed by fellow racer Don Nicholson.

A New Ride

Later in Detroit, the team of Sox & Martin took possession of their new ride for 1964: one Comet Caliente hardtop and one Comet station wagon. Buddy and Ronnie quickly chose the hardtop, and the station wagon went to Don Nicholson, who believed it to have better weight transfer characteristics. By early 1964, the car was back at home in Burlington and lettered with "Maintained by Ronnie and Buddy" identification.

The Mercury Comet 427–package cars were based on the same concept and engineering as the Ford Fairlane 427 Thunderbolts. They were all built and finished by Dearborn Steel Tubing and intended for use in the NHRA Super Stock and A/Factory Experimental classes. Ronnie and Buddy actually went to the Dearborn Steel Tubing facility and assisted with the construction of their car. The Comet two-door hardtops were based on the 114-inch-wheelbase Caliente models and the station wagon was based on the 109.5-inch-wheelbase Comet 202 wagon.

Both models were available only in white finish and had lightweight interior trim schemes in red vinyl and red carpet with pleated Bostrom companion bucket seats. These seats were identical to those used in the 1964 and

This is a copy of the original Account Invoice from Ford Motor Company transferring the ownership of a 1964 Mercury Comet dragster to Buddy Martin. The sum of $3,000 was due at the end of the 1964 racing season. Note that Buddy's address is that of Sox Sinclair Service in Burlington. (Photo Courtesy Randy Hernandez)

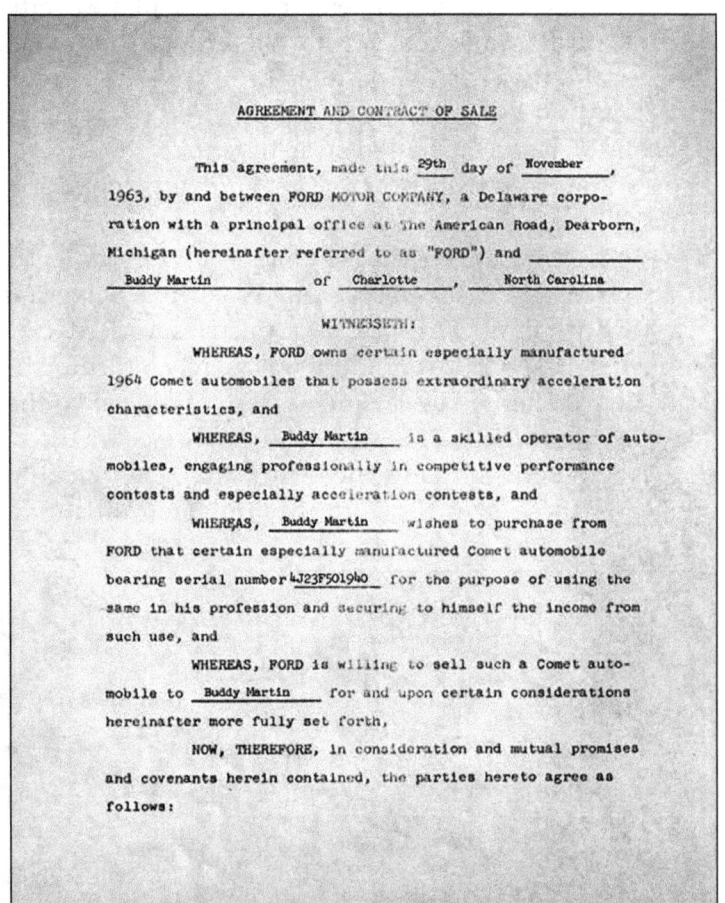

This is a copy of the original contract between Ford Motor Company and Buddy Martin. It spells out not only the ownership of the race car but also stipulates exactly what was expected of Sox & Martin during the 1964 racing season. Competition at an appropriate event was required at least once per month. (Photo Courtesy Randy Hernandez)

1965 Dodge and Plymouth Super Stock Hemi sedans. All were equipped with a 4-speed manual transmission because Ford and Mercury did not yet have an automatic as strong and functional as the 3-speed aluminum-case Chrysler TorqueFlite.

The engine was the Ford 427 High-Riser V-8 based on the FE-series block. The FE, or Ford Edsel, block was first used in a 332-ci version in 1958. The 427 was a side-oiler design and used a high-riser intake manifold with two inline 4-barrel carburetors. With its special high-dome pistons, the 427 had a compression ratio of 14:1. Ford never issued a power rating for these racing-only designs but they were in excess of 425 hp in this configuration. The engine was attached to a Ford-design 4-speed transmission, popularly known as a Toploader because the components went in from the top-mounted access plate. A Hurst Competition Plus shifter was used with this application.

> **Ronnie and Buddy soon had the Comet's performance under control and began campaigning the car all over the East and Midwest.**

Sox & Martin's First Winternationals

Ronnie and Buddy soon had the Comet's performance under control and began campaigning the car all over the East and Midwest. Early in 1964, they decided that the NHRA Winternationals at Pomona, California, on February 14–16 was a goal, but finding the money to get there was a problem. It was solved when Mercury called and told them, "Listen, we are supplying the car and the parts, and we want you out there." The Winternationals was the debut race for the new 427 Comets and Mercury wanted them well represented.

The Comets had only been tested for the first time at Lions Drag Strip in Long Beach the week before the "Big Go West." Ronnie and Buddy had to work quickly to get what they needed, but they were finally able to borrow the travel expenses from their sponsor, Brinsfield Lincoln-Mercury in Greensboro, North Carolina. They were soon mounted up and on their way west.

The long trip west was not without its troubles and excitement. Before the pair made it through Alabama, one of the extra racing slicks (mounted on a wheel) bounced off the trailer and they had to search all over the area to find it. The tire and wheel had bounced onto the Comet windshield and cracked it. Buddy and Ronnie were not too concerned about it but when they arrived at the track at Long Beach, NHRA tech officials did not allow them to run in qualifying with the damaged glass.

They were told they had to replace the glass to run on Monday but the officials eventually relented and allowed them to qualify. They posted lowest A/FX ET of the event at 11.08 seconds. Of course, someone protested because of the windshield. The glass was replaced at Bill Stroppe Racing's shop in Long Beach and the car was back in contention in the class.

Incidentally, the 1964 NHRA Winternationals was the first time the now standard "Christmas Tree" starting light system was used at a national event.

Here is the 427 Comet during one of its winning races at the NHRA Winternationals at Pomona, California. The trip to get there was eventful but it all worked out well in the end for Sox & Martin. (Photo Courtesy Randy Hernandez)

Chapter 1

Racing in 1964

While they were on the West Coast, Ronnie and Buddy made some new friends, including fellow Mercury Comet driver Jack Chrisman. They stayed at his home during the meet and enjoyed his hospitality. Their encounter with Parnelli Jones and Bill Stroppe, both winning Mercury road course racers, as well as Stroppe's work, became more important to Ronnie and Buddy after they returned to North Carolina.

By the time Ronnie and Buddy made it back home, the popular and profitable match race season had begun. Most of the cars were A/Factory Experimentals but under the "Run What Ya Brung" rules, almost anything was acceptable. This was especially true in the southeastern part of the country where southern-style match racing

1964 Winternationals

The Sox & Martin Comet did not win the 1964 A/FX class runoffs. That was won by Bill Shrewsbury in his Comet at 11.78 seconds and 120.16 mph against Tom Sturm, who missed second gear in the final.

Because anyone who wanted to do so could compete in the Eliminator categories on Sunday, Ronnie Sox had a second chance at glory. He won Factory Stock Eliminator with a holeshot, turning in an ET of 11.49 seconds at 123.45 mph against "Dyno Don" Nicholson in his white Comet wagon running an 11.47.

Ronnie told *Hot Rod* reporters, "I really like the Mercs." For their efforts, Ronnie and Buddy received a new 1964 Dodge 440 hardtop, compliments of George Hurst. Unfortunately, they had to sell the Dodge prize to pay for the trip back to North Carolina.

George Hurst of Hurst-Campbell awarded Ronnie and Buddy a huge trophy and a new 1964 Dodge 440 hardtop for winning the 1964 Winternationals. The new Dodge (left) had to be sold for the money to get back home to North Carolina. (Photo Courtesy Diane Sox)

Ronnie Sox drove the Comet to a decisive victory at Pomona in early 1964 and began a career that put Sox & Martin Racing on the map and in the minds of race fans across the country. Here he beats one of the 427 Ford Thunderbolts at the Winternationals. (Photo Courtesy Randy Hernandez)

Buddy and Ronnie pose with Miss Winternationals 1964 and display their trophy and checkered flag proudly. The white 427 Comet won Factory Stock Eliminator with a blast of 11.49 seconds at 123.45 mph for a holeshot win against Don Nicholson's wagon running 11.47. (Photo Courtesy Randy Hernandez)

was king. The rules limited minimum weight and maximum cubic inches but every team had its own idea of how to arrive at those standards. Many racers, Sox & Martin included, were given appearance money just to show up and be featured on the ads and flyers for the meets.

In addition to the match races scattered around the country, special invitational events were also put on by *Drag News* and other sponsors. *Drag News'* second annual Invitational at Detroit Dragway on June 19–21 was considered a preview of what would be seen at the NHRA Nationals at Indy in September. For the 1964 race, all of the big names were there, including Don Nicholson and his Comet, The Ramchargers' Hemi Dodge, Phil Bonner and his Thunderbolt, and of course, Sox & Martin and their Comet.

The Sox & Martin Comet looked a little different by this time. Instead of the original white finish that was standard on all factory 427 Comets, the car was now a striking red, white, and metallic blue. It seems that while their windshield was being replaced at Bill Stroppe's race shop at Long Beach, Ronnie and Buddy talked about how nice the Parnelli Jones cars looked with their Guardsman (Corporate) Blue roofs with Rangoon Red and Wimbledon White bodies.

When he returned to North Carolina, Buddy then had to fly to Louisville to pick up a new truck. While he was gone, Ronnie had the car repainted in the iconic red, white, and metallic blue scheme that became the image of the team from then on. At about this time, the Sox & Martin Comet was chosen to be on the cover of the first issue of *Super Stock and Drag Illustrated* magazine, which soon became the most important source of news for fans and racers. Buddy decided to make the car more spectacular for the cover shot by having the Jere Stahl header collectors painted with red, white, and blue stripes to complete the look. Buddy had to work closely with Jere Stahl at his shop to get it finished on time.

Jake King Arrives

The colors were not the only changes Ronnie made around that time. Needing a mechanic to take responsibilities away from Buddy, who became more and more involved with the business needs of the team, Ronnie hired John Preston "Jake" King Jr., who was already an experienced Ford racer and competed with his own 1964 Ford Thunderbolt. King's 427 Fairlane was raced out of Atwater Ford in Burlington and was a familiar sight in the area. Jake was born on January 8, 1929, and grew up on a farm near Burlington. He worked around the small garage that his father and uncle ran beginning when he was very young. His first car was a 1936 Ford, and he began his involvement in racing around 1950.

When Jake joined the Sox & Martin team, he gave up his own desire to open and operate an automobile repair shop. Because he already had racing and car building experience with his own Ford Thunderbolt, he had an advantage when dealing with the new 427 Comet.

Ronnie Sox once said, "Jake was a perfectionist. He was very laid back, very quiet. He would not put an engine together unless it was the absolute best he could do, and he took his time." Jake became the third important spoke in the Sox & Martin wheel and proved to be a significant contributor to their continued success.

Ronnie Sox completes a burnout in the 427 Comet in front of the fans. The cloud is more likely from the powdered resin used at that time rather than burning tires. The wheels were changed to dished aluminum from the previous plated spoke front and painted rear used earlier. (Photo Courtesy Diane Sox)

The tremendous torque of the 427 V-8 lifts the front wheels of the Comet as it leaps off the line at a Southeastern track. The traction off the line is helped by the wide slicks and large traction bars visible beneath the rear axle. The inner headlight openings are air intakes to the carburetors. (Photo Courtesy Randy Hernandez)

Chapter 1

Ronnie Sox tries to look over the large hood scoop as he steers the 1964 Comet to another wheelstand during a match race in the South. The plain-finish Tyree headers have replaced the red, white, and blue striped set. Buddy is looking over the action behind the car. (Photo Courtesy Randy Hernandez)

Ronnie said in a later Chrysler press release, "I would put Jake up against anybody building a car; we wouldn't be in the running without him."

Each member of the Sox & Martin team was specialized and concentrated on that job, allowing the others to do theirs.

Hot Rod's First Annual Drag Championships

Ronnie Sox and the Comet did not win the *Drag News* event but continued to compete in match races and special races across the country. Ronnie and Buddy took the car to Riverside in Southern California for the *Hot Rod* Magazine first annual Drag Championships to prove themselves against the top dogs. The Hemi Dodges and Plymouths of Al Eckstrand and Hayden Proffitt were there, along with Don Nicholson in his new Comet, *Ugly Duckling*. "Fast Eddie" Schartman came along to drive Nicholson's Comet wagon.

The Sox & Martin A/FX Comet made it through the competition, beating Jim Thornton and the Ramchargers Dodge in the semi-final. The final pitted Sox against Roger Lindamood's *Color Me Gone* Hemi Dodge. Ronnie decisively beat Lindamood out of the hole; he was charging ahead when, uncharacteristically, he missed second gear, letting the Dodge pass him for the win.

British International Drag Festival

One of the most interesting and unusual events of the 1964 season was the British International Drag Festival. Because drag racing was already a popular sport in the United Kingdom, NHRA head Wally Parks and British Drag Racing Association president (and famous sports car builder) Sydney Allard organized a meet featuring some of the best American racers. The event consisted of a tour of six British dragstrips between September 19 and October 4, 1964.

The Comet was transported to New York on a trailer that was rented from Bill Ingoll and Larry Nichols. It was loaded, along with Buddy, Ronnie, and Jake and the rest of the American racers and their cars, on the British ocean liner RMS *Queen Mary*. The 1,019-foot-long 81,961-ton vessel was one of the fastest with a top speed of 32 knots, appropriate for the drag racing passenger list and cargo. Formerly the flagship of the Cunard line, *Queen Mary* carried troops and supplies across the Atlantic during World War II; she was retired after 1967.

Some British tracks were on airport runways and military installations and the events drew large crowds wherever they went. The tour included such prominent American racers as "Big Daddy" Don Garlits, "Ohio George" Montgomery, Dave Strickler, "TV Tommy" Ivo, Tony Nancy, K. S. Pittman, and of course, Sox & Martin. They were called the United States Drag Racing Team and each car carried decals identifying them as such.

Buddy said that the British racers and events were much different from their American counterparts. The British cars ran smaller, high-RPM engines that made for some unusual sounds at the strip. Proper British courtesy was always paramount, of course. At lunch time, everything stopped and everyone was taken back to the hotel on a bus for a meal.

This portrait of Jake King shows the quiet intent of a man who was as responsible as anyone for the long success of the Sox & Martin racing efforts over many years. (Photo Courtesy Buddy Martin)

The Beginning

The Sox & Martin 1964 Comet lined up with other competitors during the British tour in 1964. At left is Don Garlits' Wynn's Jammer 392 Hemi-powered dragster. (Photo Courtesy Lynn Wineland Archive, quartermilestones.com)

The event was run on a cumulative point system for each round that determined the final overall winner. The racing was fast; Sox ran a best time of 11.72 in the Comet and Strickler ran 11.54 in his Hemi Dodge. Although Strickler was the overall points winner with 337 to Sox's 309, Sox & Martin represented their country well with their red, white, and blue paint scheme along with the neat and bright uniforms. The header collectors had been changed to plainer Tyrees before the tour but the colorful Comet still attracted a lot of attention.

Move to Chrysler

Ronnie and Buddy had fully intended to stay with Mercury for the upcoming 1965 racing season. Buddy negotiated the deal with Fran Hernandez and told him what they needed, based on their successes and results during 1964. The arrangement included sponsorship by the Lincoln-Mercury Division and by the Washington, D.C.-area Lincoln-Mercury dealers. When Ronnie and Buddy went to Washington to meet the dealers and Hernandez, they were given the new contract, which did not include the previously agreed upon personal cars for Ronnie and Buddy.

The pair thought it was important for them to have these two cars so after discussing the matter, they decided not to sign the contract. Fran told them, "This is all we can do." Fran was displeased and returned to Detroit.

When he returned to Burlington, Buddy called Dale Reeker, who was the Factory Experimental representative under Bob Cahill, head of Chrysler Drag Racing Programs, and told him that they would consider moving to Mopar. Dale said, "I'll call you back."

Dale called Buddy in a couple of hours and told them to get on a plane to Detroit right away. Buddy and Ronnie signed with Chrysler for the 1965 season and the rest is history. The two personal cars were not a problem at Chrysler. Mercury Division called them a couple of days later and said it had worked it out to give the team what they wanted, but it was too late.

The Sox & Martin 1964 Comet and operation were so important to the 1964 drag racing season that an action shot of the car was featured on the cover of Volume One, Number One of *Super Stock & Drag Illustrated* magazine, undeniably the most popular publication of its time on the subject.

At the end of the season, the Sox & Martin 1964 Comet 427 was sold to Oswego, New York, racer Dave Goodrich who repainted and re-lettered it as *Thunderball*. Goodrich did the tuning, and driving duties were trusted to fellow New Yorker Wally Bell.

The 1964 Comet was equipped with shorter Jere Stahl headers and collectors while on the U.K. tour for the United States Drag Racing Team. At one point, they were painted with red, white, and blue stripes. (Photo Courtesy Lynn Wineland Archive, quartermilestones.com)

1965–1967 Chrysler Super Stock and Funny Cars

Buddy and Ronnie were called to Chrysler headquarters in late December 1964 to view the prototype Plymouth for the 1965 altered-wheelbase (AWB) Hemi hardtop program. They began their Mopar career with some of the wildest race cars ever built by a manufacturer. (Photo Courtesy Diane Sox)

The 1965 season actually began early for Ronnie and Buddy. Although Buddy had already been to Detroit to meet with Chrysler, on December 23, 1964, Chrysler sent a letter calling all of their team members into a special presentation and seminar in Detroit.

CHAPTER 2

The following year meant not just a change in support and manufacturer, it meant a brand-new concept in drag racing strategy and technology. Because Ford and Mercury had already pushed the rules envelope with their 1964 427 Thunderbolts and Cyclones, Chrysler had to be sure that it was doing the competition one better. Chrysler's target for 1965 was the Factory Experimental classes.

Chrysler placed more emphasis and money on drag racing than it had in previous years because NASCAR had banned the powerful and dominant 426 Hemi engine from competition on the long tracks. The new-for-1964 Hemi beat just about everything the competition had. NASCAR felt that the Hemi created an unfair advantage for Chrysler. This meant that Chrysler transferred all efforts and engineering to drag racing.

The A990 426 Hemi engine had a compression ratio of 12.5:1 and was used in all of the 1965 factory Super Stock sedans and Factory Experimental hardtops; it was similar to the winning A864 Hemi engine used through 1964. The new and improved version was lightened by using an aluminum water pump housing, oil pump cover, alternator brackets, and Alcoa cylinder heads. The large cross-ram intake manifold was changed from cast aluminum to cast magnesium, taking more weight from the front of the car. The new Hemi was still rated at an unrealistically low 425 hp; it was likely much closer to 565 at the flywheel when in use.

NHRA Factory Experimental rules were much the same as 1964 but both Ford and Chrysler were already making plans to push these rules to their limits, and beyond, for 1965. When Ronnie and Buddy arrived in Detroit they saw for the first time the radical concepts that forever changed the sport. The teams were brought to the engineering building for the first showing and the car was brought over in a covered trailer. Once in the garage, the engineers pulled off the cover and everyone was shocked at what they saw. The white Plymouth Belvedere II hardtop was the most unusual stock-bodied drag car they had ever seen.

The 202 legal Super Stock sedans were not the only factory-built or authorized Hemis built for the 1965 season. At about the same time that the R01/W01 Hemi sedans were being built, at least 11 of them were delivered to the Chrysler Engineering Product Planning garage (under factory Account Number 7364) to be used for a more radical purpose.

The NHRA attempted to level the playing field in 1965 with rule changes requiring at least 100 units built to qualify for Super Stock. Chrysler satisfied that with 202 R01/W01 cars. However, for 1965, Ford dropped out of Super Stock to attack the A/Factory Experimental class. The Factory Experimental battle between Ford and Chrysler had been going on for years, and Chrysler fired its last shot in 1964 when it released the mild altered-wheelbase (AWB) Dodges and Plymouths to counter the Ford and Mercury Super Stocks.

1965 A/FX Program

When Chrysler found out that Ford planned to field the smaller Mustangs and Comets stuffed with overhead cam (OHC) 427 engines in 1965, it chose to attack from a different direction. Rather than drop the Hemi into the smaller Barracudas and Darts, Chrysler decided to keep the more marketable image of the B-Body cars and use the Coronet and Belvedere two-door hardtops. Chrysler based its decision partly on the assumption that most of these cars would be used in unofficial match races rather than strict class-rules racing. Chrysler did not bother to inform the NHRA of its plans.

The NHRA FX rules allowed a wheelbase move of no more than 2 percent. But since Ford had not really followed that rule very closely with the 106-inch-wheelbase Mustangs, Chrysler probably figured that it might as well push it a little further. The results of this assumption were the fantastic

Chapter 2

1965 AWB Hemi hardtops. The development of these cars began almost as soon as the 1965 models were available. But when NHRA officials finally viewed the cars before the beginning of the 1965 season, they went away shaking their heads in disbelief thinking, "No way." The cars were not legal for NHRA competition.

At the seminars, an engineer went over each of the details for which he was responsible and explained its purpose and intent. Holley specialists went over the carburetors. Prestolite engineers covered the ignition system and Roger Lindamood explained the transmission modifications. Each specialist or engineer went over the operation, maintenance, and recommendations of each part of the car; they wanted to ensure that the teams knew how to get the most out of the package.

Department head J. J. Fodermaier and chief engineer W. R. Rodger laid out the initial development of the Chrysler 1965 A/FX program, which H. J. McNichol Jr. authorized in confidential division technical report 4208.7. The 32-page document detailed the construction of some of the wildest race cars ever to come out of a factory. The purpose of this project was "to provide weight distribution more favorable for drag racing and to document the procedure in such a manner that the car could be duplicated with a minimum of fixturing."

At the start of the program, the decision was made to build only 11 AWB cars: six Dodges and five Plymouths (plus the Plymouth mule car).

The Dodges went to Dick Landy (*Landy's Dodge*), Jim Thornton (the Ramchargers), Roger Lindamood (*Color Me Gone*), Bob Harrop (*The Flying Carpet*), Bud Faubel (*Hemi Honker*), and Dave Strickler. The Plymouths went to Tom Grove (*Melrose Missile*), Butch Leal (*California Flash*), Forrest Pitcock and Al Eckstrand (mule car and *Golden Commandos*), Lee Smith (*Hustlin' Hemi II*), and Ronnie Sox (*Paper Tiger*).

Spec Changes

The basic idea was to move the rear axle forward 15 inches and the front wheels forward 10 inches, essentially reducing the wheelbase from 115 to 110 inches.

In addition to the wheelbase change, the new A/FX entries also used a number of fiberglass parts for a significant weight reduction. This included the front fenders, hood, higher A/FX scoop, front bumper, doors, instrument panel, and deck lid. The K-member was also a specially built, lightweight, thin stainless piece with two front reinforcements for the strut connections.

The modified two-door hardtop body was a chemically milled body-in-white steel shell with no front-end components, K-member, or interior. (The one exception was the experimental Belvedere mule car, which was intentionally built using a standard steel shell.) The components (except for the K-member and rear springs) needed to complete the cars were taken from 11 complete white R01/W01 Super Stock sedan donor cars that were stripped of their interiors, engines, rear axles, and suspensions.

The majority of the cars were built in the facilities of Amblewagon, an ambulance builder in Troy, Michigan, under Chrysler engineering direction. A few teams, including the Ramchargers, Golden Commandos, Roger Lindamood, and Dick Landy, built their own cars using an acid-dipped body-in-white, parts, and a donor car supplied by Chrysler.

Butch Leal said that the factory-built AWB cars were assigned to drivers ahead of time, but that did not always work out as planned. "Sox got my car; I got his. We were snowed-in in Indianapolis and could not get to Detroit in time."

A Few Tweaks

Ronnie and Buddy quickly picked up their new Plymouth and transported it to Burlington to prepare it for

Ronnie is driving the 1965 AWB Plymouth racing against Dave Strickler in his 1964 Hemi Dodge sedan, probably at the 1965 Winternationals. The Plymouth did not keep this Chrysler Pentastar logo on its doors for very long. (Paul Hutchins Photo)

Ronnie poses with the 1965 Plymouth AWB hardtop at the staging line. At this time, the car is equipped with American Racing mag wheels and steel rear wheels. (Photo Courtesy Diane Sox)

the upcoming winter meets in California. The cars were basically ready when received but, like most teams, Sox & Martin and team mechanic Jake King pulled the factory engine and rebuilt it to their standards.

He painted it Ford Engine Blue as he did with all of their competition engines. Front and rear wheels as well as tires were replaced and the body was painted in the familiar red, white, and blue Sox & Martin livery. Later, "Gate City Motor Company" was painted on the doors in white letters indicating sponsorship. However, for the 1965 winter meets, a large blue and white Pentastar was the only decoration. "Sox & Martin Racing Team" appeared only on the front fenders in smaller letters. The *Paper Tiger* name appeared only on the rear deck panel. The entire underside and suspension of the car was painted white to make servicing easier at the track.

Surprisingly, *Melrose Missile* was the only factory AWB 1965 Plymouth donor sedan delivered with 4-speed equipment, which means that the Sox & Martin donor car originally had a TorqueFlite. Of course, it was replaced with a 4-speed for Ronnie's use while the AWB Hemi hardtop was being built. This was the lowest donor car VIN assigned any 1965 Plymouth AWB hardtop, which indicates that it was the first one selected.

The Rush to Compete

Because of the time involved in modifying the AWB hardtops, some of them were not ready for the AHRA Winter Championships and the NHRA Winternationals early in 1965. The first car completed was Bud Faubel's *Hemi-Honker*. So, the only modified cars at those events were *Hemi-Honker*, the Dodges of Landy and Harrop, plus the Plymouths of Lee Smith, the Golden Commandos, Butch Leal, and Sox & Martin. Dave Strickler's A/FX entry was not yet completed. At the AHRA Scottsdale meet, the Golden Commandos' AWB Ultra/Stock Plymouth (with Hilborn fuel injection), driven by Forrest Pitcock, was not yet fully painted and sported only plain lettering on its white body.

Four of the not-yet-completed AWB cars were hurriedly put together as NHRA-legal 2-percent A/FX cars and brought to both western meets. The four Hemi hardtops appeared in relatively stock form, although they sported fiberglass parts as on the AWB cars. These four cars were *Melrose Missile*, *Golden Commandos* (second car with Al Eckstrand driving), *The Ramchargers*, and *Color Me Gone*. When the two western events were completed, three of these cars were shipped back to Detroit for full 10/15-inch modifications; *Melrose Missile* had the same alterations made in California.

The Winter Meets

As usual, the AHRA Winter Championships at Scottsdale, Arizona, January 29–31, was the earliest major event for Super Stock and A/FX competition. Most of the more than 800 entries were stockers. The event drew almost 60,000 spectators at Bee Line Dragway and it was

> "The event drew almost 60,000 spectators at Bee Line Dragway and it was the first drag racing event to be taped for closed-circuit television, airing in 42 major eastern cities."

the first drag racing event to be taped for closed-circuit television, airing in 42 major eastern cities. This was the first opportunity for the major Detroit automakers to put their 1965 entries on display.

AHRA rules differed from the NHRA, and allowed a variety of new cars to run. AHRA rules included classes for S/S-1 at 3,200 pounds with a stock wheelbase, S/S-2 at 3,200 pounds with a 2-percent wheelbase change,

Chapter 2

and U/S (Ultra Stock) at 3,000 pounds with a 12-percent adjusted wheelbase. The U/S cars were legal at NHRA meets.

The only Ford in Top Stock competition was Phil Bonner's 427 wedge U/S Falcon. His new Hemi Mustang was left on the trailer because Ford did not allow its Mustangs to race the radically altered Dodges and Plymouths. The Ford corporate rule affected the outcome of U/S and F/X competition for the remainder of the season. Bonner's 10.83-second qualifying run made him the real threat to the Mopars, but engine problems put him out early.

Eight 3,000-pound U/S and U/SA 12-percent AWB Dodge and Plymouth hardtops qualified at this meet. They included Bud Faubel (*Honker*), Dick Landy (*Landy's Dodge*), Butch Leal (*California Flash*, painted dark blue for this meet only), Lee Smith (*Learner Plymouth*), Forrest Pitcock (*Golden Commandos*, fuel-injected), Bob Harrop (*Flying Carpet*), and Ronnie Sox (*Paper Tiger*). These were the factory 110-inch wheelbase hardtops with the rear wheels moved forward 15 inches and the front wheels moved forward 10 inches, with fiberglass hood, deck lid, doors, and larger hood scoop.

Mr. Stock Eliminator competition was drawn from the 16 fastest qualifiers from the six classes of standard- and automatic-transmission cars. Of course, all of the first-round winners were Dodges and Plymouths; Bud Faubel turned in the quickest ET at 10.92 seconds at 128.33 mph. In the second round, Bud Faubel beat Roger Lindamood at 10.87 seconds at 128.93 mph. Unfortunately, all four of the 4-speed drivers were forced out with problems but Ronnie Sox turned in a 10.76-second low ET of the meet. The Ramchargers Dodge driven by Mike Buckel was the Top Stock Eliminator.

The 1965 Plymouth was equipped with Keystone chrome wheels and the new door lettering advertising sponsor Gate City Motor Company. Keystone was a longtime sponsor of Sox & Martin. The location is Dover Drag Strip. (Photo Courtesy Diane Sox)

The 100-inch-wheelbase Mopars did not run at the NHRA meet at Pomona in February. Only the 4-percent Mopars ran at Pomona. These were not the cars that Chrysler wanted to put against the Ford entries.

Test of the New Rules

A number of events were held across the country throughout early 1965. One of the more exciting was the Super Stock extravaganza held at York US 30 Drag-O-Way in York, Pennsylvania, on May 15. This was a preliminary experimental trial run of the new rules set up expressly for the big *Super Stock* Magazine Nationals planned for August 7, 1965. The cars were classed by weight, with the big Ultra Stock cars (injection and/or superchargers) and carbureted car classes at 2,800, 3,000, and 3,200 pounds.

"Dyno Don" Nicholson was always one of Ronnie's most fearsome competitors. Nicholson in his 427 Comet and Sox in the Plymouth launch off the line together at Gainesville, Florida. (Photo Courtesy Diane Sox)

Ronnie gets on the big Hemi hard as he launches the 1965 Belvedere AWB Hemi hardtop. The Plymouth was still running carburetors at this race in early 1965.

1965–1967 Chrysler Super Stock and Funny Cars

A Step Up to Fuel Injection

Soon after the first few AWB cars were completed, Chrysler engineers were already planning their next attack. The factory prototype AWB mule car was the white Golden Commandos' Plymouth; it had the standard-thickness steel body so it was used as a testbed to experiment with the new Hilborn fuel-injection setup. Test driver Forrest Pitcock found that although power increases were significant, he experienced problems making the setup work without loading up with the low-RPM TorqueFlite starts.

Development on the new system began well before the Scottsdale event but it took some further experimental work to make it work well. Chrysler engineers knew that the Hilborn setup boosted ETs by at least .2 second and increased trap speeds accordingly. The solution was a series of special bypass jets that prevented loading-up. This was especially important with TorqueFlite-equipped cars. The Hilborn design was intended to work at wide-open high speed and at more continuous RPM. Chrysler engineers also developed tuned-length, flared tubes and settled on 14 inches for the TorqueFlite-equipped engines and 7¼ inches for the 4-speed cars.

One of the first factory cars to receive the perfected unit was Sox & Martin's AWB Plymouth hardtop. Factory engineers were on hand to install and tune the unit and by mid-April 1965 had it working well enough that Ronnie Sox forced Arnie Beswick's blown Pontiac GTO into the 9s; Ronnie lost with a 10.04. The following week, on April 24, 1965, at York US 30 Drag-O-Way, the Sox & Martin team had the system refined and Sox ran 9.98 against Beswick, becoming the first unblown, stock-bodied automobile to run in the 9s.

Soon, the Ramchargers and almost all of the other factory A/FX teams were running the Hilborn injection setup and blowing away most of the competition in match races. Later in the season, increasing the inlet tube diameter to 2½ inches and increasing the size of the internal jets and passages a further 12 percent improved the original Hilborn injection setup. These changes brought the already impressive ETs even lower.

Photographer Charles Milikin caught Ronnie at speed at Cecil County Dragway. The 1965 Plymouth hardtop was now Hilborn fuel injected. The hood was removed and American Racing mag wheels were on the front again for this run, which was probably a match race. (Charles Milikin Jr. Photo)

Early in 1965, Ronnie met NASCAR great Richard Petty, who was also from the Piedmont area of North Carolina. Both were leaders in their sport but in 1965 Richard was drag racing his 1965 43 jr and Outlaw Plymouth Barracuda.

Ronnie and Buddy took the Plymouth to the 1965 Super Stock *Magazine Nationals at York, Pennsylvania, and entered it in the 2,800-pound class. The car had the small fuel tank in the grille and Keystone chrome wheels on the front. (Photo Courtesy Diane Sox)*

Chapter 2

Match Racing Backup

Early in the spring of 1965, it was evident to Ronnie and Buddy that match racing was going to be their primary business with the AWB Plymouth. With three or four races scheduled each week, they decided that it was important to have a second car available to fill in for double-booked events and also in case of problems with car number one. Another factory-built hardtop was not possible but a standard white Hemi Super Stock sedan was still available so Buddy requested one from Chrysler.

This car was intended to be an AWB donor because it had the correct Factory Engineering delivery code and factory experimental account number; Chrysler made it available to the team sometime in March. This donor car, as with the first, was built with a TorqueFlite but was soon converted to 4-speed and painted in the same familiar red, white, and blue livery as the hardtop. It was named *Paper Tiger Too*.

In early 1965, Sox & Martin needed a second car to satisfy its match race commitments. A standard 1965 Hemi sedan was located and soon converted to AWB specifications. The car used a special stainless front crossmember to reduce weight. (Geoff Stunkard Photo)

The 1965 AWB Hemi sedan is restored today but it is equipped with an incorrect later steering wheel. Ronnie liked to use blue tinted glass and headlights on many of his race cars. (Geoff Stunkard Photo)

Both of the 1965 Sox & Martin Plymouths used a variety of wheels depending on the situation. The chrome-dish rear and American Racing magnesium fronts were used frequently for match racing. (Geoff Stunkard Photo)

The interior of the restored 1965 AWB sedan is in standard 1965 Hemi trim but Ronnie used a shorter Hurst Competition Plus shifter rather than this stock 1965 shifter handle. (Geoff Stunkard Photo)

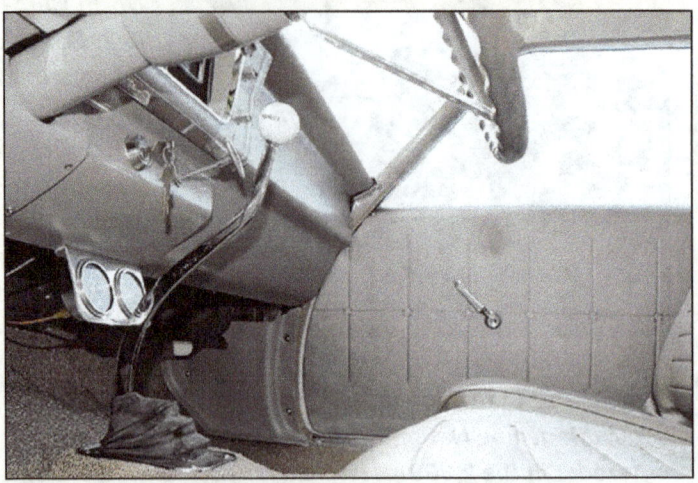

1965–1967 Chrysler Super Stock and Funny Cars

The engine compartment of the 1965 AWB sedan was much like that of a standard 1965 Hemi except for the relocated engine mounts and front crossmember. The shorter Hilborn fuel injection stacks were used with the 4-speed. (Geoff Stunkard Photo)

The stainless front crossmember for the AWB cars is identified by the rectangular reinforcements at the strut rod connections. The crossmember was moved forward 10 inches from the stock location. (Geoff Stunkard Photo)

The Gate City Motor Company team rolled in style for 1965. Highway tractor-trailer rigs and enclosed trailers had not yet been considered and showing off the cars was a priority.

Dodge and Plymouth Super Stock and FX cars clearly dominated the meet with five AWB cars making up the Ultra Stock class, including Bud Faubel's *Honker* Dodge and Sox & Martin's *Paper Tiger* Plymouth. Ronnie Sox made a 10-second 136.02-mph pass in the class run but was put away by Faubel in the final overall eliminator run when Faubel ran a 10.30 at 134.50 mph.

East Coast Drags

A premier event for 1965 was the introductory NHRA Springnationals held the first weekend in June at the brand-new ultramodern track at Bristol, Tennessee (later called Thunder Valley). This was the first major drag racing event in the East and represented an opportunity for East Coast and Midwest drivers to show their stuff.

The Springnationals was the inaugural event of NHRA's new semi-official Funny Car or Match Bash class, so it was filled with nearly every top A/FX car in the country. Mopars were well represented with the factory AWB hardtops of Lee Smith, Bud Faubel, Sox & Martin, the Golden Commandos, Bob Harrop, and Dave Strickler in attendance.

Ronnie Sox ran a best time of 10.47 but red-lighted in the first round. Although "Dyno Don" Nicholson's Comet and Dick Brannan's Mustang turned in the best pre-race times, Dave Strickler won the class with a run of 10.64 seconds at 131.57 mph with his 1965 Dodge AWB hardtop. The Sox & Martin Hemi sedan made it to the final round in Super Stock but lost, uncharacteristically, to the holeshot of William Andress in the Serbay Motors 1965 Plymouth.

Chapter 2

A beautiful view across the pits and the fields surrounding York US 30 at the 1965 Super Stock Magazine Nationals. The Sox & Martin 1965 AWB Hemi sedan is at the lower left.

On June 18, 1965, Ronnie and Buddy hauled their Plymouth sedan to Charlotte Motor Speedway for the first Manufacturer's Championship; it was promoted by Ed Otto and Bob Bartel and sanctioned by the National Automobile Timing Association Championships (NATAC). Sox & Martin were surprised that the new track was on the back straight of the famous Charlotte Speedway and it was only 1/8 rather than 1/4 mile in length.

After the Springnationals, *Paper Tiger Too* was damaged at a race at Old Dominion Dragway in Manassas, Virginia. It was then decided to send the sedan to Dick Branstner's shop in Detroit to have the rear wheels moved forward, which shortened the wheelbase to 95 inches. Fate must have been with Ronnie because "Dyno Don" Nicholson (in his Comet) beat him in the first round, only to be reprieved when Nicholson was disqualified for being 28 pounds underweight.

Ronnie next outran Moline, Illinois, native Lee Smith in his 1965 Plymouth AWB hardtop at 6.23 seconds at 118.43 mph. Ronnie's first appearance at an eighth-mile track was successful. He won a large trophy and $1,300 of the $5,000 purse posted by the promoters. Nicholson fervently challenged the disqualification, but to no avail.

The First Super Stock Nationals

Many fans consider the most memorable event of 1965, and maybe ever, to be the *Super Stock* Magazine

Every member of the Sox & Martin team had an important job. Jake King took his responsibility for keeping the 426 Hemi working perfectly very seriously. Here, Jake works on the AWB Hemi hardtop at the 1965 Winternationals. (Photo Courtesy Jake King Collection)

Nationals at York US 30 Drag-O-Way in York, Pennsylvania, on August 7. With $5,000 cash plus equal amounts of merchandise awards up for grabs, the event was sure to draw the top cars in the country. At the time, no one could have known that this was the biggest single day of drag racing in the history of the sport up to that time. The official count of spectators through the gate was 21,650, but many more were turned away and countless others tried to storm the fences and blocked traffic for miles just to be part of the action.

The Classes

Five classes of competition ranged from the "Run What Ya Brung" Unlimited class to the 2,700-, 3,000-, 3,200-, and 3,400-pound weight classes. The Unlimited class had no weight or cubic-inch restrictions and was intended for cars with rear engines, blowers, or those running on fuel. This class included Mopars from Dick Landy, Al Eckstrand, Bob Harrop, Jim O'Conner, and Bud Faubel; all were running nitromethane mixtures.

The 2,700-pound class was essentially the same Funny Cars running on gasoline. Competitors included Ronnie Sox, Dave Strickler, Butch Leal, and Lee Smith driving AWB Mopars against two Chevelles and a Mustang. Lee Smith lost in the first round to Phil Bonner's Mustang and Dave Strickler put away both Chevelles with times of 9.97 seconds and 11.77, respectively. Ronnie Sox took the injected *Paper Tiger* AWB hardtop down for a solo run at 9.94, the low ET for the class. Dave Strickler knocked out Butch Leal for a Strickler-Sox final. Due to a couple of bad starts and the late hour, the final decision was made to halt it there and split the winnings.

The 3,000-pound class was made up of what were essentially AWB cars with added ballast, running on gasoline with carburetors or injection. This class included Bill Jenkins' *Black Arrow*, Sox & Martin's carbureted sedan (with the moved rear wheels), and Cecil Yother in the *Melrose Missile* Plymouth. A few OHC Mustangs and some others were also in the class. The final round saw Sox beat Billy McDuell's 1964 Comet with a 10.37-second ET at 131.96 mph.

Necessary Mods

As usual, the action for the fall season was highlighted by the 11th annual NHRA National Championship races (The Nationals) held at Indianapolis Raceway Park over the Labor Day weekend. With more than 1,200 entries, the 1965 Indy show was heavy with competition

Ronnie Sox usually took on the responsibility of spreading the resin dust traction compound at his many match races. This routine was an important part of the show. (Photo Courtesy Diane Sox)

The Jo Han Company was one of the first to produce a 1/25-scale plastic model kit of a Sox & Martin race car. Unfortunately, in this case they chose an incorrect Fury hardtop.

Chapter 2

"The Boss" and the "King" got together a number of times during the 1965 drag racing season when the 426 Hemi was banned on the long NASCAR tracks. They were almost neighbors back in North Carolina so the friendship was natural. (Photo Courtesy Diane Sox)

from Stock, Super Stock, Factory Experimental, and Funny Cars. Because many of the radically altered 1965 machines did not fit into any specific NHRA class, they were relegated to competing in fuel dragster, altered, and gas classes. Others, including Sox & Martin, chose (or were instructed) not to attend at all.

> **The weight of the big Belvederes could not compare to the lighter Mustangs and Comets showing up at races.**

Because no legal NHRA classes were offered for AWB cars, many previous exhibition match and Funny Car drivers showed up (or were advised by Chrysler to compete) at the Nationals with legal Super Stock sedans put together specifically for the meet. Three of the more prominent new Hemi Super Stock sedans were raced by Bob Harrop, Dave Strickler, and Butch Leal. Strickler borrowed his 1965 Coronet sedan from racer Bob Lawliss, who had purchased the car new from Grand Spaulding Dodge just for the engine. Strickler put the stripped shell into racing condition, installed a Hemi with a 4-speed, lettered it, ran it for this one weekend only, then returned it to Lawliss.

Butch Leal received his R01/A990 sedan from Dabbs Motor Company in Clarksville, Tennessee. The dealership had not been campaigning the car actively so Chrysler advised Leal to use it. Leal drove from Sox & Martin's shop in Burlington, North Carolina, to pick up the new car. He brought it back to their shop to have the preparations, paint work, and lettering finished in time for the Indy competition and the remainder of the season.

This was an excellent example of the Chrysler teams' cooperation. Although fierce competitors at the track, Leal worked out of the Sox & Martin shop from August to October 1965 before traveling back to California for the winter. Bob Harrop and his Dodge won the Super Stock final at Indy with an 11.39 at 126.05 mph.

Match Racer to Funny Car

Toward the end of the wild 1965 match racing season, Ronnie and Buddy decided that they had extracted all of the performance they could out of the two AWB Belvederes. The weight of the big Belvederes could not compare to the lighter Mustangs and Comets showing up at races. Buddy said, "We just don't want to spend the 1966 season chasing 2,000-pound fiberglass wonders. We knew we would have to come up with something lighter and faster than our quickest 1965 Plymouth. The lightest weight that AWB car ever ran was 2,600 pounds and our best ET with it was 9.54."

The team's winning 1965 AWB hardtop and sedan were sold to Buckeye Phillips and Vernon Rowley from Baltimore, Maryland. They continued to campaign both cars under the Buckeye & Vernon Racing Team name. The hardtop still ran with red and white livery, but the blue roof was repainted red.

Barracuda Alterations

Buddy and Ronnie came up with the answer to their match race dilemma by building a new Hemi-powered Barracuda and naming it *Baccaruda*. It was based on a 1966 Barracuda steel fastback body-in-white from Chrysler, minus doors, deck lid, front fenders, and glass. They lightened the body shell further by removing the inner body panels, fenderwells, cowl, and floor. Aluminum inner panels were formed into the body and used to replace stock floorpans, fenderwells, and firewall. The grille was molded fiberglass and both front and rear bumpers were aluminum that were molded into the body panels. Plexiglass replaced all of the glass.

Once the original steel floorpanels were removed from the body, the chassis was rebuilt and reinforced to receive the Hilborn fuel-injected 426 Hemi engine and 4-speed transmission. Both front and rear wheels were moved forward 8 inches but maintained the original 106-inch wheelbase. Because the new chassis was 4 inches too narrow to accept the lightweight stainless K-member used in the Belvederes, the stock front suspension was replaced with a straight tubular front axle and two-leaf longitudinal leaf springs on each side. Vertical tube-type shock absorbers provided the axle bounce control. No front brakes were used. The engine was moved back 10 inches from the stock location to improve weight distribution.

The rear suspension consisted of a standard leaf-spring setup and shock absorbers as well as the heavy-duty Dana 60 axle taken from the 1965 *Paper Tiger* Belvedere hardtop. The entire chassis side rails were integrated into the

Ronnie made it a policy to check the seating and steering wheel position of any car built in the Sox & Martin shop. Here, the 1966 Baccaruda *is being finished to compete against the match race cars of Mercury, Pontiac, and Chevrolet. It is already equipped with a Dana 60 rear axle. (Photo Courtesy Smyle Collection)*

roll cage; they added stiffness to the chassis and suspension. A rectangular channel was welded into the chassis side rails to provide a mounting point for the stock-type pinion snubber to control axle wind-up on acceleration.

When the metal work was finished, the car was painted and lettered in the familiar red, white, and blue livery. It featured the Gate City Motor Company name on the front fenders and Sox & Martin on the doors. A large painting of a silver barracuda fish was placed just below the Sox & Martin name.

Buddy Martin, Ronnie Sox, and Jake King check out the final assembly of the body on the 1966 Baccaruda *match race funny car. Its original construction featured a relatively stock wheelbase but it was extended later in the year to improve handling at speed. (Photo Courtesy Smyle Collection)*

An action rear view and portraits of Buddy and Ronnie appeared on their publicity materials for the 1966 Baccaruda. The parachute was needed to help stop the car at the end of the track. (Photo Courtesy Buddy Martin)

Chapter 2

The 1966 Baccaruda *was equipped with Hilborn fuel injection and Doug's Headers. Gate City Motor Company of Greensboro, North Carolina, continued as the sponsor. The silver Barracuda painted on the side was a bit of artistic decoration. (Photo Courtesy Buddy Martin)*

Testing and Fine-Tuning

The new *Baccaruda* was completed and ready for testing in early February 1966. Because of the deep snow common in North Carolina winters, to play it safe, Ronnie and Buddy hauled the car to Carlsbad Drag Strip in California for testing and adjustments. The plan was to make it to the Bakersfield and Long Beach meets early in the year for the new car's debut. With the 1965 hardtop recording a .750 match race win average and times in the 9-second range, they had no doubt that this new car would be more than competitive against the Fords and Mercurys.

The short wheelbase of the *Baccaruda* soon showed that wheelstands would be a constant detriment to winning races. Not long after the car's introduction, the front end was lengthened and the front wheels moved forward to improve the weight distribution. This also improved the car's handling. Ronnie's iconic 4-speed transmission was installed when the car was built, but it was found that the impact on the drivetrain and suspension was too much. A TorqueFlite soon replaced the 4-speed to make the car more manageable and reliable.

The car was eventually sorted out; by the end of the 1966 season, it won 70 out of 90 match races. Ronnie steered the car to a low ET of 8.74 seconds at 159 mph before the end of the season. Like the 1965 Belvedere, *Baccaruda* was sold to Buckeye & Vernon at the end of 1966. It was refinished in blue and white with blue tips on the injector tubes, which Buckeye & Vernon lengthened to work better with the TorqueFlite they used. When he was available, Ronnie sometimes drove the car during match races and exhibition shows.

NASCAR Winter Drag Championships

One example of Ronnie competing in the Buckeye & Vernon *Baccaruda* was the second annual NASCAR

Drag racing photographer Charles Milikin Jr. captured this shot of the 1966 Sox & Martin Baccaruda funny car. The wheelbase has been extended so this was later in the 1966 season. (Charles Milikin Jr. Photo)

Later in the season, the 1966 Baccaruda was equipped with wider aluminum rear wheels and wider racing slicks to handle the high power and lack of traction.

1965–1967 Chrysler Super Stock and Funny Cars

Usually, Buddy and Jake had to help push Baccaruda while Ronnie steered the car back to the pits. There were always some fans to help out. The long injection tubes indicate an automatic transmission at this time. (Photo Courtesy Dave Christie)

The Buckeye & Vernon team continued to race the ex–Sox & Martin 1965 Plymouth AWB Hemi sedan well into 1967. By the time of this picture, Vernon's name had been removed. (Alan Lewis Photo)

Winter Drag Championships. It was held at Deland, Florida, February 24–26, 1967, and run in conjunction with the Daytona Speedweeks. Racers and fans were hoping for a warm Florida weekend, but to their dismay, the temperature on Saturday night dropped to 26 degrees, bringing out bonfires and blankets.

Ronnie Sox made this a historic weekend, winning both the Handicap Eliminator and Heads-Up Eliminator, the first in a NASCAR Grand Stock circuit event.

The original 1965 Hemi sedan was delivered to Sox & Martin in March 1965. It was soon taken to Dick Branstner's shop near Detroit to have the rear wheels moved forward. Buckeye & Vernon raced the car after the 1965 season ended. (Alan Lewis Photo)

Ronnie started the weekend off a bit lower when he lost the Ultra Super Stock class to Dick Smith and his 1965 Hemi Plymouth Belvedere. Ronnie's 10.45 at 124.63 could not make up for Smith's winning 9.97 at 139.49. The Handicap Eliminator runoffs found Ronnie Sox defeating Dick Smith in the second round. He beat Silver Springs, Maryland, racer Chick DeNinno and his 1966 Dodge in the next round to advance to the final. The final round saw Sox beat Hubert Platt of Atlanta, Georgia, in the Paul Harvey Mustang at 9.97 seconds and 139.49 mph in the Buckeye & Vernon Barracuda.

When the time came for the Heads Up Eliminator, Ronnie beat defending champion Bill Lawton from Cranston, Rhode Island, with a 9.91 at 139.42 mph to Lawton's 10.01 at 141.73. In the finals, Sox ran a quick 9.86 at 145.10 mph against James Lake's 10.05 at 137.19.

Sox's efforts pushed the Dodge-Plymouth team to a 40 to 0 lead in the Manufacturer's Championship. The Sox & Martin team took home $2,600 in winnings for the weekend. Ronnie and Buddy also used this opportunity to present one of their early Supercar Performance Clinics at local dealers. Because the 1967 RO23 car probably was not ready, they may have used a modified standard production Belvedere or GTX for the program.

New Super Stock Package

Near the end of the 1966 season, it was clear to Chrysler that their drag racing support was not contributing to

Chapter 2

Supercar Clinic Program

The Chrysler Supercar Performance Clinics were a revolutionary new idea for 1967 and Sox & Martin and Dick Landy were instrumental in its development. The program was an opportunity for the drag racing teams to meet personally and up close with customers and enthusiasts at local dealer showrooms and racetracks. The clinics introduced the new high-performance vehicles to the public and allowed them to see how the professionals modified and used these cars to win races.

In 1967, one of the cars was equipped with a TorqueFlite transmission so that public relations people could drive a Super Stock car down the strip. A question-and-answer session was usually conducted in the dealer showroom. The clinics were presented by Dick Landy and Bill Tanner for Dodge and Don Grotheer, Ed Miller, and Sox & Martin for Plymouth from 1967 through 1970. John Petrie operated a similar program for Dodge in Canada.

The Sox & Martin 1967 Plymouth RO23 Hemi hardtop was displayed prominently at dealer showrooms during the Supercar Clinics. A stock 1968 Barracuda is alongside for contrast. A large banner advertised to the public that the team of Sox & Martin is in town. (Photo Courtesy Buddy Martin)

Linda Vaughn poses with Buddy and Ronnie to promote a Plymouth Supercar Clinic. The special large Plymouth brochure Linda is holding was available to attendees in the showroom during clinic presentations. (Photo Courtesy Buddy Martin)

Ronnie (right front) and Buddy (left front) pose with George Hurst (right rear) and their 1967 Plymouth Belvedere hardtop for a promotional photo in early 1967. This Plymouth is stock and has no hood scoop. (Photo Courtesy Buddy Martin)

Buddy Martin and Ronnie Sox give away one of their racing jackets to a woman attending one of their Supercar Clinics in 1967. Drawings and prizes were also part of the clinics in addition to performance information and race cars. (Photo Courtesy Buddy Martin)

the development and sales of cars to the public, which was, of course, the main point of their efforts. It was this situation at the end of the year that caused Bob Cahill, head of Drag Racing Programs, to call Buddy and Ronnie into his office in Detroit.

As Buddy put it in a later interview, "We sat down at his desk, he looked straight at both of us and said, 'We did not sell a single Barracuda Funny Car this year. If we are going to spend the money that we are spending, we want to spend it on something that represents what we are doing.'" Cahill made it clear that the company wanted to put its emphasis and money back into Stock and Super Stock classes that represented what the public was buying.

By early February 1967, production began on the new packages. The development had actually been held up for nearly a year. The original plan was for a new Super Stock package car to be available for the 1966 season. Frank Wylie of Dodge Public Relations sent out a press release in January 1966, announcing a Dodge Super Stock package. The document described a car based on the standard Coronet two-door sedan with fixed quarter windows and special L1T tan interior trim like that in the 1965 Hemi cars. The engine planned was a 12.5:1 compression ratio 426 Hemi with aluminum crossram intake manifold. The car was to be equipped with standard 15 x 6K wheels.

It is likely that a similar program was planned for Plymouth Division.

Although this would have been a competitive Super Stock car, it was a moot point as a letter dated late March 1966 announced the cancellation of the program. Reasons given were that production delays prevented the manufacture of the aluminum heads in time for the 1966 race season. This proposal and subsequent cancellation drew little notice from most drivers who were still more than competitive with their 1965 Hemi sedans and hardtops. Many had moved to the more profitable match racing circuits and avoided NHRA Stock and Super Stock altogether.

The NHRA did work to improve the racing competition for 1967 by creating the new Super Stock division with 10 classes of Super Stock from SS/A to SS/E and SS/AA to SS/EA. Super Stock entries were basically identical to Stock except that they could use any camshaft, any intake manifold of stock configuration, and any size tire that fit in the stock wheel opening of at least 7-inches wide and 1/16-inch tread depth. Factory Experimental was eliminated from NHRA competition for 1967.

Chapter 2

Other sanctioning bodies, including the American Hot Rod Association (AHRA), the National Association of Drag Strips (NADS), and the United Drag Racers' Association (UDRA), all had their own rules; most followed those similar to the NHRA. The AHRA used a weight to cubic-inch displacement formula in Stock classes and generally allowed more modifications to simplify classification.

Back to Stock

Planning for the 1967 Dodge and Plymouth drag package cars began early in 1966, but the initial order for the first 30 cars of each brand was not issued until January 18, 1967. Rather than the more radical Super Stock and FX cars of 1964 and 1965, the 1967 drag package was initially directed toward legal NHRA A/Stock class. This was later revised to B/Stock because of the class weight requirements. The cars ended up actually running in NHRA Super Stock/B class. The production date for the first 30 Coronets and 30 Belvederes was scheduled for Sunday, February 12, 1967, at the Lynch Road plant. An additional 25 units of each was scheduled to be built the same day. Once the cars were built, they were forwarded to a modification center for "specialized handling." To make the cars legal for NHRA Super Stock, they were given a special VIN and body identification number of RO23 (Belvedere) and WO23 (Coronet).

Body and Interior

The 1967 drag package cars were directed more toward product marketing than the earlier package cars, and they were built using a high-line two-door hardtop body rather than the lower-line sedan. The company was more interested in selling the more profitable Belvedere II and Coronet 440 hardtops than cheaper two-door sedans. The adage, "Win on Sunday, sell on Monday" was clearly the motivation.

The bodies were stock, except that all sound deadener and insulation was deleted. A lightweight steel scoop, similar to the one used on the 1965 Hemi Super Stock, was mounted on the hood, but the new scoop was flatter at the rear edge to match the new hood shape. An aluminum hood adapter assembly was furnished in the trunk and was used to replace the standard air cleaner. The trunk also housed the heavy-duty Super Stock battery mounted transversely in the right rear as it was in 1965.

The 1967 RO/WO cars were more standardized than the 1965 Hemi cars. They were available in only one model and body type, and in only one color. Every RO/WO hardtop was finished in WW1 white with a black vinyl or cloth and vinyl bench seat interior trim. All cars had the heater deleted. Each car had special order 7.75 x 15–inch black sidewall tires and body color 15 x 6JK steel wheels with the hubcaps deleted.

Transmission

The rear axle and suspension were essentially standard Street Hemi equipment with heavy-duty leaf springs and shock absorbers along with a Sure-Grip differential. The TorqueFlite-equipped cars used a Chrysler 8.75-inch ring gear with standard 4.86:1 gears; the 4-speed cars (like the ones Ronnie Sox drove) used a 9.75-inch Dana

Three Sox & Martin Hemi-powered race cars are displayed at an outdoor Chrysler/Plymouth exhibit prior to the road races at Riverside, California, in early 1968. (Alex Gabbard Photo, Courtesy John Mahoney)

Team Sox & Martin brought a pair of GTXs to Minnesota Dragways to compete in SS/B and SS/E. As you can see here, the SS/B car (nearest) has a hole cut in the underside of the hood for carburetor clearance; the SS/E car's hood remains unaltered. (John Foster Jr. Photo)

60 unit with 4.88:1 gears. Brakes were 11-inch drums on the rear and 10-inch drums on the front, replacing the standard disc brakes. Both transmissions used in the 1967 drag package were special race units. The A-727 TorqueFlite had the manual-shift reverse-pattern modifications first used in 1964. It used heavy-duty friction materials for the front clutch and kickdown bands and was designed for 7,000-rpm shifts. The transmission was operated with a standard column-shift but the quadrant was not changed as it had been in 1965.

When a 4-speed manual transmission was ordered, the drag package cars were equipped with a 2.66:1 low-gear Chrysler cast-iron case A-833 that was modified to Slick Shift specifications. This modification involved removing the synchronizers and machining every other tooth off the engagement gears. This modification made normal street driving difficult but full-power shifts were much easier.

An 11-inch high-strength pressure plate and high-burst speed disc were used with a heavy-duty torque shaft. A special steel flywheel was built for these engines by experienced Super Stock driver and builder "Akron Arlen" Vanke and his father in their RC Industries shop in Ohio. An NHRA-approved cast-steel RC426 flywheel housing was standard. A special short (12-inch) handle DP-FX-65 Hurst Competition Plus shifter with reverse Loc-Out was mounted on a special steel remote mounting bracket that moved the shifter back and up from the stock position through the modified shifter hump in the floor.

> **The most significant improvement to the engine used in the RO/WO package was the intake manifold.**

Hemi Engine

The heart of the 1967 SS/B package was, of course, the underrated 425-hp 426 Hemi engine. The Hemi was essentially a stock A-102 Street Hemi with a cast-iron block and heads. All internal components were identical to those used on the standard Street Hemi, including the 10.25:1 compression ratio pistons. The camshaft was the standard solid lifter Street Hemi design with .467-inch lift (intake), .473-inch lift (exhaust), 276-degree duration, with a 74-degree overlap.

The most significant improvement to the engine used in the RO/WO package was the intake manifold. Although the basic manifold was a standard aluminum Street Hemi inline dual 4-barrel unit, it was modified

Chapter 2

extensively by fellow Plymouth racer Arlen Vanke and performance tuner Bill Stiles.

The dividing walls were removed from the plenum and front carburetor flange and partially removed from the rear. The primary bores were increased to 1.6875 inches. A small dam was welded in the rear plenum. The intake ports were machined to match the head intake ports. The manifold was designed to use two Carter AFB carburetors with a model 4139 in the front and a 4140 in the rear. Different primary clusters, needle, and seat, and accelerator pump clusters and jets were required to modify the carburetors.

This manifold showed a loss of torque below 3,000 rpm, but from 3,000 to 7,000 rpm there was a significant gain of torque and about 20 extra hp.

When delivered, the Hemi was equipped with the standard cast-iron Street Hemi exhaust manifold and 2.25-inch-diameter exhaust system with dual mufflers and tailpipes. However, a set of headers was included in the trunk.

The ignition system was enhanced by the same Prestolite transistorized system used on the 1965 Hemi Super Stock sedans. The finned black heat sink box was mounted horizontally in the center of the inside of the firewall for 1967. The special wire harness exited through the upper passenger side of the firewall in the engine compartment.

Of course, the Sox & Martin team put their own touches to the car, improving whatever could be improved upon within the confines of the rules.

His helmet is in place and Ronnie Sox is ready to go with the new 1967 Plymouth Super Stock/D hardtop. The interior trim says this is a GTX, but the chrome body molding says this is a Belvedere II, most likely an RO23.

1967 Racing Events

The team brought the 1967 RO23 Plymouth, the 1967 GTX 440 delivered in November 1966, and the 1967 Hemi GTX delivered in December 1966 to the 1967 Winternationals. Ronnie won the SS/E class at the Winternationals with an 11.95 ET.

Ronnie continued to drive the Buckeye & Vernon 1966 *Baccaruda* at the Florida NASCAR meet in late February.

The Sox & Martin 1967 Plymouth RO23 Hemi hardtop. This Plymouth is equipped with the chrome Keystone wheels for which Sox & Martin were well known.

With its red, white, and blue finish, Keystone wheels, blue-tinted headlights, and silver lettering, this 1967 RO23 Hemi Plymouth is an iconic representation of what was Sox & Martin Racing.

1965–1967 Chrysler Super Stock and Funny Cars

NHRA Springnationals

The first important meet to see the new 1967 cars run was the third annual NHRA Springnationals at Bristol, Tennessee, June 8–11. Ford Motor Company was on hand in strength with 14 Fairlanes. Chevrolet's contingent included Bill Jenkins' Camaro. Chrysler brought its big guns with Dick Landy, Jere Stahl, Arlen Vanke, Ron Mancini, and of course, Sox & Martin.

By this time Buddy had received the new RO23 Hemi Plymouth through Gate City Motors in Greensboro and had it prepared to race. The Mopar drivers knew that Ford didn't have enough to beat them for this event and their only concern was to not break out of their ET bracket.

Landy was out of the running by Saturday but hung around through Sunday to watch the rest of the event. Ronnie Sox made it through five rounds, including beating Bill Jenkins' big-block 396-powered SS/C Camaro to win the Super Stock title in his Hemi Plymouth RO23 SS/B Belvedere, *The Boss*. The winning time was 11.34 at 123.45 mph. Sox also won SS/E in the 1967 GTX 440.

Daytona 500

Although the primary 1967 Belvedere hardtop was an actual RO23 Hemi, the other two or three cars were either a stock Belvedere II 383 hardtop or a stock GTX prepared for drag racing. At least one early photo of the cars performing a parade lap at the 1967 Daytona 500 race shows two Belvederes side by side with standard hoods and no scoops. One of these two or three additional cars was a standard Plymouth RS23 GTX with a scheduled build date of September 15, 1966, so it was probably delivered to the team much earlier than the later built RO23.

Because this GTX was pulled from regular stock on the lines, there was no opportunity to select any of its details, so the car was built as a QQ1 Dark Red Metallic with a red and white interior trim. It was originally equipped with a standard 440-ci wedge engine and a single 4-barrel carburetor attached to a 3-speed TorqueFlite transmission. However, the engine and transmission were replaced with a 426 Hemi and a 4-speed so the car could run in SS/D class.

> "The Mopar drivers knew that Ford didn't have enough to beat them for this event and their only concern was to not break out of their ET bracket."

Super Stock Nationals

The next important event for 1967 was the popular *Super Stock* Nationals, presented by *Super Stock & Drag Illustrated* magazine. This year's event was held June 23–25 at Cecil County Dragway in Maryland, a favorite track of many East Coast racers.

These two 1967 Plymouths circled the track at Daytona for the 1967 running of the Daytona 500 NASCAR race. The cars were painted almost identically but neither one had any type of hood scoop at this time. The 1967 RO23 was not yet produced when this photo was taken. (Photo Courtesy Buddy Martin)

Chapter 2

GTX Lookalikes

Both the Dick Landy and Sox & Martin teams fielded three and sometimes, four 1967 B-Body racers in 1967 in SS/B, SS/D and SS/E. The Sox & Martin Plymouths were all finished with painted GTX badges on the rear quarters and although only one was apparently a "real" GTX, others may have had GTX rear deck panels, gas filler caps, hood badges, and rear-seat logos.

The actual RO23 and Belvedere II Plymouths can be identified easily by the chrome trim moldings on the upper fender line which a real GTX did not have, although even this detail could have been added at some point simply for appearance.

Chrysler wanted to emphasize the High, Premium, or Sport lines of cars for marketing rather than a less expensive Belvedere. This was a clear indication of the importance placed on the value to the company of Super Stock drag racing.

Ronnie leans forward in the GTX, possibly gathering momentum between shifts. This image is from Aquasco Speedway, the first quarter-mile dragstrip on the East Coast. (Alan Lewis Photo)

This 1967 Super Stock/D Plymouth hardtop is identified on the quarter panel as a GTX but the upper body molding shows it to actually be a Belvedere II. Chrysler/Plymouth wanted to promote the premium sport GTX model so all of the drag race cars were lettered this way. (Mike Galewski Photo)

A big controversy ensued this year over the handicap system, which made for some strange times being turned in among qualifying, class run-offs, and eliminator matches. NHRA class rules applied but the eliminator handicaps were determined by averaging the ETs of the cars qualified for each class. There were no ET breakout limits in Super Stock.

The Mopar Performance Clinic teams of Dick Landy and Sox & Martin were in attendance, filling up four of the five SS/B and SS/EA entries. Butch Leal and Lee Smith were chosen to drive two of the three Sox & Martin 1967 Plymouths.

Ronnie Sox started the event by shaking up the Mopar factory representatives with a class win of 11.86 against Dick Landy's 12.08 followed by an accidental pre-final run of 11.43 against Jerry Gross. Sox lost the final race to Dick Arons running an 11.02 at 125.87 mph in his SS/B car against Arons' SS/EA Camaro at 11.63 and 118.60 mph. Arons had won his class running 12.62, an indication of the sandbagging involved.

The meet had a somewhat low spectator attendance at 17,000 but was otherwise considered successful.

One of the Sox & Martin 1967 Plymouth Hemi Belvedere hardtops is displayed at a car show in the Midwest. This is the Super Stock/D car owned by John Mahoney in Kansas. (Mike Galewski Photo)

NHRA Nationals

The NHRA Nationals at Indianapolis on Labor Day weekend was the biggest and most important event of the year. The Mopar domination of Super Stock was becoming a thorn in the side of the competition and they were beginning to fight back. Hubert Platt had a new 3,320-pound 427 Fairlane running 10.96, while Bill Jenkins 396 Camaro was running 11.45.

The NHRA finally made an attempt to put a stop to the dangerous neutral starts, a practice of punching low-gear from neutral at high RPM. Chrysler Corporation was prepared for any contingency; it brought a truckload of TorqueFlites built especially to hold up to the practice. Ronnie Sox beat Iowan Gary Ostrich for the SS/E class win and turned in the low ET in SS/B with an 11.08. Super Stock Eliminator was eventually won by Jenkins and his Camaro with an 11.55 ET at 115 mph.

In addition to winning the Super Stock class at the NHRA Springnationals and NHRA Nationals, the Supercar Clinic program had grown significantly and had become an important part of the Sox & Martin team's income. The success of the clinics allowed Sox & Martin to improve and grow in other areas and set them on the road to becoming a household name in drag racing. The move back to stock classes also proved to be profitable for Chrysler and Plymouth.

The 1967 and 1968 Sox & Martin Hemi cars are shown side by side at a Midwest car show. Both of these cars are owned by Clark and Colleen Rand of Fair Grove, Missouri. (Mike Galewski Photo)

1968–1969
Super Stock Domination

The Sox & Martin Supercar Performance Clinic team always arrived at the dealer in this impressive custom-built Dodge D700 hauler. Another car was hauled behind on an open trailer. (Photo Courtesy Buddy Martin)

Chrysler began development of the new 1968 package cars late in 1967 but they were not available in the field until early 1968. Ronnie and Buddy continued to run the four 1967 Belvederes in Super Stock. They also continued with the very popular Supercar Clinic Programs prior to the race events.

CHAPTER 3

These clinics always attracted a crowd of fans and enthusiasts and there is no doubt that sales of new cars and parts were a result of their efforts and professionalism.

The Importance of Team Image

The Sox & Martin team was already well-known for their neat appearance and clean, attractive uniforms, sometimes with white pants and shoes. If anyone's uniform or hands became dirty for any reason, they immediately cleaned themselves and changed clothes as soon as possible. The trucks, trailers, and every part of the race cars were washed and polished at every opportunity. Ronnie was also seen, at times, washing the frame and undercarriage of a car or truck.

All of this attention to appearance was Buddy's idea and served to put them above the rest of the pack. Other important team members included Danny Graves who took care of parts, Mark Graves who later worked with Bird Schoffner, and of course, the women in the front office. Buddy even refused to hire anyone who smoked because that was not a proper clean image for his professional team. Buddy still says he was lucky and blessed to have such fine people and that many of them remain great friends today.

The group of Plymouth Supercar Performance Clinic participants and drivers met at Chrysler headquarters in Detroit to talk about the goals and operations of the program. This group consisted of (front row, left to right): Wiley Cossey, Ed Miller, and Coordinator Dave Koffel, and (back row, left to right): Don Grotheer, Buddy Martin, Ronnie Sox, and Arlen Vanke.

Buddy and Ronnie were always dressed in clean, bright, neat uniforms at the racetrack and at all public appearances. Buddy knew from the beginning that good appearance meant that they would be remembered positively later and it presented a good image for the public. (Photo Courtesy Buddy Martin)

Chapter 3

Plymouth Drag Race Game

Chrysler continued to add new materials to their marketing efforts, taking advantage of every opportunity to use the racing success and image of Sox & Martin racing. Chrysler directed promotional and marketing materials to every demographic group. In late 1967 or the beginning of 1968, one of the new products was a board game. The game was based on drag racing and was called the Plymouth Drag Race Game.

The game was distributed by J. Day Co. in Hollywood; it came in a well-designed and colorful 9⅞ x 18¾–inch box with a Sox & Martin Plymouth GTX on the lid. It contained a heavy game board that folded horizontally and even featured game cards with the front of a Barracuda in red and white. Material inside told about Sox & Martin, drag racing, and the Performance Clinic program.

A black-and-white publicity photo was published around the same time showing Ronnie and Buddy playing the game.

A popular promotional item for 1968 was the Plymouth Drag Race Game. The 1968 Sox & Martin Hemi GTX was a sure way to attract interest to the game and to Plymouth. This example is part of John Mahoney's memorabilia collection.

Buddy and Ronnie found time between their race dates and clinics to try out the new Plymouth Drag Race board game. This was a great way to attract young people and families to Plymouth through racing. (Photo Courtesy Buddy Martin)

It was around this time that Tom Richardson came on board at Sox & Martin. Tom was Public Relations Director for Hurst and worked out of its Warminster, Pennsylvania, headquarters. Tom met Buddy and Ronnie at races and, like many others, they frequently used the Hurst facility at Warminster to work on their cars. Tom was soon invited to join the Sox & Martin team and moved to Burlington.

Tom remembers the Sox & Martin shop as a small, one-stall setup with only a pay phone for communication. He had to stand outside the shop to talk and avoid the hectic sounds of work in the garage.

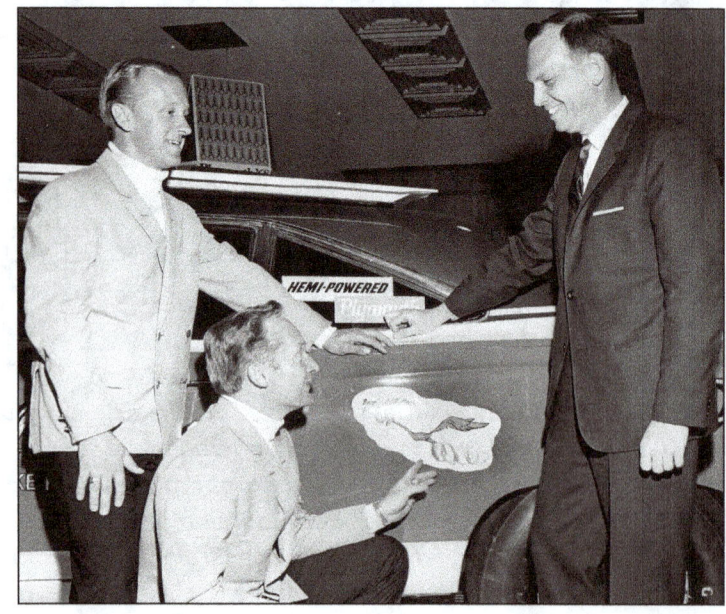

Buddy Martin points out the distinctive Road Runner decal on the side of the 1968 Plymouth Road Runner race car during a dealer supported clinic program. (Photo Courtesy Buddy Martin)

This poster was used to announce the upcoming Plymouth Supercar Performance clinics at Plymouth dealers. Copies were issued by Plymouth Division and posted around towns to be sure that everyone knew about the coming event and Sox & Martin. (Photo Courtesy John Mahoney)

This Supercar Clinic poster announcing the appearance of Sox & Martin and their cars at the local Plymouth dealer was sure to draw crowds. The design is similar to the colorful psychedelic paintings done by artist Peter Max at the time. (Photo Courtesy John Mahoney)

Tom was immediately put in charge of all Sox & Martin public relations requirements and directed the clinic program. To promote and schedule the clinics, Tom traveled for weeks at a time to locations in the United States and Canada. He coordinated with dealers and arranged advertising for the clinics. Tom's work eventually put the Sox & Martin team on the cover of every motorsports publication in the country.

Clinic Popularity

The Chrysler Clinic Program had been successful during 1967 so the program head, Jerry Gross, increased its exposure for 1968. The two teams, Sox & Martin and Dick Landy, were unable to cover all of the dealers so it was decided to increase the number of teams so there was one for each region. The team members were Chrysler racers who were already campaigning in their chosen area and had proven their ability.

Each team was set up with a set of color slides or films showing the Sox & Martin Plymouth or Dick Landy Dodge team conducting a clinic. The slides gave hints on tuning, chassis setup, etc.; the teams could add their own observations and answer questions. For example, Don Grotheer conducted the clinics in his area around Oklahoma City.

The start of the clinic program was slow at the beginning of 1967 because the dealers had to put up their own money for the advance advertising program. They also had to empty their showroom for a couple of days to allow setup of clinic materials and then the actual conducting of the clinic. The chosen dealer in any particular region was the one who promised to do the most advertising.

Chapter 3

Each of the 1968 Dodge and Plymouth Performance Clinic teams had its own special brochure that was made available to the public at the clinics. The brochure explained the purpose of the program and told about Sox & Martin. It also included some printed performance tips.

An additional color brochure was available at the participating dealer to promote Plymouth cars and products. It included technical information on the performance parts and packages and included photos of Sox & Martin race cars.

Anytime Buddy and Ronnie posed with the race car everyone focused their eyes and attention on them. Here the pair is next to the 1968 Hemi Barracuda at the track. (Photo Courtesy Dave Christie)

Buddy talks to another group of clinic attendees with two of the Sox & Martin race cars in a dealer showroom. Two of the young men are reading copies of the February 1968 issue of Hot Rod containing a feature on the Road Runner. (Photo Courtesy Buddy Martin)

1968–1969 Super Stock Domination

This is the view that Buddy and Ronnie may have had while they were addressing a group at a Supercar Performance Clinic at a dealer showroom. The 1968 Hemi Barracuda was displayed in the center of the room with the hood on the roof so that everyone could see the car and its engine. (Photo Courtesy Buddy Martin)

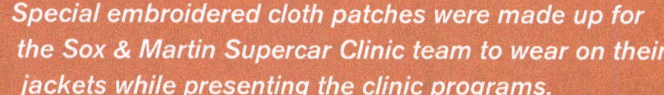

Special embroidered cloth patches were made up for the Sox & Martin Supercar Clinic team to wear on their jackets while presenting the clinic programs.

An attentive and interested group of high school–age young men in front of a Sox & Martin 1967 Belvedere listen to Ronnie and Buddy talk about increasing the performance of their cars. Crowds such as this filled Plymouth dealer showrooms around the country. (Photo Courtesy Buddy Martin)

SOX & MARTIN   53

Chapter 3

This 1968 Barracuda is equipped with a 340-ci engine and competed in the E/Stock Automatic class. It was driven from North Carolina to the West Coast for the race. (Photo Courtesy Buddy Martin)

Later in the year this changed because of reports of as many as 1,000 enthusiasts in attendance. In addition, an increase in used and new car sales convinced the dealers that this was profitable. By the end of the year, the only drawback was that there were not enough teams to conduct the clinics for the dealers who wanted them. The 1968 and 1969 program solved that problem.

1968 Drag Racing Season

The 1968 season cemented Sox & Martin into drag racing history. The iconic 1968 Hemi Barracuda went to event after event, and was the vehicle of recognition when recounting their former years.

The Winternationals

As always, the NHRA Winternationals at Pomona was the premier NHRA drag racing event and was the season opener. The 1968 Winternationals took place on February 2–4, 1968, at Pomona, California. Sox & Martin brought their 1967 Belvedere RO23, 1967 Hemi GTX, and 1968 440 GTX Plymouths all the way from North Carolina and, of course, presented their Supercar Performance Clinics at local dealers before the race weekend. They had planned to bring a 1968 Road Runner 383 to the meet to run in Stock class. However, they were not able to get it to run better than 13.12 at 106 mph so they decided to leave it in North Carolina.

In addition to the B-Body cars, a member of the Sox & Martin team drove the stock 1968 Barracuda 340 Formula S to the West Coast, towing a U-Haul parts trailer. The Barracuda was prepared; the heater was removed and headers were installed in California by Jake King and driven by *Hot Rod* magazine editor Jim McFarland. The Barracuda won E/SA defeating "Smoky Joe" Coletti in his Barracuda 340 in the class final and was runner-up for Stock eliminator. Public relations man Tom Richardson drove the car back to Burlington after the race.

The Dodge and Plymouth brigade carried the show in many of the stock classes. Ronnie Sox won SS/D in a 1967

This 1968 Plymouth GTX is running in Super Stock/E class and is equipped with the standard GTX hood. The fender-well headers indicate that it is equipped with the 440-ci RB V-8 engine. (Photo Courtesy Buddy Martin)

The 1968 440-powered GTX gets out to a lead against what looks to be a 1965 Hemi Dodge in the far lane at Union Grove/Great Lakes Dragway, Wisconsin. (Photo Courtesy Mark and Laura Bruederle)

1968–1969 Super Stock Domination

This 1968 Plymouth Road Runner is being tested early in the season and is still equipped with the stock Road Runner hood. Like most Sox & Martin cars of this era, it is equipped with Keystone chrome-spoke wheels. (Photo Courtesy Buddy Martin)

Plymouth at 11.12 seconds and 106.76 mph and SS/F in a 1968 Plymouth 440 GTX at 12.17 seconds and 105.01 mph. The speeds were low compared to the ETs; this is an indication of some slow-down at the traps. Sox & Martin's 1968 E/SA 340 Barracuda, driven by Jim McFarland, took runner-up in Super Stock Eliminator on Sunday.

Two Road Runners and a Barracuda

At around the same time, the AHRA Winter Championships were held at Lions Drag Strip in Long Beach, California, on February 24 and 25. The Super Stock Eliminator runoffs were dominated by the big Mopars of Dick Landy and Sox & Martin, with fiberglass front ends and the back seats removed for AHRA competition. Ronnie Sox, in the 1968 Road Runner, red-lighted in the final and Landy rode to the win at 10.49 seconds. By this time, they had both a 440-powered SS/E 1968 Road Runner and a Hemi-powered SS/B 1968 Road Runner coupe. Of course, both were equipped with 4-speeds.

The 1968 Road Runner SS/B car was built by the team especially for the 1968 winter AHRA event and was designed with a lightweight fiberglass front end. The engine was a 426 Hemi with 12.5:1 compression ratio and 1965 aluminum cylinder heads. The Road Runner's weight was pared down to 3,400 pounds from about 3,589 and Ronnie was able to make runs in the 10.80s.

Ronnie and Buddy barely had time to make it back to Burlington to prepare for a performance clinic and an exhibition at the New York Auto Show held on March 30. The first scheduled build date for the new 1968 Hemi Barracudas was February 23 but an unplanned strike at the Hamtramck Plant (where the base cars were built) caused changes and a split in production schedules.

Other than the racing slicks and deep oil pan, this 1968 Plymouth Road Runner appears essentially stock. It could be equipped with either a 383 V-8 or a 426 Hemi. (Photo Courtesy Buddy Martin)

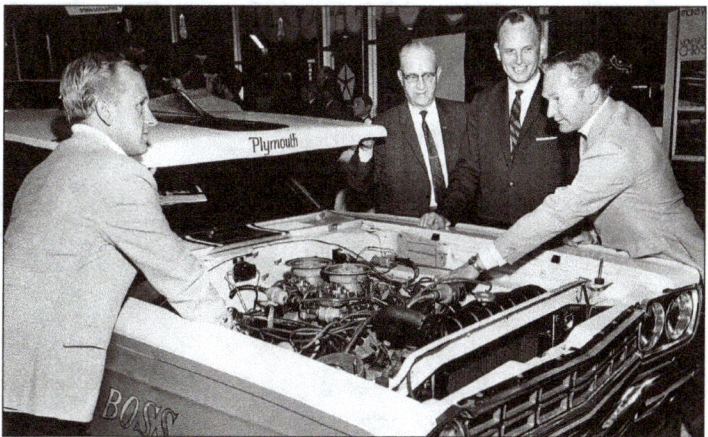

Buddy and Ronnie point out the features of their 426 Hemi-powered 1968 Plymouth Road Runner to officers of a dealership where they were conducting a Supercar Performance Clinic. The Plymouth has been modified with a cool can, tachometer drive, and high-performance plug wires for racing. (Photo Courtesy Buddy Martin)

Chapter 3

Only the fastback version of the 1968 Barracuda was used for the BO29 Hemi Super Stock package. The car was delivered to owners in gray primer and black gelcoat. This 4-speed car is equipped with a Dana 60 heavy-duty rear axle.

This 1968 Hemi Barracuda is owned by Clark and Coleen Rand and is restored to exactly as it looked for the 1969 World Championship race. The Keystone chrome wheels were a Sox & Martin trademark.

The 1968 Hemi Barracuda Super Stock package cars were delivered with lift-off fiberglass hood and front fenders. The large fiberglass scoop was molded integrally with the hood.

A side view of the 1968 Hemi Barracuda shows the arch of the special Super Stock rear springs and the height of the hood scoop. The decals identified sponsors who provided parts and funds to operate the race team throughout the season.

1968–1969 Super Stock Domination

The trunk of the Sox & Martin 1968 Hemi Barracuda was used to carry the heavy-duty battery mounted to the rear passenger's side of the floor with a steel plate and white plastic tray. The rear roll bar supports were welded to the rear floorpan for strength.

A Jake King–built 426 Hemi can always be identified by its Ford Blue engine paint rather than the more familiar Hemi orange. This restored engine is finished exactly like the original with cast-iron cylinder heads and cross-ram intake manifold.

The original stock Barracuda front seats were replaced with these lightweight Bostrom companion seats covered in black vinyl and mounted on aluminum brackets. The 4-speed shifter is a Hurst Competition Plus unit with reverse Loc-Out.

Most owners had to drive to Detroit and pick up their cars when they were ready. But some of the factory-supported teams received their cars earlier and sometimes in unfinished condition to allow them to be completed for special events or shows. The first Sox & Martin 1968 Hemi Barracuda was such an example.

The car was delivered directly from the Hamtramck assembly plant to the Sox & Martin shop in Burlington in primer without its engine or transmission. The rear axle, front brakes, and suspension had not been changed and the interior was not finished. The seat brackets were sent with the car and actually came in a mixed-up set with three lefts and one right.

The team included Ronnie Sox, Buddy Martin, Jake King, Levi Hester, Red Gibson (paintwork), and Carl Clayton. The car had to be completed in time for the show in New York and they had about 72 hours to put the car in shape. The story of the build was a feature in the June 1968 issue of *Super Stock and Drag Illustrated* and the Sox & Martin Barracuda was the cover car.

The A-Body Terror

In a five-page letter to dealers issued February 20, 1968, the new Hemi-powered Barracuda and Dart Hemi Super Stock packages were announced. The cars were based on the new A-Body designs first created for the 1967

Chapter 3

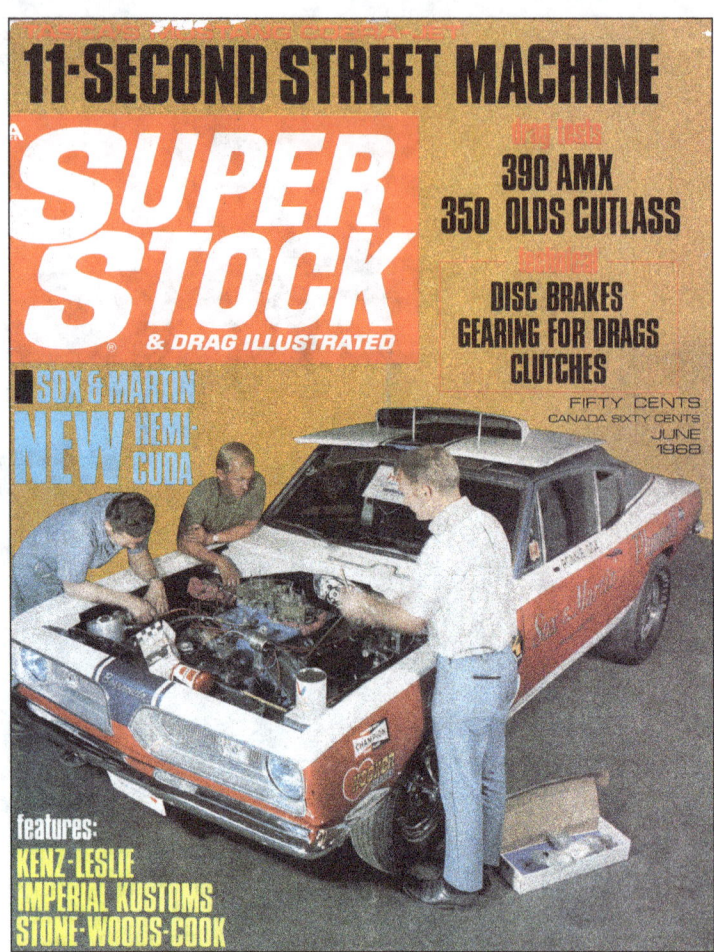

The June 1968 issue of Super Stock and Drag Illustrated featured the newly delivered 1968 Sox & Martin Hemi Barracuda. The story told in words and pictures how the car was received and completed in 72 hours for a New York Auto Show display.

The paint and striping variation differentiate this Super Stock/B Hemi Barracuda from the previous version. It appears to be racing at Union Grove Drag Strip in Wisconsin.

> " The lift-off hood had no hinges and was secured with four chrome-plated pins and clips. "

model year, and were available in March. They weighed approximately 3,000 pounds and met the specifications of sanctioning bodies including the NHRA. The cars had been developed under the direction of Dick Maxwell and Bob Cahill and engineering work was accomplished by Robert Tarozzi in Special Vehicle Engineering.

The first car, a 1967 Barracuda, was ready for testing in January 1968 and taken to Irwindale Raceway in California. Tests proved that the car was clearly capable of mid- to high-10-second times. It was a surprise to some drivers, including Ronnie Sox, that the design worked well with both manual transmission– and TorqueFlite-equipped cars.

As with the 1967 drag packages, the cars were given their own VIN with an "O" code for Super Stock to be sure they were accepted as factory stock cars. The VIN began with LO23 for the Dart and BO29 for the Barracuda. (The Barracuda was based on the standard Barracuda S two-door fastback sport hardtop.) The NHRA class homologation requirements had been reduced for 1968, so 80 Darts and 70 Barracudas were built. All 1968 Hemi Super Stock cars were assembled with basic components at the Hamtramck assembly plant with a 383 4-barrel engine. However, the Hemi installation and final assembly was performed at the Hurst Performance facility in a rented warehouse near Hazel Park, Michigan. The completed cars were transported back to the U-drive storage lot near the Chrysler Lynch Road plant for delivery to customers or for shipping to dealers.

Post-Build Mods

The 1968 Super Stock packages were built with the idea that racers would finish the cars in their own paint and lettering scheme, so they were delivered with the entire body in light gray primer with the front fenders and hood in flat-black gel-coat fiberglass. The lift-off hood had no hinges and was secured with four chrome-plated pins and clips. The doors and front bumper were lightweight .024-inch-thick chemically milled steel. The doorjambs, inner front fender panels, and engine compartment (including the firewall) were painted gloss black. The right inner fenderwells were modified to clear the wide Hemi engine.

The interior panels of the 1968 Hemi drag cars were stock Barracuda black vinyl with the rear seat deleted and replaced with a black, grained cardboard panel. The standard front bench seat was replaced with a pair of Bostrom Companion seats similar to those used in the 1965 Hemi sedans except they were covered in black vinyl. The seats were mounted on lightened, welded-aluminum brackets similar to those on the 1965 seats, but these were unpainted.

The rear quarter windows were stationary and made of .080-inch-thick Corning Chem-Cor tempered glass. The door glass was also made of .080-inch tempered glass and operated with a seatbelt-type black woven nylon strap that attached to a snap at the bottom of the inside door frame when the glass was in the up position. The black plastic instrument panel was stock but had standard plastic block-off plates to cover the deleted standard heater and unused optional radio opening.

The rear axle for the Sox & Martin 4-speed Barracuda was a narrowed Dana Spicer 60 with 4.88:1 gears and a Sure-Grip differential. The front brakes were disc and the rear brakes were standard drum units. The brake master cylinder was moved to the left with a special machined offset aluminum mounting bracket to provide more engine clearance.

The 4-speed transmission was the standard cast-iron-case A-833 used since 1964, but it had the shift-improving Slick Shift modifications first used on the 1967 Hemi package cars. The 4-speed was accompanied by the steel clutch housing and special heavy-duty 10.5-inch clutch disc and flywheel. The special floor shifter unit was a Hurst Competition Plus unit with a short 12-inch chrome-plated flat handle, reverse Loc-Out lever, and black pleated rubber boot.

The heart of the 1968 Super Stock package was the A-102 426 Hemi engine. The Hemi was basically a standard Street Hemi block with cast-iron cylinder heads and black crackle-finish rocker arm covers, but the pistons provided a 12.5:1 compression ratio like the previous drag-package cars. The aluminum dual 4-barrel crossram intake manifold was identical to that used on the 1964 Hemi although some 1968 Hemi A-Body cars were equipped with the 1965 Magnesium manifold. The carburetors were Holley 4150 (List 4235/4236) 4-barrels with 1.6875-inch bores topped with unsilenced air cleaners. The supplied camshaft was a standard 1968 Street Hemi solid lifter unit because engineers knew that racers would change it for a competition version anyway.

The Hemi engine was enhanced by a high-capacity oil pump, deep-groove drive pulleys, an aluminum seven-blade fan with viscous drive, and a heavy-duty radiator. The exhaust was handled by competition Hooker headers and two straight exhaust pipes with small, round, glass-pack mufflers that exited down and under the car in front of the rear axle. The dual-point distributor worked in conjunction with a Prestolite transistor ignition box similar to that used in the 1964, 1965, and 1967 drag cars, but the 1968 finned aluminum heat sink box was blue rather than black. The ignition system included a light blue coil.

A pair of 1968 Barracudas do battle at Great Lakes Dragway in 1968. No 1968 coupes were available with the 426 Hemi. (Photo Courtesy Mark and Laura Bruederle)

Chapter 3

Springnationals

One of the first major meets for the Sox & Martin A-Body Hemi Barracudas was the AHRA Spring Nationals held at Bristol Dragway in May. This was the first AHRA meet held at Bristol. Ronnie won Super Stock Heads-Up Eliminator and Super Stock Handicap Eliminator at this event. The AHRA Heads-Up Eliminator class was the forerunner to Pro-Stock, which followed in 1970. The fans and the racers liked this kind of racing because it brought the sport back to where it started.

One of the Sox & Martin Hemi Barracudas in action. This one is competing in the Super Stock/B class at the 1968 Springnationals. The NHRA competition number (784) on the quarter windows helps to identify the car. (Photo Courtesy Diane Sox)

Buddy Martin, Ronnie Sox, and Jake King pose proudly in front of the huge trophy that they won at the 1968 AHRA Spring Nationals. This 1968 Hemi Barracuda has blue stripes on the scoop lettered with "Hemi 426." (Photo Courtesy Jake King Collection)

Buddy Martin points out the Champion Spark Plug decal on the front of the 1968 Hemi Barracuda. Champion was just one of the important sponsors that helped them win the 1968 AHRA Winter Nationals. (Photo Courtesy Buddy Martin)

Buddy, Ronnie, and Jake have beautiful company at the 1968 AHRA Winter Nationals winner's circle. On the left is Miss Bristol International Dragway, center is Miss Spring Nationals, and on the right is Miss AHRA. (Photo Courtesy Buddy Martin)

Sox & Martin unloaded nearly 0.60 faster than the national record at the Springnationals in Englishtown. Ed Hedrick had driving duties with the Nova that weekend while Grumpy concentrated on his Camaro. (Alan Lewis Photo)

NHRA Springnationals

The next major meet was the 1968 NHRA Springnationals at Englishtown, New Jersey, on June 14–16. As with all national events in 1969, Sox & Matin conducted a Supercar Performance Clinic at a local dealer prior to each race. The team took four cars to the event, eventually winning SS/B in a new Hemi Barracuda and SS/D in a 1967 Hemi GTX. Ronnie also took Super Stock Eliminator in the Hemi GTX at 11.20 ET. Ronnie drove the Hemi Barracuda to top qualifier spot with a 10.49 ET. He then won SS/B with a 10.52 ET at 131.19 mph against Arlen Vanke's Hemi Barracuda. Unfortunately, in the second round of Super Stock Eliminator against Hubert Platt's black and silver SS/E 428 Cobra Jet Mustang, Ronnie came off the line hard enough to tear out the screws that held the left rear slick to the rim and had to shut down and coast off the track.

Herb McCandless drove the SS/D 1967 GTX Hemi, the same one that Ronnie took to Super Stock Eliminator at the 1967 Springnationals. Herb qualified the car in the 16th spot with an ET of 11.26, which put it in Super Stock Eliminator contention. Herb made it to the fourth round, but because Ronnie was out of the Hemi Barracuda, he decided to drive the GTX for the two final rounds. Ronnie faced Fellow SS/B Hemi Barracuda driver Don Grotheer in the final. At the lights, both drivers broke out, but since Sox broke out less, according to NHRA rules, he was awarded the win.

NHRA Nationals

Later in 1968, James Leonard "Bird" Shoffner was added to the Sox & Martin team. Bird was also from Burlington and worked on engine building, maintenance, and other aspects of building race cars.

In 1962, Bird drove a black 409 Chevy Impala hardtop that was owned by Junior Clark and tuned and maintained by Ronnie Sox. It was also tuned by Larry Wilson, who owned another car that Ronnie and Buddy maintained. This Chevy was sponsored by Ronnie's dad's Sox Sinclair Service in Burlington and was called *Carolina Thunder II* (after Ronnie's similar red car named *Carolina Thunder*) and *Mr. 409 II*.

As always, the most important and crowning event of the season was the NHRA Nationals held at Indianapolis Raceway Park over Labor Day weekend. The 1968 Nationals were bigger than the event the year before, but the problems with eliminator handicapping from national

The 1968 Hemi Road Runner (with 1969 grille) ran multiple classes. Here it has a wide Hemi hood scoop and runs in B/Modified Production class. (Photo Courtesy Don Moats)

The Dodge D700 hauler carrying the 1968 Sox & Martin Hemi Barracuda was an excellent way to attract public attention as the team traveled from city to city. Of course, it was painted red, white, and blue just like the race cars. (Photo Courtesy Diane Sox)

Chapter 3

Clinic Schedule Repercussions

By this time, the Chrysler Supercar Performance Clinics, managed by Dave Koffel, consisted of three to five teams for each make, with Plymouth represented by Sox & Martin in Burlington, Don Grotheer (Oklahoma), Wiley Cossey (Pomona, California), and Ed Miller (Syracuse, New York). The Dodge teams were Dick Landy (Sherman Oaks, California), Bill Tanner (Atlanta, Georgia), and John Petrie in Canada. The schedule could be grueling for the team but the additional money gave them the ability to build and race the best equipment.

The pressure from the races and clinic events became so heavy that sometimes it got to them. On one occasion, Ronnie was traveling with Jake in the hauler and trailer rig. They had just passed through El Paso, heading west, when they had to stop alongside the road in the black of night. Ronnie, who was driving, jumped out; he was soon back inside and took off. About 25 miles down the road, he leaned back to say something to Jake. Ronnie didn't know that Jake had gotten out on the passenger side of the truck. Ronnie had left him at the side of the road in the dark.

Only the sharp eyes of Pee Wee Wallace, a fellow Mopar racer from Virginia, following a few miles back in his own rig, saw Jake and picked him up. Pee Wee caught up with Ronnie and the hauler at the next town. Pee Wee pulled up alongside Ronnie at a stop light and asked him if he was traveling alone.

Ronnie replied, "No, Jake's in the back seat sleeping."

The Plymouth Belvedere Road Runner was usually posed at the dealer or on display with one of the distinctive Warner Brothers' cartoon Road Runners. This Plymouth has an unusual hood scoop design, one of a number of different styles used. (Photo Courtesy Buddy Martin)

Pee Wee said, "I don't see him."

Ronnie turned to look in the back and saw that Jake wasn't there. They all laughed when Jake sat up in the seat of Pee Wee's truck and surprised Ronnie.

It was almost like a major Hollywood premier when Sox & Martin and their race cars arrived at a dealer for a Supercar Performance Clinic event. This dealer hired searchlights and large banners. (Photo Courtesy Buddy Martin)

The Sox & Martin team always arrived at the track with an impressive appearance that was just right for the times. A Dodge D700 hauler with an extended wheelbase and ramp carried the Super Stock Barracuda safely, but allowed it to be seen by the public when they were traveling. (Tommy Erwin Photo)

1968–1969 Super Stock Domination

The Sox & Martin 1967 Plymouth Hemi GTX launches hard at the 1968 NHRA Nationals at Indianapolis Raceway Park. The car ran in Super Stock/D class at this time. (Photo Courtesy John Mahoney)

records were increasing. The Chrysler racing powers in attendance wanted an additional Mopar in Super Stock Eliminator, so they directed class winner Ronnie Sox to throw the race.

To make sure that the spectators and other competitors knew that the red light was intentional, Ronnie left far enough ahead of the green to be obvious about it and ran .3 second under the record. The NHRA somehow let Ronnie get by the scales for inspection and he drove straight to the trailer and they loaded the car.

Mopars still dominated the meet with Wiley Cossey winning SS/B in his Hemi Barracuda at 12.80 seconds

Number 783 Finds a New Home

At the end of the 1968 NHRA Nationals, Competition Number 783 non-RO23 SS/D GTX 1967 Plymouth was sold to racers Phil Collins and Dale Jones from Champaign, Illinois, for $4,200. Phil and Dale did not bring a trailer to the meet so someone from the Sox & Martin team delivered the car to them at Champaign. The car was equipped with the standard twin-scoop GTX hood when Phil and Dale took possession of the car; Ronnie offered the extra RO23 hood to them for $100, which they declined.

Phil and Dale raced the Plymouth in the Midwest, Florida, and as far away as the Southwest, repainting and lettering the car for their purposes. In 1985, the car was located in the Kansas City area where Phil had moved. The car was then purchased by collector John Mahoney, who subsequently restored it to its proper appearance.

Mahoney replaced the GTX hood with an original RO23 hood from another car. He contracted a local painter, but hired original Sox & Martin painter Carl Clayton to fly to Kansas City to apply the silver-leaf lettering as it appeared in 1967.

Jake King was not available to build a new Hemi for the car, so John hired Herb McCandless.

This 1968 Hemi Barracuda's wider rear tires and different paint and striping scheme identify it as the B/Modified Production and match race car. The legal Super Stock car had dual blue stripes on the hood. (Photo Courtesy Diane Sox)

By 1990, the restoration was complete. In 1994, the Revell Model Company used the car to create and issue a 1/25-scale plastic model kit of the Plymouth SS/D GTX.

Chapter 3

Ronnie and Buddy pose proudly in front of the facility in Burlington along with one of their iconic 1968 Hemi Barracudas. They always dressed and presented Chrysler, themselves, and their team professionally. (Photo Courtesy Jake King Collection)

Ronnie Sox and Buddy Martin pose with two of their race cars at one of the smaller dragstrips in the Southeast. The 1968 Hemi Barracuda is in front and one of the 1968 Belvederes is in the rear. (Photo Courtesy Buddy Martin)

and 66.91 mph. Ronnie Sox took SS/D in his big Plymouth Street Hemi GTX with NHRA competition number 783 at 12.22 seconds and 86.12 mph. The mismatch of ET versus trap speed was a clear indicator of the braking action going on at Indy in 1968. This was the last time that Ronnie drove that SS/D car.

Title Wins

Ronnie and Buddy continued their success through the remainder of the 1968 season, finishing with wins in Super Stock Heads Up Eliminator at the AHRA Summer Nationals and the AHRA All-American Championships, both in the 1968 Hemi Barracuda. Ronnie won AHRA Driver of the Year and his award was presented at the 1969 AHRA Winter Nationals at Beeline.

The team won the Drag World Championship race in Super Stock Eliminator and were the *Hot Rod* Magazine Championship runner-up in Super Stock Eliminator.

> **Ronnie won AHRA Driver of the Year and his award was presented at the 1969 AHRA Winter Nationals at Beeline.**

They also won the Heads Up Eliminator and 3,000-pound class gas Eliminator at the *Super Stock* Magazine Nationals at York US 30 Drag-O-Way, the Super Stock Eliminator at the *Cars* Magazine Super Stock International, the Super Stock Eliminator at the Drag Racing Championship, and the Super Stock Eliminator at the Olympics of Drag Racing.

1968–1969 Super Stock Domination

Ronnie Sox lines up with the 1968 Road Runner. To his left, Buddy Martin is ready for action in the 1968 Hemi GTX. Both cars brought excitement to Super Stock drag racing fans across the country in 1968. (Photo Courtesy Buddy Martin)

One of the Sox & Martin 1968 Hemi Barracudas lifts the front wheels during some cool weather action at Shuffletown Dragway near Charlotte, North Carolina. (Photo Courtesy Buddy Martin)

Buddy Martin and local volunteers push the 1968 Hemi Barracuda out of the pit area to the staging lanes during a race. There were always crowds of helpful fans around when help was needed.

Sox & Martin were becoming increasingly popular and well-known during the 1968 racing season. It is rumored that a clearly visible Sox & Martin Racing cloth patch was sewn on Opie Taylor's jeans on one of the *Andy Griffith Show* episodes. I have not found any verification of this, but it is entirely believable.

1969 Drag Racing Season

Ronnie, Buddy, and Jake began 1969 by moving from their small Chapel Hill facility on Highway 54 to a new, modern 14,000-square-foot shop at the corner of 3167 Tucker Street Extension and Anthony Road in Burlington. The address was known thereafter as 426-P Tucker Street Extension. Their business had grown significantly and they were not just building cars for themselves, but also for other racers around the country.

The 1969 match race Hemi Barracuda lifts the front wheels at Cecil County Dragway in Maryland. The car was equipped with lighter mag wheels, a parachute, and no front brakes. The right rear quarter panel is noticeably damaged in this photo. (Bob McClurg Photo)

Chapter 3

The grand opening at the new facility included a gala and open house. In attendance were luminaries including Miss Hurst Golden Shifter Linda Vaughn and Glen White, Chrysler Corporation vice president and general manager as well as representatives from the NHRA, Chrysler-Plymouth Division, *Super Stock* magazine, Valvoline Oil, Hooker Headers, and others. A cocktail party and dinner was held at the local Holiday Inn and the building opened to the public at 10:00 am the next morning.

Sox & Martin were considered Burlington's chief claim to fame in the sports world.

AHRA Winter Nationals

The 1969 AHRA Winter Nationals took place at Beeline Dragway near Phoenix, Arizona, on January 24 where competitors were treated to a brand-new track surface. Ronnie Sox started well with a low-qualifier time of 10.67 seconds in his Hemi Barracuda, now updated to the 1969 appearance. Ronnie lost the first round due to a broken clutch eye bolt. He managed to win Top Stock Eliminator with the Hemi Road Runner with a 10.94 and 128.38 over Dick Hallahan in the final.

Two men who Ronnie and Buddy would say were two of the most important members of their team. Jake King (left) and Dave Christie (right) are the mechanic and builder who made the red, white, and blue cars do their job. (Photo Courtesy Dave Christie)

The victory came just before a serious incident on the way to Pomona. The Sox & Martin truck and trailer rig were wrecked and both the Hemi Barracuda and B/MP Road Runner were badly damaged. The Road Runner had some fender and front-end damage, but the Barracuda's problems were more extensive. With the truck and trailer out of commission and both cars needing

> **The Sox & Martin truck and trailer rig were wrecked and both the Hemi Barracuda and B/MP Road Runner were badly damaged.**

repair, Buddy contacted Wiley Cossey. Wiley brought his two rigs from Pomona to take the cars and what equipment they could gather to Hooker Headers in Ontario, where he worked. Buddy also called California Mopar racers Joe Fisher (scheduled to drive the B/MP car at the NHRA Winternationals) and Dave Christie to help.

Dave and Joe worked with Ronnie and Jake at Hooker to repair the cars while Buddy was having the truck repaired; he brought it to the shop a few days later. Dave said later that this was where he first met Jake King, who became a mentor to Dave and a big influence on his life and career. Ronnie and Buddy were so impressed with Joe and Dave's work and experience that they invited both of them to move to Burlington and hired them to become a part of the Sox & Martin team.

NHRA Winternationals

The 1969 season-opening NHRA Winternationals event at Pomona saw Ford attempt to make a strong showing with 12 entries in the 32-car Super Stock field. Chrysler was ready for the fray with seven Plymouths and eight Dodges, mostly of the 1968 A-Body Hemi variety. Some contenders were new faces. Factory team drivers Ronnie Sox and Dick Landy chose (or were told) not to compete until the NHRA came up with a reasonable answer to the "breakout" (disqualification for running below the class record) rules and a plan for heads-up racing.

They both competed in the sportsman A/Modified Production class, where Sox and his Barracuda put Landy

1968–1969 Super Stock Domination

Ronnie gives up a lot of ground with a 10.39 dial in SS/B. You can see the tail of a Jenkins Competition Camaro at left. (Alan Lewis Photos)

away with a 10.53-second ET at 134.53 mph against Landy's red light. Herb McCandless drove Landy's similar car for the B/MP race and won at 11.01 and 116.88 mph over Joe Fisher, in the repaired Sox & Martin Road Runner, running a losing 11.49 at 108.56. That dropped the class record by .24 second.

The Road Runner was later updated with a 440 wedge 6-barrel setup. It was mostly stock with three 2-barrel Holley carburetors and an Edelbrock aluminum intake manifold. The camshaft was an Iskenderian 1012B with solid lifters. The engine used 13:1 ForgedTrue piston and Hooker headers. Of course, the Plymouth was equipped with a 4-speed A-833 Slick Shift transmission. The hood was fiberglass and was later equipped with a 1965–1967-style wide Hemi hood scoop.

NHRA Springnationals

The next major NHRA event in 1969 was the fifth annual Springnationals, held at Dallas International Motor Speedway. Thirty-one cars, including the Mopars of Arlen Vanke, Dick Landy, Ron Mancini, and Don Grotheer, competed for the Super Stock Eliminator title, but the final came down to Ronnie Sox's Hemi Barracuda against Barrie Poole's 1969 Mustang. Sox took the win with an ET of 10.63 seconds at 111.50 mph, making him the first driver to win three consecutive Super Stock Eliminator titles.

Super Stock Nationals

August 9 and 10, 1969, saw the fifth running of the Super Stock Nationals, presented by *Super Stock & Drag Illustrated*, again at York US 30 Drag-O-Way in Pennsylvania. This three-day event was originally limited and ran only four classes: Unlimited Fuel Funny Car, Injected Fuel Funny Car, NHRA Super Stock, and NHRA Stock. In 1968, a fifth class had been added: Experimental Super Stock. It was a heads-up class designed for exhibition match racers.

For 1969, the event was run with an Enduro Eliminator system with no qualifying. Eliminations were open to

Ronnie gets ready to heat up the tires for his next run. Future Sox & Martin employee Chick DeNinno and his Dodge Charger ran against Ronnie in Factory Experimental. (Alan Lewis Photos)

Chapter 3

Factory Experimental was another class in which Sox & Martin regularly fielded cars. More classes meant more opportunities to bring home more money. (Alan Lewis Photo)

anyone and you raced until you were beaten; points were awarded according the number of rounds completed. Many Fuel Funny Car racers were unwilling to compete under this system because of the expense, so the race became essentially a Super Stock event.

> "It was common knowledge at the time that most, if not all, manufacturers wanted to be certain that their drivers had the best possible advantage in Super Stock racing."

Sox & Martin ran in the Experimental Super Stock Eliminator along with fierce competitor Bill Jenkins. Jenkins pushed his way through the field, winning the Friday eliminations with low ET and top speed of the day at 141.93 mph for 9.94 seconds. Ronnie Sox took runner-up in his Hemi Barracuda at 10.13 and 135.13 mph in the final.

This pattern repeated itself on Saturday. Jenkins' lead could not be hurt and by the end of the meet on Sunday he had high points at 34 to runner-up Ronnie Sox at 14.

NHRA Nationals

The 1969 NHRA Nationals were held on Labor Day weekend at Indianapolis Raceway Park, bigger and better than ever. The NHRA was well aware of the handicap system shortcomings in Super Stock Eliminator. It offered solutions to the ever-increasing brake lighting, sandbagging, and other efforts by the drivers to fight the system.

The previous Eliminator setup was made up of a field with 18 class winners and 14 low qualifiers. A maximum .10-second breakout was permitted with the exception of the final round where drivers ran as quickly as they could, creating new class ET records in the process. It was hoped by everyone involved that this new system would produce equal factory participation and good racing for the fans.

With the new plan, the two low qualifiers from each class ran in Eliminator. If their best time trials were below the class ET record, the car was dialed in for that class car. There were no breakouts and each car was allowed to run as far below the dial-in class marks as they desired. The new low time did not become the new class record, nor did their dial-in change. Only in the final round of eliminations did a sub-record run become the new class record.

Chrysler Mini-Nationals

It was common knowledge at the time that most, if not all, manufacturers wanted to be certain that their drivers had the best possible advantage in Super Stock racing. Chrysler became so well known by its efforts that it was announced over the public address system at the 1969 NHRA Nationals that they were trying to stack the Eliminator field in their favor. This accusation was due to the fact that all Super Stock/B, BA, and CA Mopars attended a "Chrysler Nationals" session at Tri-State Dragway in Hamilton, Ohio, the Friday before the "Big Go" at Indianapolis.

Here, each of the Dodge and Plymouth Super Stock entries ran as hard as they could, out of sight of the NHRA. The quickest two cars in each of the three classes

1968–1969 Super Stock Domination

Buddy Martin was selected as Crew Chief of the Year and was presented with a trophy recognizing him as a member of the 1968 Car Craft Magazine All-Star Racing Team. Others in the group included Don Garlits, Dick Landy, Don Nicholson, Roland Leong, Keith Black, and George Hurst. (Photo Courtesy Buddy Martin)

were selected. These six "winners" returned to the Nationals on Saturday and qualified at above-record times, while the "losers" dominated their classes and put away the competition.

The purpose was, of course, to defeat the NHRA attempt to have the cars running off times relative to their true potential. This extra race was not created by Chrysler, but by the racers to give themselves an advantage to win. Ronnie Sox ran 10.25 with his SS/B Barracuda at Tri-State, but at Indy, he dialed in on the 10.61 record with a .36-second cushion. His Eliminator best was a below-potential 10.40. Sox won Super Stock Eliminator with a 10.890 at 124.82 mph. With the new NHRA rules, no class eliminations were held in the Super Stock bracket.

Because of the inequities of the NHRA system, a group of Super Stock racers, representing each of the manufacturers, met on Tuesday following the 1969 NHRA Nationals to discuss what needed to be done. The Chrysler group members included Buddy Martin and Bill Bagshaw.

The drivers agreed that there were too many Super Stock classes under the current system. They also agreed that a better approach should be created by the racers and presented to the NHRA to set up some sort of heads-up Super Stock class or Eliminator. A committee was organized to present their ideas to the NHRA at the rules board meeting at the Dallas World Finals in October.

AHRA U.S. Open Championships

In early fall 1969, the AHRA held its first annual U.S. Open Championships at Rockingham International Dragway in Rockingham, North Carolina. Super Stock competition found Ronnie Sox winning the first round against Dyno Don Nicholson; his 10.14 at 135 mph beat Nicholson's losing 10.50. In the second round, Sox won against Ed Skelton's red light with a 10.14 ET. In the semi-final round, Sox had the front wheels in the air as he beat Al Joniec's Ford with a 10.12 ET. The final round was all Sox with an AHRA Super Stock record-breaking 9.22 at 135.95 mph putting away the red-lighted attempt of Arlen Vanke, who tripped the lights at 10.16 and 135.74 mph.

The Sox & Martin team also participated in Top Stock. Don Carlton drove the Sox & Martin Road Runner but was bested in the first of two final rounds by Hubert Platt's Mustang. Because both drivers broke out, the race was run again and Platt repeated his first race results by beating Carlton the second time.

On October 17, 1969, Ronnie and Buddy received another pair of "company" cars for their personal use, as had become customary since the beginning of their

Chapter 3

Chrysler Corporation always made sure that at least one of the Sox & Martin race cars appeared at an important auto show in Detroit or New York at the beginning of each year. This is the 1969 Road Runner in front of a Plymouth Rapid Transit Authority display. (Photo Courtesy Don Moats)

relationship with Chrysler Plymouth. Ronnie received a red 1970 'Cuda equipped with a 383 V-8 and a TorqueFlite and Buddy took possession of a black 'Cuda with a 440 V-8 and TorqueFlite. Both cars were delivered through Central Motor and Tire Company in Burlington.

The Birth of Pro Stock

After the dissatisfaction of the NHRA Super Stock drivers in 1968 and 1969, it was clear that something needed to be done about the handicap and breakout system. Heads-up no-handicap racing with no breakout disqualification was the only answer. It was better for both the fans and the drivers. The UDRA had been running Super Stock under a heads-up system with a 3,200-pound weight minimum in the Midwest since 1965, and the AHRA had changed its Super Stock classes to heads-up racing, so the NHRA was lagging behind. In addition to the heads-up advantage, the UDRA system was intended to even the competition of the field and reduce costs for racers.

A number of important NHRA Super Stock drivers and owners, including Buddy Martin and Bill Jenkins, met with NHRA officials in Dallas, Texas, after the October NHRA World Finals. They presented a plan for a set of rules that satisfied the desires of drivers and the needs of the NHRA. Most of the requested rule requirements were accepted by the NHRA and the association presented the official announcement of a new heads-up category in the October 31, 1969, edition of *National Dragster*. The announcement was part of the NHRA Super Season for 1970 and

Ronnie lines up against the Competition TorqueFlite 1964 Plymouth during Super Stock eliminations at York US 30 Drag-O-Way in Pennsylvania. The Sox & Martin Plymouth is probably equipped with a 383 engine because there is no hood scoop. (Alan Lewis Photo)

1968–1969 Super Stock Domination

Buddy is talking to the crowd gathered for a clinic and is telling them about a prize drawing. It was unusual for Jake to attend these affairs but he can be seen in a suit and tie at the lower right of the photo. (Photo Courtesy Buddy Martin)

included four new categories, most important of which was a new heads-up Super Stock Eliminator category.

The new class was called Pro Stock when introduced at the 1970 Winternationals, and featured American cars of 1968 and newer manufacture with a minimum displacement of 7 pounds per cubic inch (lbs/ci) and a minimum weight of 2,700 pounds. The engine had to be the same make as the car; any internal modifications were allowed with a maximum displacement of 427 ci. Lightweight body components were allowed for the front fenders, hood, and deck lid, but an original steel body was required. Carburetion was limited to two 4-barrel American-made automobile carburetors.

The Sox & Martin team topped off its 1969 schedule of 92 race dates and 103 clinics by winning the NHRA Super Stock World Championship, the Olympics of Drag Racing, the Mid-South Super Stock Championships, the Great Lakes Championships, and a win in Pro Stock at the *Cars* Magazine Super Stock Championships.

George Hurst put up $5,000 for anyone who could win the NHRA World Finals in Super Stock. Sox & Martin

> **"The new class was called Pro Stock when introduced at the 1970 Winternationals, and featured American cars of 1968 and newer manufacture."**

needed one round of points to be eligible. Buddy called starter Buster Couch to see where they could run and the only division points race available was at Orange County in California. They hauled the Barracuda to California, won the first round and hauled it back East, and qualified for the Nationals at Indianapolis.

From left to right in this photo: A representative from Hurst; Jake King contemplating the win and celebrating with some bubbly; Linda Vaughn; Ronnie Sox holding his Wally trophy; Miss NHRA; and Buddy Martin. Their 1968 Hemi Barracuda is in the background. (Photo Courtesy Jake King Collection)

1970–1972
Pro Stock 4-Speed Era

Ronnie Sox pulls the front wheels off the ground with the 1970 Pro Stock Hemi 'Cuda on this launch at Rockingham sometime in late 1970. (Photo Courtesy Dave Christie)

By the beginning of 1970, the Sox & Martin operation in Burlington continued to grow and prosper. They were now one of two authorized performance parts and equipment direct distributors for Chrysler; the other was Richard Petty Enterprises in nearby Randleman, North Carolina.

CHAPTER 4

Petty concentrated on NASCAR products and racing while Sox & Martin were oriented to drag racing.

Sox & Martin, Inc.

An illustrated 55-page catalog and information brochure was one of the first publications produced by the team to introduce the public to the capabilities of Sox & Martin, Inc. The book included photos of their machine shop, offices, and race car building facilities. The catalog was designed and produced by Sox & Martin public relations director Tom Richardson. Tom also took all of the photographs in the publication.

The rest of the catalog and price list included pages of parts and services offered by Mopar, and by Sox & Martin. Everything from camshafts, pistons, and transmissions to complete race engines assembled under the direction of Jake King were now available to any racer who wanted the best and wanted to win. The back of the catalog was filled with advertising from the sponsors of the team.

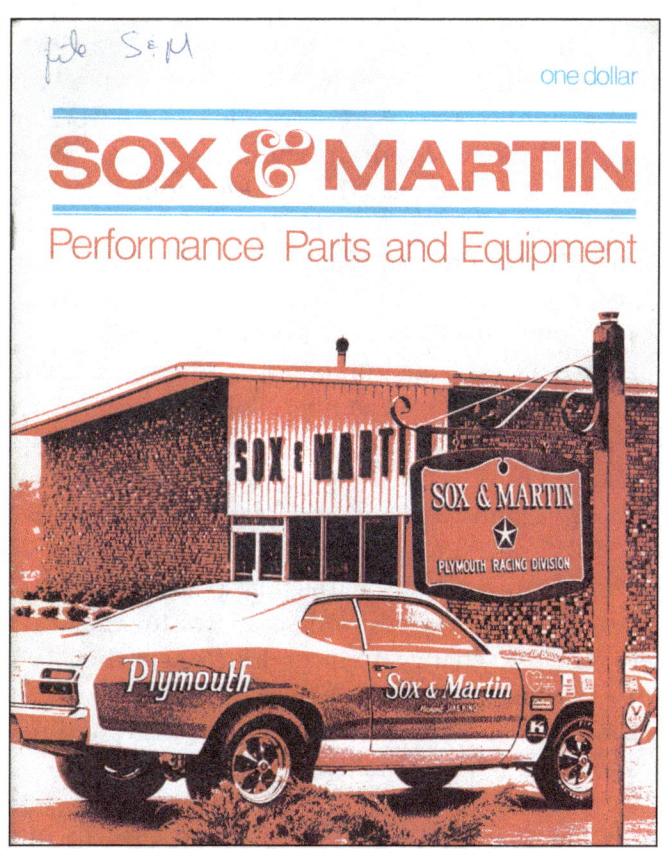

The Sox & Martin parts catalog was designed by Tom Richardson and published in 1971. It offered everything from parts to a completely built drag race engine put together in the Sox & Martin shop in Burlington. The 1970 Hemi Duster was featured on the cover.

The back cover of the catalog was decorated in colorful psychedelic style with an image of the Plymouth Supercar Clinic and Rapid Transit System logos. The Sox & Martin Duster and Barracuda were displayed prominently. The same image was used on Performance Clinic posters.

SOX & MARTIN

Chapter 4

Ronnie lifts the front wheels on a launch off the line at a match race event at Maple Grove Dragway as Buddy watches. The opponent was Bill Jenkins in one of his Grumpy's Toys *Camaros. A close race was always assured when these two met. (Carl Rubrecht Photo)*

Each ad featured photos of Ronnie, Buddy, and their race cars and told potential customers how much confidence they had in their sponsors' parts and equipment.

In addition to direct sales from the Sox & Martin shop through Chrysler, other shops also signed on as distributors. The first, in 1969, was Chick DeNinno's chassis building and speed shop in Maryland. Chick had first met Ronnie and Buddy as early as 1963 while involved in match racing with Malcolm Durham and others. From that time, Chick and Ronnie had maintained a friendly relationship so that in 1970, when the time came for the staff to be enhanced, Chick was one of the first choices to come to Burlington and join the team. He sold his speed shop and took the plunge.

This shot shows Buddy and Ronnie in business attire in their office in Burlington. The picture was used in their 1971 parts catalog. The pictures on the wall remind them of what their business is all about.

Changes for 1970

The opening 1970 NHRA Winternationals at Pomona saw a new excitement for fans and drivers thrilled by the sounds and competition of the stock-bodied American cars. The cars that had previously been relegated to Modified Production classes were now allowed to represent the manufacturers in heads-up action.

This was also the year that NHRA adopted its now familiar "Wally" trophy for winners at national events. Interestingly, the original Wally figure was actually not modeled after Wally Parks. The model for it came from a photo of NHRA Top Gas racer Jack Jones.

Because of the large number of red-light starts with the old four progressive amber light system, a new Pro-Tree start system was adopted in 1970. This new system is still in use.

For 1970, most drivers and teams that had 1969 Super Stock cars and equipment made few changes. The 1968 Hemi Darts and Barracudas (some with 1969's updated appearance) had been so successful that there was no reason to change, so most drivers kept their 1968 mounts. Factory-supported drivers, including Ronnie Sox, Dick Landy, and Don Grotheer, moved to the new Hemi-powered E-Body Challengers and Barracudas.

The 1970 season started a little slow for Chrysler when Bill Jenkins, in his 1968 Camaro, took the first Pro Stock win and the $10,000 purse at the Winternationals at Pomona January 30 through February 1. He ran a 9.99 ET over Ronnie Sox's second-place 10.12. Don Carlton drove the Sox & Martin 1968 Barracuda at this race, equipped with a destroked 408-ci Hemi and less weight but it could not run as quick as the new 1970 car.

1970–1972 Pro Stock 4-Speed Era

On rare occasions, top Pro Stock driver Don Carlton drove for Sox & Martin. Here, he is driving the 1969 match race Hemi 'Cuda at Orange County in California. (Photo Courtesy Dave Christie)

The Pro Stock field included eight Dodges and Plymouths. Ronnie drove the SS/A car to a 10.44 at 117.03 mph class win. He won the 1970 AHRA Winter Nationals meet on January 22–25 at Beeline in Scottsdale, Arizona. He beat Mike Fons in the final round in 10.08 at 137.61 to Fons' 10.54. Dick Landy's 16-plug Hemi Dodge had clutch and transmission problems and did not qualify.

In previous-season starts from 1965 to 1968, the team usually had to wait until spring for the new factory Maximum Performance packages to be introduced and built, but the new Pro Stock cars were based on modified standard new cars that would have been available in the fall of the previous year. Because the new NHRA rules were announced in October 1969, development and work had already begun and the new cars were ready for the Winternationals.

The new E-Body Barracuda (Identified as the sportier 'Cuda model for marketing purposes) was different from the 1968 and 1969 cars in a number of ways. Nevertheless, Ronnie, Buddy, and Jake were on top of what was needed to win.

The E-Body Hemi Pro Stock

The new stock E-Body 'Cuda was built on a 108-inch wheelbase, like the 1968–1969 A-Body Barracuda. The chassis and the engine compartment were wider and more like the B-Body Dodge and Plymouth, allowing more room for the 426 Hemi, which made servicing easier. The tread width was increased from 58.4 to 60.2 inches in the front and from 55.8 to 60.7 inches in the rear. These changes increased the weight of the basic standard car from about 3,005 pounds in 1968 to about 3,395 pounds for 1970.

Chrysler racers did not rest on their laurels; a serious Pro Stock development program was already underway by the beginning of the 1970 season. As always, Chrysler Engineering Special Vehicle Development, Department 7590, was on top of the game under Tom Coddington and Allen Adam. Pro Stock was Chrysler Corporation's major drag racing effort for the 1970 season. This class allowed extensive engine and chassis modification, and achieved significant performance levels of 9.60- to 9.80-second ETs and 138- to 142-mph trap speeds. Obviously, this provided a great deal of impressive product display to the public.

Test the Transmission

Two cars were used for testing of the Pro Stock program. An E-Body 1970 Dodge Challenger served as the

Ronnie made many test runs in the newly built 1970 Hemi 'Cuda to make sure that everything from the engine to the tires was in the best adjustment and condition before taking it to its first race.

Chapter 4

Ronnie pulls to the starting line in the 1970 Hemi 'Cuda. This first E-Body 'Cuda was built from a body-in-white and parts off a new showroom 'Cuda from a dealer. (Ray Mann photo, quartermilestones.com)

test mule for the ClutchFlite transmission. This car was named *Motown Missile* (coined by Arlen Vanke) with Richard "Barney" Oldfield as the principal driver. The ClutchFlite was developed by engineer Fred Wiggins in the Chrysler Racing transmission lab. It used a special dry clutch with oil pressure supplied to the transmission by a modified power steering pump. It had already been determined that the standard A727 TorqueFlite was not competitive in a race car of this weight and performance level.

Chrysler knew that outside of Ronnie Sox, Arlen Vanke, Larry Griffith, and Herb McCandless, no one had enough 4-speed skill to win consistently.

The 4-speed manual transmission test mule was an A-Body Hemi-powered 1970 Plymouth Duster driven by Arlen Vanke. Because other drivers, notably Dick Landy and Ronnie Sox, had full schedules due to their clinic programs, Vanke was the best choice for several reasons. He was not only a winning driver, he had worked with Chrysler Engineering testing and development for a number of years, and was located in nearby Akron, Ohio. The Duster was similar to the successful 1968 A-Body Hemi Darts and Barracudas, and it incorporated many of their design principles.

The lessons learned from this testing were spelled out to select Pro Stock drivers and owners in a confidential letter published October 2, 1970. This letter, from Tom Coddington and Al Adam in Special Vehicle Development, listed the departmental chassis recommendations for a 1970 A-Body and E-Body Pro Stock race car.

The letter specified the details of the front suspension, rear suspension, braking system, chassis stiffening, and roll cage construction accompanied by sketches, layouts, parts source lists, and part numbers. It was clear by the information included in this letter that, as always, Chrysler was playing the game to win.

Start with a Stock 'Cuda

The first 1970 Hemi 'Cuda was delivered to Sox & Martin's shop in Burlington late in 1969 but it was actually two cars rather than one. To save time and work, a completely stock, brand-new 1970 Hemi 'Cuda titled to Buddy Martin was the starting point. Chrysler also sent a 1970 Barracuda body-in-white; this shell was used to construct the actual race car.

It was considerably easier to take the needed components off the stock car and install them on the new body than it was to remove everything not needed from the stock car and rebuild it. (This was actually standard practice with most race car construction shops.) This procedure had already been proven in the construction of the 1965 AWB Dodges and Plymouths from 1965.

This stock 1970 'Cuda was the last Hemi-powered car delivered to the team with a VIN. The stock 'Cuda was stripped further and used later in the season to build a second car.

Assemble a Team

The procedure began by setting up the new 3,800-pound 'Cuda on stands and removing the wheels and tires. The Barracuda body-in-white was already finished and painted in the body shop and then parked on stands alongside the new car to make removal and replacing of necessary parts as simple and efficient as possible. By this time, the Sox & Martin shop employed a full staff, each with a specific job responsibility. As many as 33 people worked in the Sox & Martin shop at its peak around this time.

Of course, Jake King was responsible for the engine building and he had his own special shop within the shop to keep his delicate work separate. Jake was assisted capably by Bird Shoffner. Red Gibson did the red, white, and blue paint and Carl Clayton applied the lettering, working in silver leaf. Shop foreman Joe Fisher oversaw the day-to-day shop operations and Tom Richardson worked on public relations and publicity. Mechanic Dave Christie was responsible for chassis building and tuning.

Make a Few Mods

The stock 'Cuda front crossmember, including the steering, spindles, and brakes, was removed intact from the factory car and installed on the new bare body without problems because, according to the 1970 NHRA Pro Stock rules, it was required to all be stock. The NHRA required four-wheel brakes but when running in the AHRA, just the rear brakes could be used when accompanied by a parachute.

Buddy believed in the solid stopping power of the four-wheel brakes and stuck with that setup. Of course, a Lakewood Industries roll bar was installed before beginning the build.

The heavy-duty Dana 60 rear axle was used from the standard Street Hemi car but used 4.89:1 gears, as did the 1968 Barracuda. Proven 1968 Hemi Super Stock rear springs were adapted to the 1970 chassis with front-spring mounting spacers.

Fiberglass body components were not available early in the 1970 season so the car ran standard steel parts. Later in the year, A&A Engineering had appropriate fiberglass fenders, hood, and deck lid to replace the stock parts. The finished weight of the car with the steel body parts was 2,980 pounds so the change to fiberglass lightened it even further.

The 426 Hemi engine that was installed in the 1970 'Cuda was similar to those used in the 1968–1969 cars but modified further according to the new Pro Stock rules. It used Chrysler 12.5:1 pistons with Dykes rings and Chrysler forged crankshaft and connecting rods, all of which turned on Federal-Mogul bearings.

> **The finished weight of the car with the steel body parts was 2,980 pounds so the change to fiberglass lightened it even further.**

The Pro Stock engine was equipped with aluminum heads from 1965. Because these heads were no longer manufactured, a steady supply of heads and components had to be found and kept on hand. Later in the year, new aluminum cylinder heads became available from Mopar and they were added to the engine. These new heads had cast-in bosses that allowed conversion to dual spark plug use and they used standard Street Hemi–type rocker arm covers and gaskets. A fabricated eight-quart oil pan and Milodon swinging pickup was employed to keep a steady supply of oil to the upper and lower end.

Fine-Tune a Little

Although the 'Cuda ran for a while with a standard 1965 Hemi cast-magnesium cross-ram intake manifold with two 780-cfm Holley 4160 4-barrel carburetors, a new specially designed Pro Stock intake was being developed by Chrysler engineers. This manifold was built around fabricated short welded tubes that fed two huge NASCAR-type Holley 4500 4-barrel models flowing 1,250 cfm each. This new manifold mounted the two carburetors inline and was largely responsible for the drop in ET and increase in top speeds that proved to be the norm once the setup was worked out.

The engine was finished with 2⅛-inch-diameter Hooker headers and a Chrysler transistorized ignition tach-drive distributor. A Lakewood steel clutch housing connected the engine to a Chrysler A-833 Slick Shift 4-speed transmission and Hurst Competition Plus shifter with reverse Loc-Out.

Chapter 4

Initial testing showed ETs around 9.70 seconds and trap speeds of 140 mph for the new 'Cuda.

Another change initiated with the 1970 Pro Stock cars was the familiar red, white, and blue finish. Since mid-1964, all Sox & Martin race cars had been painted with Ford factory colors, but beginning with the 1970 models, similar Chrysler Corporation shades of red, metallic blue, and white were used.

1970 Pro Stock Competition

By 1970, the majority of Sox & Martin racing activities and income involved match racing. These events numbered three to four per week and were usually set up as part of a regular circuit and, if possible, were run on the way to or returning from other major events to save expenses and make the most of the shows available for the public. The races usually meant facing such personalities as Bill Jenkins and Don Carlton. Many match races were held at Maple Grove Raceway, about 14 miles south of Reading, Pennsylvania.

An important race in the 1970 NHRA season was the inaugural Gatornationals held on February 13–15 at Gainesville, Florida. Bill Jenkins repeated his Winternationals win against Ronnie's runner-up finish in the 'Cuda.

Super Stock Magazine Nationals

The sixth annual *Super Stock* Magazine Nationals was held at York US 30 Drag-O-Way, its permanent home. May 8–10, 1970, saw an impressive collection of Super Stock and Pro Stock competitors, all prepared for the event's first battle in the new Pro Stock category. The 1970 event was called a "racer's meet" because the racers themselves set up the rules of the weekend. Each eliminator chose a liaison, whose job was to see that the rules were fair for everyone. The Pro Stock competitors accumulated points each day, with 46 cars making the first round each day. The overall points were determined by totals.

On Friday's time trials, Ronnie Sox drove his 1970 Hemi 'Cuda to consistent mid-9.8-second times at more than 138 mph. Don Carlton was close behind in the second Sox & Martin car and kept his Hemi Duster in the low-9.9s.

Saturday saw one problem after another. The first was caused by a crew member leaving the carburetor covers on Don Carlton's Duster, which caused him to lose to Dave Strickler's Camaro.

Next, Ronnie had to fight to get the 'Cuda to the line. He was changing a transmission in the staging lanes between rounds, and just made his spot for the win against Mike Fons in the semi-final. He made up for the problems by beating Strickler in the final round with a 9.934 ET to Strickler's losing 9.954.

Joe Fisher went four rounds in Super Stock Eliminator in the SS/E Superbird before finally losing to John Elliot's Mustang. The 11.13 was the best time for the Plymouth; it represented the most successful outing for the Superbird and the run effort for SS/E class.

Sunday's finals began with Ronnie Sox beating Jenkins' Camaro with a 9.94. Dave Strickler was considered a favorite but he red-lighted against Wally Booth in the semi-final. It would have been a great race because Strickler went through the lights at a 9.96 to Booth's 9.97. In the same round, Ronnie was put away by Dave Lyall's

Ronnie Sox waits at the end of the track at Maple Grove, next to his 1970 Hemi 'Cuda after a match race with Bill Jenkins and his Camaro. (Carl Ruprecht Photo)

Team driver Joe Fisher pulls the front wheels off the ground in the 1970 Sox & Martin Plymouth Superbird. The Superbird raced in Super Stock/E in this configuration. (Photo Courtesy Don Moats Collection)

1970–1972 Pro Stock 4-Speed Era

Herb McCandless Comes Onboard

A native of Memphis, Tennessee, Herb McCandless began his drag racing career in 1962 when he drove a 1962 Chevrolet 409. By 1964, he was racing a Chevrolet in B/MP Z11 and learning his trade.

Although Herb was driving the Z11 Chevy, he had repeatedly beaten a racer who was an assistant regional manager for Chrysler. After a number of defeats, this fellow offered Herb a factory racing parts deal if he purchased a new 1965 Hemi Plymouth sedan. Herb, of course, chose a 4-speed version and once he moved into a winning Mopar, he never looked back.

Herb attended the Chrysler drag racing school in Detroit and with his natural skill and under the tutelage of Tom Hoover, Robert Cahill, and Dick Maxwell, soon became known as "Mr. 4-speed." Herb continued his success and, in 1967, purchased and raced a 1967 Hemi Coronet, followed in 1968 by a Hemi Dart. He won the AHRA points title that same year.

Over the winter of 1967–1968, Herb heard that Sox & Martin were planning to take two cars to the Winternationals at Pomona so he called Buddy and offered his services driving the second car. Herb had to quit his job, but left for California and drove the 440 GTX to an NHRA Super Stock win. Later that year, he won the Bristol race in the Road Runner. During

Herb McCandless sits in the staging lanes in the 1970 GT-1 Hemi 'Cuda waiting for his class at the 1970 NHRA Springnationals at Bristol, Tennessee. This car is equipped with a hood scoop similar to that used on the 1968 Hemi Barracuda. (Tommy Erwin Photo)

this time, Herb continued campaigning his own Hemi Dart. By May 1970, Ronnie and Buddy decided to run two cars permanently and hired Herb as a full-timer driver for the team.

Mustang with a 9.86 at 138.46 mph. Wally Booth ended up being the final-round winner with a 10.00 holeshot to Ronnie's 9.95, leaving Sox in second place.

AHRA Spring Nationals

On May 24, 1970, the AHRA ran its Spring Nationals as part of the AHRA's Grand American Series. The event was held at Bristol International Dragway in eastern Tennessee, wedged between the mountains. Sox & Martin arrived at Bristol with three Dodge haulers and four cars, prepared for battle.

They brought a Hemi 'Cuda and a Hemi Duster to run in AHRA Super Stock, the equivalent of NHRA Pro Stock, and another 'Cuda prepared with a single 4-barrel carburetor to run in GT-1 class. They also brought a 340 Duster to run in F/Stock class.

Herb drove the Hemi Duster and the GT-1 'Cuda; Ronnie drove the points-leading Hemi 'Cuda in Super Stock. Chief mechanic Jake King was kept busy making sure that all four entries were at the top of their game.

Super Stock qualifying found Ronnie just behind Dick Landy's Dodge with a 10.16 to Landy's 10.13 ET. Herb McCandless took the Hemi Duster to a 10.24, matching the time of Plymouth teammate Arlen Vanke.

Even this lowly 340 Duster was a Sox & Martin entry at the 1970 NHRA Springnationals at Bristol Dragway. The car was an F/Stock class competitor. (Tommy Erwin Photo)

Chapter 4

The 1969 Plymouth Road Runner and 1968–1969 Hemi Barracuda always drew the most attention when the Sox & Martin team pulled into the pits. Here, the team prepares for the 1970 Spring Nationals at Bristol. (Tommy Erwin Photo)

Bill Tanner's Dodge and Don Grotheer's Plymouth filled fifth and sixth places.

The first round of Super Stock was all Mopar. Herb beat Bill Hielscher, Ronnie Sox put away Larry Shepard in a Fred Gibb Camaro, and Grotheer defeated Fast Eddie Schartman. Herb also beat David Atkins' *Mr. Bardahl* Camaro in GT-1.

In the second round of Super Stock, Ronnie beat teammate Joe Fisher in the Hemi Duster with a 10.28 at 136.36 mph over Joe's 10.28 at 132.46 mph. Herb was supposed to drive the car, but he could not get back in time from his previous run. Herb was still in the running in GT-1, beating the Atkins/Hielsher Camaro. Herb capped off his day in GT-1 by winning the final eliminator with a win over Jay Wheatley at 10.95 at 126.58 mph to Wheatley's 11.10 at 124.48. Ronnie took the money in Super Stock with a holeshot 10.23 at 136.45 mph win over Landy's losing 10.21 at 135.13.

NHRA Springnationals

The 1970 NHRA Springnationals were held on June 12–14 at Dallas International Motor Speedway, where Ronnie won Pro Stock Eliminator in his 1970 Hemi 'Cuda. He qualified in the 32-car field at 9.93 on Saturday

The Sox & Martin team always drew a crowd when they arrived in their three trucks and trailers with three to four cars entered for competition. (Tommy Erwin Photo)

The 1969 Hemi Plymouth Road Runner is being prepared for another run at Bristol in 1970. This car was entered in the Super Stock/E class. (Tommy Erwin Photo)

Herb (in the 1970 Hemi Duster) lines up with Ronnie (in the 1970 Hemi 'Cuda) for a match up in Pro Stock competition. (Ray Mann photo, quartermilestones.com)

Team Expansion: Superbird and Duster

By mid-1970, Sox & Martin had expanded their team race cars by adding a 1970 Plymouth Road Runner Superbird set up for Super Stock/E and a new Pro Stock 1970 Plymouth Valiant Duster.

The 426 Street Hemi-powered Superbird was mostly stock, of course, but was equipped with the new tub-type two-piece Edelbrock Rat Roaster intake manifold. Usually driven by shop foreman Joe Fisher, the 3,840-pound Superbird ran 11-second ETs and held the NHRA class speed record at 124.83 mph. This unusual car was built in just four weeks in the team's shop.

The first race for the Superbird was a World Championship Series (WCS) divisional meet at Phenix City, Alabama, on April 5 or 12. Tim Richards also ran a 1970 Superbird in SS/EA and this may have been the most successful of the winged Plymouths. The Sox & Martin winged cars were not alone. Jack "Mr. 5 and 50" Werst also drove a Hemi Superbird in the 1970 season.

The new 2,900-pound Sox & Martin Hemi Duster, usually driven by Don Carlton, and later by Herb McCandless, was a bit more sophisticated. It was set up much like the A-Body 1968 Barracuda and was equipped with the same black Bostrom lightweight seats and aluminum brackets.

The body was based on a standard steel body-in-white sent from Chrysler. The hood and deck lid were replaced with

The 1970 Pro Stock Duster was built using the technology of a 1968 Hemi Barracuda and replaced that car through most of the 1970 season. The engine, the hood scoop, and the chassis construction was similar. (Tommy Erwin Photo)

pieces from A&A Fiberglass held in place with chrome pins and clips. An additional 100 pound lead-filled ballast bar was welded into the rear of the inside of the trunk behind the rear-mounted battery.

The engine was a 426 Hemi built by Jake King. It had dual inline 4500 Series Holley 4-barrel carburetors on a custom S&M intake manifold and Hooker headers. A special .606-inch lift camshaft worked the valves, putting out the impressive power for which the team was known. The Hemi reportedly made around 700 hp. Of course, a Hurst Competition Plus-operated, Slick Shift Chrysler A-833 4-speed changed the gears.

The 1970 Pro Stock Hemi Duster was posed in front of the Sox & Martin facility in Burlington. The picture was used later for the cover of the Sox & Martin parts catalog. (Photo Courtesy Buddy Martin)

Ronnie occasionally drove the F/Stock 340 Duster in competition. He appreciated all types and sizes of race cars and drove them all exceptionally well. (Photo Courtesy Don Moats)

night while Herb, in the second S&M car, ran a 10.07. Ronnie pushed through the field and beat red-lighting Wally Booth's Camaro in the final in 10.02 seconds for the $14,000 prize. Joe Fisher was entered in the Road Runner Superbird in SS/E at this meet but did not run.

NHRA Summernationals

The team's winning streak did not stop for the inaugural NHRA Summernationals held in July 1970 at York US 30 Drag-O-Way in Pennsylvania. Although a Sox & Martin car did not win the race, Herb, driving the Sox & Martin Hemi Duster, worked to an impressive second spot against Dick Landy in the Pro Stock final.

AHRA Nationals

August 28–30, 1970, saw the AHRA Nationals at Center Moriches on Long Island, New York. The event was scheduled for the previous weekend but was rained out. Because the AHRA World Championships were held the same weekend at Bristol in Tennessee, it was difficult for those working toward the season points leads and who had to make both events.

Herb drove the Pro Stock Duster at Bristol and Ronnie handled the Super Stock and GT-1 cars at Long Island. Sox took Super Stock Eliminator with a 9.84 ET at 139 mph and won GT-1 at 10.80 at 130.

NHRA Nationals

The 1970 NHRA Nationals came together as usual at Indianapolis Raceway Park on Labor Day weekend for the 16th annual event. The Nationals were permanently based at Indy beginning in 1961, a facility fully capable of handling the crowd of 140,000 spectators and 1,500 race cars attending in 1970.

The fans' interest in the new Pro Stock Eliminator category was evidenced by the crowd standing and cheering when the cars pulled from the staging lanes. A number of mishaps and missteps during this year's event began with Bill Jenkins being turned away by an NHRA tech for an unapproved hood scoop and Bob Banning's Dodge hitting Bo Law's Camaro when his throttle stuck during a burnout.

In the final round, Herb McCandless in the Sox & Martin Hemi Duster beat Arlen Vanke on a holeshot with both cars turning identical ETs of 9.98 seconds at 138.03 mph.

Ronnie followed this Nationals win by winning Pro Stock at the NHRA World Finals in Dallas.

NHRA Mattel Hot Wheels Supernationals

On November 21–22, 1970, the inaugural NHRA Mattel Hot Wheels Supernationals was held at the newly completed Ontario International Speedway in California. This invitational race was one of the first NHRA events with a named sponsor, an arrangement that become the norm in later years. The event's finals saw Ronnie Sox win the Pro Stock title in the updated 1971 Hemi 'Cuda.

End of Season Tally

By the close of 1970, the Sox & Martin team accomplished an amazing string of wins that represented a great season. In addition to the races already described,

The 1970 Duster, equipped with a 340-ci V-8, waits on the trailer at the track. This Duster competed in the F/Stock class. This car is now owned by Don Moats in Pennsylvania. (Photo Courtesy Don Moats)

Herb drove the 1970 Pro Stock Duster a number of times during the 1970 racing season. Here, he waits in the staging lanes for his next run. Notice the approved roll bar design for the times. (Photo Courtesy Smyle Collection)

1970–1972 Pro Stock 4-Speed Era

Ronnie Sox won the 1970 NHRA Pro Stock World Championship and Super Stock Eliminator at the AHRA Points Finals. He was runner-up at the AHRA Grand American race in Boston and Super Stock Eliminator at the AHRA Grand American at Rockingham. The GT-1 Hemi 'Cuda won at that same event.

By the close of 1970, Chrysler realized more every day the value of the wins and the public image of drag racing as well as the Dodge and Plymouth racers Don Grotheer, Arlen Vanke, Herb McCandless, and of course, Ronnie Sox and Buddy Martin.

The entire Sox & Martin gang poses for a great photo while at the 1970 NHRA Mattel Hot Wheels Supernationals, which was held at Ontario International Speedway in California. Left to right is: Vaughn Currie, Dave Christie, Jake King, Ronnie Sox, Buddy Martin, and Herb McCandless. (Steve Reyes Photo)

> **Because the 1970 Superbird was no longer a current model, it was decided that a new 1971 Road Runner was the appropriate replacement.**

Chrysler Plymouth Division contracted Dan Gurney Productions to produce a 22-minute promotional video called *Pro*. The video told the history of drag racing for the general public, but it was obvious throughout the presentation that Sox & Martin were number one and the center of attention. After the succession of national Pro Stock wins in 1970 by the team, the choice was clear.

New Power For 1971

The Sox & Martin race car stable had some changes for 1971. Because the 1970 Superbird was no longer a current model, it was decided that a new 1971 Road Runner was the appropriate replacement. Both the Plymouth and the Dodge B-Body lines featured radical styling changes for 1971 so the new Plymouth stood out from the crowd and from the previous models.

The bodies were longer and wider. A full-width, chrome-bordered grille opening dominated the massive front-end view. This, and the swept-back roof-styling gave the car a heavier appearance. Nevertheless, it was important for the team to show the new car to support Chrysler-Plymouth marketing efforts for the model year.

The Road Runner was prepared, not only for show and Performance Clinic use, but for real competition in

The long hairstyles make it clear that this photo of Buddy Martin and Ronnie Sox was taken sometime in 1970 or 1971. They always appeared professional with uniforms and a clean and neat appearance. (Photo Courtesy Diane Sox)

Chapter 4

Jake looks away, but the white towel keeps dirt and prying eyes from the two big Holley carburetors on the 426 Hemi engine in the 1972 Pro Stock 'Cuda. (Photo Courtesy Dave Christie)

the NHRA B/Modified production class. The body was essentially stock but a large Pro Stock–style hood scoop was necessary to cover and feed fresh air to the larger than normal intake manifold and carburetors. The body was finished in the iconic Sox & Martin red, white, and blue colors by Red Gibson. This included Jake King's silver-leaf lettering on the doors finished by painter Carl Clayton.

Ronnie elects to rest on his hands as his fellow teammates use the Plymouth Duster as a backrest. About the only downtime for these guys was waiting in staging for their class runoffs. (John Beach Photo)

Of course, the power for the Road Runner was provided by a 426 Hemi fed by a custom-built inline tunnel-ram induction system topped with a pair of 1,150 cfm Holley 4500 series 4-barrel carburetors. Stock cast-iron heads were used, as was a Chrysler Cam Craft 590 high-performance camshaft. TRW pistons and connecting rods were connected to a stock Chrysler forged steel crankshaft. A Sox & Martin nine-quart oil pan held oil circulated by a Milodon oil pump. Exhaust gases exited through Hooker headers and ignition was controlled by a Prestolite unit pushing spark through Champion N-64Y

The 1971 Sox & Martin Road Runner was mainly used for clinics, but did turn a 10.50 at 130.00 in B/Modified. (Bob McClurg Photo)

A very intent Jake King looks on as Ronnie Sox surveys the action at the dragstrip. Each of these men believed the other was the most important part of the Sox & Martin team. (Photo Courtesy Jake King Collection)

Cricket Economy

One of the most unusual cars to come into the Sox & Martin shop was a 1971 Cricket. In addition to the positive publicity that Chrysler received from the drag racing wins of Sox & Martin, the company also realized that the team could be beneficial to its product development program. The four-door Cricket was a badge-engineered import sold by Chrysler in Europe as the Hillman Avenger. The small economy car was intended as competition for the Chevrolet Vega and Ford Pinto.

In stock form, it was equipped with a 91.4-ci 70-hp 4-cylinder inline engine with a single-barrel Stromberg CDS carburetor. Chrysler enlisted the experience and aid of the Sox & Martin team to test the possibilities for performance improvement of the little car for the American market. Quarter-mile times of 19.72 at 67.66 mph were not exactly impressive, even with the economy of 22.2 mpg on the road.

Once the Cricket was in the Sox & Martin garage, the team put their unique spin on its capabilities. A special high-performance twin-carb parts package was produced in England, but not sold in the United States, so Chrysler sent one to Sox & Martin for the car's conversion. The package consisted of a replacement cylinder head, a new camshaft and timing chain, clutch, distributor, high-compression pistons, Hooker headers, and a dual-carburetor intake manifold. Additional modifications also included a change in rear axle ratio from the stock 3.90:1 to 4.30:1.

The new cylinder heads featured larger 1.47-inch-diameter intake valves and dual-coil valvesprings to improve breathing. The replacement pistons were part of the twin-carb package and provided a higher 9.0:1 compression ratio. The new camshaft was a Holbay 1725 that offered improved valve timing and performance. Quarter-mile dragstrip times were greatly improved; the car now showed a 16.6-second ET. The little car was finished with mag wheels, Firestone road racing tires, and of course, the iconic Sox & Martin red, white, and blue paint job.

The car was used for pit service and shows. It also towed the 1970 Superbird back from the scales on the return road at the 1971 NHRA Winternationals at least once.

---

spark plugs. A battery was mounted in the rear passenger's side of the trunk using the steel mounting plate and plastic tray from the 1964–1968 package race cars.

A Chrysler New process A-833 4-speed transmission and stock clutch controlled by a Hurst Competition Plus shifter sent power to a Dana 60 rear axle with 5.13:1 gears. The axle was supported by Hurst shock absorbers and a Sox & Martin pinion snubber. Keystone wheels mounted with 12.25 x 13 x 15–inch Firestone slicks put the power to the ground. The modified Road Runner posted times at the quarter-mile track of 10.50 at 130 mph, so it carried its mass well.

1971 Pro Stock Domination

The 1971 season was a successful one for Sox & Martin. With six major event wins and a perfect match race record, the team was on top.

NHRA Winternationals

As it had for a number of previous years, the 1971 drag racing season opened with the NHRA Winternationals in Pomona on February 5–7. Due in large part

Mechanic Jake King (left) and driver Ronnie Sox (right) check over the new Hemi 'Cuda at Pomona at the beginning of the 1971 season. Mechanic Dave Christie looks on (lower left). (Photo Courtesy Dave Christie)

Chapter 4

Ronnie Sox brings his Hemi-powered 1971 (updated 1970) 'Cuda to the starting line. He drove this car to Pro Stock Eliminator in the first two major races of the 1971 season. (Photo Courtesy Dave Christie)

to the high standard and image set by the Sox & Martin team, drag racing became more and more professional in appearance and businesslike.

For 1971, the NHRA had made great efforts to increase the starting line traction but these efforts were yet to show any progress at this early event. Track conditions were still on the slippery side, much to the disappointment of many competitors.

For this first anniversary of Pro Stock, Sox & Martin were well-prepared for combat. Ronnie set the low qualifier times with a 9.81 at 141.50 mph in his all-new 1971 *Boss* Hemi Barracuda. The 1970 car qualified at 9.94 seconds at 140.18 mph. Sox won the event with a 9.86 and 141.20 mph against Wally Booth's losing 10.02 at 139.53 in his Camaro.

> **It was evident to everyone that the Mopars, and especially those built by the Sox & Martin team, were unbeatable.**

AHRA Winter Nationals

The AHRA Winter Nationals at Phoenix was, as usual, the next race. The weather was cold this year and that, plus a bit of rain, brought records for carbureted cars that liked the cool temperatures. The AHRA called the class Pro Super Stock and the same times from the same cars found at the NHRA event were prevalent here. Don Carlton, driving Billy Stepp's Challenger was low qualifier at 9.75, followed by Ronnie Sox in his 1971 'Cuda at 9.78.

Carlton's power did not take him past round one; he red-lighted against Bill Jenkins, turning in a 10.01 in his Camaro. Ronnie Sox made it through round one but red-lighted in round two, moving out of contention. "Akron Arlen" Vanke took the final against Bob Lambeck's Dart.

NHRA Gatornationals

The NHRA Gatornationals at Gainesville were a repeat of the Sox & Martin power from February. Sox garnered the low qualifying run in Pro Stock with a 9.57 at 142.76 mph. He waded easily through Arlen Vanke and Wally Booth in four rounds of eliminations to face Don Carlton and *Motown Missile* in the final. Carlton somehow grabbed the wrong gear in his ClutchFlite after his burnout, allowing The Boss a win at a 9.60 ET at 141.95 mph.

Many Pro Stock cars ran the new Weiand plenum intake manifold; it appeared to make at least 2 more mph on the top end so the Sox & Martin team planned to change from the fabricated manifold and go with the crowd.

The new Sox & Martin Hemi 'Cuda sported the 1971 grille and taillights in addition to the 16–spark plug heads, dual distributors, and new Weiand intake manifold with dual Holley 4500 Series 1150 CFM 4-barrel carburetors. The higher hood scoop was also updated with a redesigned horizontal rectangular intake opening.

NHRA Springnationals

Because the International Hot Rod Association (IHRA) now owned the track at Bristol, Tennessee, the NHRA 1971 event was held at the new Dallas International Speedway in Texas. By this time, it was evident to everyone that the Mopars, and especially those built by the Sox & Martin team, were unbeatable.

This point was proven at the 1971 Springnationals when Chevy competitors Bill Jenkins and Wally Booth decided not to enter. They moved to match race opportunities where they had a chance of winning and could remove weight from their Camaros (although they did show up for the Sunday finals to watch Sox win).

Others, such as former Chevy racer Mike Fons, chose to move to the other side and switch to driving a Mopar. Ford competitors were equally outgunned with the exception of Don Nicholson.

The NHRA and reporters were beginning to fear that the Chrysler domination would prevent the class from growing and suggested that there should be some sort of weight break for the Chevy and Ford cars so that the fans saw more competition. At this year's Springnationals, 22 of the 32 cars qualifying for Pro Stock were Mopars, 8 were Chevrolets, and 2 were Fords.

Don Carlton in the now 4-speed equipped *Motown Missile* and Ronnie Sox in the Hemi 'Cuda were low qualifiers, running identical times of 9.613 and nearly identical 142.63-mph top speeds. By the end of round two, there was only Don Nicholson's Ford to battle it out with the rest of the Mopars. Sox beat Arlen Vanke in round three and Melvin Yow in the semi-finals with a 9.68 blast.

The final round was a classic match of Sox and Nicholson. Although Dyno Don and his Maverick gained half a car length on Sox out of the hole, Ronnie used his Hemi power and drove around Don for the win with a 9.70 ET at 143.08 mph to Nicholson's losing 9.78 at 140.40.

This win marked Ronnie Sox's fifth victory at an NHRA national event. Sox had never lost in class or eliminations at Dallas and had won every NHRA Springnationals since 1967. Ronnie had also not lost a match race or NHRA race in 1971 and kept his record by winning the $11,950 Pro Stock purse for this race.

IHRA Spring Nationals

The 1971 IHRA Spring Nationals was held at Thunder Valley. Larry Carrier, who owns the Bristol track, was the president of IHRA so the event was an obvious choice. This first showing saw a crowd of 55,000 at the popular venue.

The IHRA created classes and rules based on what were perceived as the best ideas of the NHRA and AHRA. One difference at IHRA events was the presentation of jet cars and exhibitions. This ended up contributing to already bad track conditions at the 1971 event because of recent repaving and weather conditions; it caused problems throughout the weekend. By Saturday the surface was lifting and checking badly.

The cars that ran in IHRA Pro Stock were gathered for what they called Super Stock and the field consisted of 15 competitors. Everyone assumed at the start that Ronnie Sox would win the event. He beat Warren Barnett in

The 1970 Sox & Martin Hemi Duster is waiting for the racing to begin in the grassy field at the track. The debris on the ground is Polaroid photo backings left by adoring fans. (Tom Kasch Photo)

the first round. Reid Whisnant in his Sox & Martin–built Duster put away Joe Satmary in the *We Haul* Camaro. Sox put out Arlen Vanke in the second round with a 9.69 and 139.96 mph to Vanke's 10.13 at 136.96. But Herb McCandless, driving the J&B Automotive Sox & Martin–built Duster was beaten by Reid Whisnant in his Duster.

Three Sox & Martin cars made it to the semi-final round to fight Don Carlton's Dodge Challenger. The final round saw Carlton's *Motown Missile* Challenger against Ronnie Sox in the Hemi 'Cuda. It was all over before it started when Carlton red-lighted, running a 9.63 at 141.28 in the process. Sox won the race with a slower 9.72 at 140.18 mph.

NHRA Summernationals

Next in the season was the second annual NHRA Summernationals, held at Madison Township Raceway Park in Englishtown, New Jersey. Crowd numbers were much improved over the previous year's event with 45,000 spectators filling the stands in 1971. As usual, a Mopar again put down the best qualifying times, but this time, it was not Ronnie Sox, but Don Carlton in *Motown Missile* with a record setting time of 9.502 and 145.39 mph. Sox had to settle for fourth position with a 9.640 ET and 143.31 mph in the Hemi 'Cuda.

Ronnie's troubles did not end there. The Hemi 'Cuda did not make it past the second round because of a flat rear tire at the starting line after a burnout. This mishap was very disappointing to the normally winning team

Chapter 4

from Burlington, especially after working all weekend to find the right combination. With Sox out and the other Mopars put away one after the other, Nicholson and his Pinto ended up winning the event for Ford.

Canadian Grandnationals

A new NHRA event for 1971 was the Canadian Grandnationals held on August 16 at the great Sanair facility at Montreal, Quebec. The fans north of the border were ready and showed up in force to the tune of 27,000. Ronnie Sox won Pro Stock with his 1971 Hemi 'Cuda, first

> "Stepp took the check, tore it up, and threw it back at Martin, along with some words of contempt, likely creating a new rivalry in Pro Stock."

putting Jere Stahl and his 'Cuda on the trailer and then beating Don Carlton in *Motown Missile* in the final with a 9.50 ET. Sox had consistently kept the 'Cuda in the 9.50 range all day long and was back on the winning track.

NHRA Nationals

The 1971 NHRA Nationals at Indy on September 2–6 proved to be another "Big Go" in every sense; each year was better than the previous. As it had been in the Summernationals, qualifying in Pro Stock was led by Don Carlton's 9.55 in the Ted Spehar–built *Motown Missile*. The first round saw, among others, Don Carlton over John Hagen, Stuart McDade over Reid Whisnant, and Herb McCandless in the second Sox & Martin car beating Northern Illinois racer Larry Griffith. Mopar racer Don Grotheer beat Warren Johnson in his Camaro and Ronnie Sox defeated Gene Graham's Dodge Demon. McCandless was put away by Carlton in the second round.

By the fourth round, all competitors were Mopar and all were the top qualifiers. This round found Sox and Carlton facing each other and poised for the most anticipated run of the day, but the lights were somehow set for a .03-second handicap start on the *Missile*'s lane, giving Sox the jump on Carlton.

Everyone at the line knew of the error immediately, and soon the announcer said that the race had to be rerun. Unfortunately for Carlton, a clutch finger broke while on the way back to the line on the return road. The crew worked frantically to fix the problem, but before they could get to the line, the announcer stated that *Missile* could not make it back on time and the results stick, making Sox the winner of the round.

In the final, Ronnie Sox faced Stuart McDade in the Billy Stepp Hemi Challenger. At the end of the race, Sox maintained his dominance by besting McDade with a 9.586 at 142.85 mph to McDade's 9.588 and 143.31, with only inches between them at the lights. *Super Stock* magazine called it, "One of the best single runs in drag racing history."

The win was made less than sweet because earlier in the event, after qualifying, Buddy Martin filed a protest against the Stepp car. The engine was torn down, checked, and found to be legal so Buddy had to hand over the protest fee to Stepp. Stepp took the check, tore it up, and threw it back at Martin, along with some words of contempt, likely creating a new rivalry in Pro Stock.

IHRA World Finals

The IHRA World Finals were run in late September at Lakeland International Dragway in Florida. Competitors were greeted with a newly finished track surface and the local officials worked all weekend to make sure it was kept up, which made for great Pro Stock times. Pro entry was restricted to only those drivers who had previously participated in at least one IHRA event over the past year.

The end of the day on Saturday found Ronnie Sox beating out Don Carlton for the top spot with a 9.63 to Carlton's 9.69. Reid Whisnant was third at 9.75. Sox was a little too anxious in his first round race against Carlton and red-lighted. Sox complained about a perceived tree malfunction but a check found it working correctly and Sox was out. Carlton ended up winning the meet with a 9.71 at 143.31 mph against Reid Whisnant in his Sox & Martin–built car at 9.84 and 140.62.

NHRA World Finals

The seventh annual NHRA World Finals race on October 23–24 was moved to the updated track at Amarillo, Texas, due to the loss of the Dallas facility to the IHRA. The World Finals could be entered only by winning 35 World Championship points for the season in a division. Show money was provided for the competitors, making for a well-attended event. Pro Stock eliminations were held in an unusual East meets West contest with the fastest East car meeting the fastest West car in the first round. The track's 3,700-foot elevation made the air thin, affecting times but the competition was still fierce.

Because of a mismatch of competitors, eight single runs were in that first round. In the second round, Stuart McDade in Billy Stepp's Hemi Challenger beat Don Carlton in *Motown Missile*, Ronnie Sox beat Dick Landy in his Dodge, and Herb McCandless in the number-two Sox & Martin car beat Reid Whisnant with a 10.30 time.

This was Mike Fons' year because, by the end of the semi-finals, he had put away two-time World Champion and NHRA Division 2 Champion Ronnie Sox with a 10.06 to Sox's losing 10.14. Fons, in his Rod Shop Dodge Challenger, followed this up with a final win for the Championship against Herb McCandless in the second Sox & Martin car at 10.05 to Herb's 10.40.

The 1971 NHRA World Finals venue was the perfect place for Mopar to present the special trademarked official racing jackets to their sponsored teams and drivers. Blue jackets were given to the Plymouth teams: Sox & Martin and Don Grotheer. Red jackets were given to the Dodge teams: Larry Griffith, Dick Landy, Don Carlton, and the *Motown Missile* crew. The jackets were emblazoned with the driver's and team member's names and the unique division logos. These jackets helped to represent the professionalism and factory support of the Mopar racing operation and recipients were happy to display them.

NHRA Supernationals

The last big NHRA event of the year was the second annual Supernationals held at Ontario International

On one of their West Coast trips, Buddy and Ronnie met with Big Willie Robinson of the International Brotherhood of Street Racers. He told them about his efforts to bring street racers off the streets and give them a safe and legal place to race. Both E-Body Hemi 'Cudas were on hand. (Photo Courtesy Doug Boyce)

Speedway in California on November 20 and 21. Some called this the "Secret Nationals" because of the lack of promotional efforts by Ontario Speedway. This failure meant that the event would probably be moved to a different venue for 1972. As in 1970, the Supernationals was an invitation-only race so only the best competed.

The Pro Stock field was supposed to be a 32-car show but only 28 cars attended. Apparently, Ronnie's consistent wins in this category kept a number of racers from coming all the way across the country just to be put right back onto the trailer by the red, white, and blue 1972 Plymouth 'Cuda (actually an updated 1971 model).

Ronnie steers the Pro Stock Hemi 'Cuda straight off the line at the 1971 NHRA Supernationals held at Ontario International Speedway in California. This event was often nicknamed the "Secret Nationals" because of the lack of promotion by the track. (Roger Phillips Photo)

Chapter 4

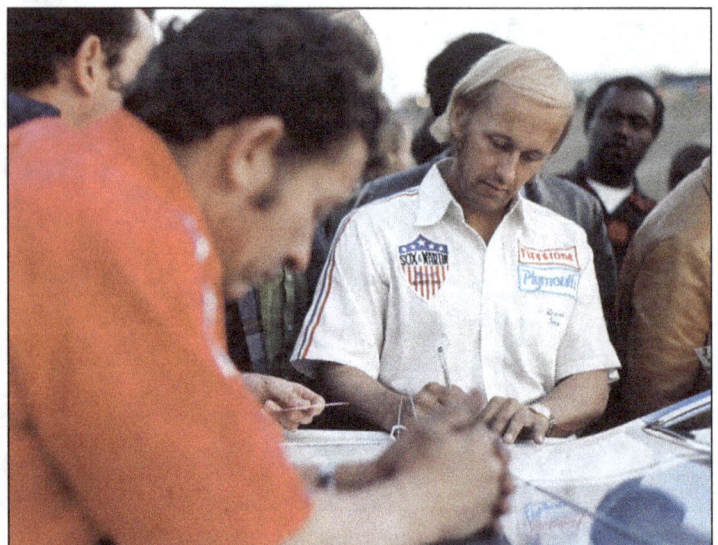

Jake King seems to be resting as Ronnie Sox signs autographs for his fans on the deck lid of the Barracuda during the 1971 NHRA Supernationals at Ontario International Speedway. (Roger Phillips Photo)

Ronnie Sox usually had a long line of adoring and loyal fans waiting for a chance to get an autograph. He was kept busy between rounds at the 1971 Supernationals. (Roger Phillips Photo)

Qualifying started off well for Californian Butch Leal with an impressive 9.53, followed by Mike Fons with a 9.57, and Don Nicholson's 9.60 in his Maverick. Ronnie Sox only made it to sixth position with a "slow" 9.66 ET. He made up for that by beating Shirley Shahan, Don Nicholson, and Dick Landy on his way to the semi-final round.

Butch Leal had been claiming that he was going to beat Sox at this race and when the semi-final round came up, he did. Leal put a serious holeshot on Sox and maintained this 6-foot lead all the way to the lights with a 9.553 over Sox's 9.558.

Leal's win was only temporary because Buddy Martin protested his weight distribution and NHRA techs found that Leal was 66 pounds overweight on the rear wheels, which disqualified him. The scales showed 57.2-percent on the rear, exceeding the NHRA 55-percent rules limit. Unfortunately for Leal, this rule was changed soon after this race.

Ronnie won in the final against teammate Herb McCandless driving the Sox & Martin–built Keystone-sponsored 1972 'Cuda owned by John Millwee and Geno Redd. Sox recorded a 9.61 at 143.31 mph over McCandless at 9.64 at 142.13. McCandless made it to the final by beating Don Grotheer in the third round with a 9.64 over Grotheer's 9.75.

On Monday, the Sox & Martin 'Cuda was questioned by NHRA tech officials regarding wheelbase and engine setback. It was found legal after extensive checking and measuring against a stock Challenger owned by Dick Landy. This was Ronnie Sox's sixth NHRA national event win in 1971.

By 1971, Chrysler introduced the new twin-spark plug cylinder heads for Pro Stock competition. The twin plugs provided improved flame propagation within the combustion chamber and allowed less spark advance. (Photo Courtesy Photographic Archives of C.A.R.S.)

Crank It Up!

Chrysler and other manufacturers continued to release innovative Sox & Martin–themed promotional and publicity materials in 1971. One was a 33⅓-rpm record album titled *Sox & Martin's The Drags*, produced by DGFA in California in association with Michael Doane Advertising for the Keystone Corporation.

The 12½-inch-square record jacket showed the then-popular red, white, and blue psychedelic title across a large photo of someone's left ear stuffed with cotton. The reverse side showed large black-and-white portraits of Buddy and Ronnie superimposed over wide red, white, and blue horizontal stripes. The long-playing record had a different theme on each side.

Side one featured Ronnie and Buddy in an interview with track announcer and television host Steve Evans, talking about what it takes to put a winning effort together. They talked about equipment, safety, team management, and what drag racing has meant to them.

Side two contained a compilation of the sounds of drag racing. The sounds were taken from several events and featured Top Fuel, Top Gas, Funny Cars, Pro Stock, and others. These sounds and their associated action were part of what drove the enthusiasm of the drag racing fans of the 1960s and 1970s. Many of the popular and important racers of the day were included.

One interesting and unusual promotional item produced in late 1971 was this record album featuring Ronnie and Buddy on one side and the sounds of drag racing on the other. (Album Courtesy John Mahoney)

The back side of the record album cover featured portraits of Buddy and Ronnie and a contents list. The record was a convenient way for fans to feel closer to the personalities. (Album Courtesy John Mahoney)

Post-Season Highlights

By the close of 1971, Sox & Martin's business operations in Burlington had grown beyond merely winning almost every race. They were heavily into the sales and distribution of Mopar Performance parts, in addition to building race engines and expensive and exotic Barracudas and Dusters for others. At the end of 1971, orders for customer cars were on a four-month waiting list.

Two very pleased Sox & Martin customers were Freeman Lee Crowder Sr. and Freeman Lee Crowder Jr., of Livingston, Tennessee, who purchased a race-ready 1971 Pro Stock Dodge Demon from the Sox & Martin shop for $14,000. They joined driver John Livingston and mechanic (and John's brother) Gerald Livingston to create a winning race team. The Livingstons already had some experience running winning Chevrolets in the area so they were great choices.

Once the new Demon arrived at the Crowder shop it was finished in white with a wide bright green stripe bordered in blue down the center of the body and the name,

Chapter 4

Ronnie gently lifts the front wheels on the launch at the open country track of Union Grove, Wisconsin. The front tires of this Hemi 'Cuda have "Ronnie Sox" emblazoned on the sidewalls. (Mark Janaky Photo)

Tennessee Thunder, emblazoned on the doors in yellow. For the 1971 season, John Livingston drove the former *Motown Missile* Challenger as the new *Tennessee Thunder*. By 2015, the *Tennessee Thunder* Demon had been found and restored to its original 1971 race appearance.

One of the most interesting events at the end of the 1971 season was when motorsports was recognized with a special meeting and reception at the White House with President Richard M. Nixon. Invited attendees included Richard Petty, Don Garlits, and of course Ronnie Sox and Buddy Martin. Ronnie even had a conversation with President Nixon about what it was like to drive his race car.

Public Relations Director Tom Richardson also garnered well deserved recognition for his work with Sox & Martin. At the end of the 1971 season, he was presented with the NHRA Public Relations Award. The town of Burlington celebrated this achievement with a parade through the town in his honor.

Rules Changes for 1972

The most significant and important news for the 1972 Pro Stock racing season was the introduction of new rules from the NHRA. First used at the Pomona Winternationals,

In December 1971, a number of motorsports figures were invited to the White House to meet the president and recognize the accomplishments of the motorsports industry. Ronnie Sox and Buddy Martin were among them. Here, Buddy shakes hands with Richard Nixon.

Ronnie Sox was in line directly behind Buddy and also enjoyed the great honor of meeting President Richard Nixon. Ronnie said later that the president asked him about driving a race car.

1970–1972 Pro Stock 4-Speed Era

Ronnie drove the 1971 Pro Stock Hemi 'Cuda at several top events and match races all around the country, including this one at Union Grove Drag Strip in Wisconsin. (Mark Janaky Photo)

the new rules changed the image of Pro Stock more than any other event since the class's inception in 1970.

Rather than the previous system of large displacement factory big-block engines, such as the 426 Hemi, 427 Chevy, and 429 Ford, the new rules allowed for three sizes of engines and cars. The new weight breaks attempted to equalize the competition by allowing fewer pounds per cubic inch for the smaller configurations.

The new weight system allowed 6.75 lbs/ci for the mini cars with wedge engines, 7 lbs/ci inch for the inclined-valve engines, and 7.25 lbs/ci for the big engines such as the 426 Hemi and Ford Boss 429. The various types of cars competed together, heads up, in Pro Stock.

These new rules were developed in December 1971 by a meeting of Chevy competitor Bill "Grumpy" Jenkins and NHRA Executive Vice President Jack Hart. Jenkins knew that he could compete with the Hemi by putting the 331-ci small-block Chevy V-8 in the smaller, shorter-wheelbase Vega package. The idea behind the NHRA's decision was that it was better for marketing purposes because the public was buying smaller cars. Chrysler protested the new rules, but the rules stood anyway.

The AHRA joined the NHRA in publishing new Pro Stock rules for the 1972 season. In addition to adding 36 stock classes, the new AHRA Pro Stock class had three weight breaks, similar to those adopted by the NHRA. Inline-valve engines were to run at 6.5 lbs/ci,

Jake King posed with the 1971 Hemi 'Cuda for this photo, which was used later for a Champion Spark Plug magazine ad. Jake was one of few drag racing crew chiefs or mechanics who was as well-known to fans as the drivers. (Photo Courtesy Jake King Collection)

Ronnie posed for photos with one of the many trophies he won at races around the country. The patches on his driving suit represent the sponsors and supporters of Sox & Martin. These sponsors helped pay for the operation of the team in exchange for advertising their products. (Photo Courtesy Diane Sox)

Chapter 4

stagger-valve engines at 6.7 lbs/ci, and the Hemi and OHC Ford engines at 7 pounds. Pony Cars with big-block engines were also required to run the 7 pound break.

Small cars were limited to 94 inches minimum wheelbase; firewall modifications necessary for engine clearance were allowed. Plexiglass windows and any rear axle housing were permitted throughout Pro Stock. The GT-1 class was also revised to allow more room for independent Pro Stock racers with 8 lbs/ci for Hemis and 7.8 for wedge engines.

Ronnie Sox's wins in 1971 put him near the top of handicapper lists for winners in 1972. *Hot Rod* picked Don Carlton as number one and Ronnie Sox number two, both at 2:1 odds. Mike Fons and Butch Leal were listed as numbers three and four, both at 4:1. Herb McCandless was placed at number seven, and Bill Jenkins was down the list at number nine.

1972 Meets from Coast to Coast

Ronnie Sox's winning streak broke in 1972. Between Jenkins' new Vega and some bad breaks, including Ronnie's own wrist, the season was a downer. Sox won only one major event, but team member Herb McCandless was on a winning streak.

NHRA Winternationals

The first major event to run under the new rules was the NHRA Winternationals at Pomona on February 6, 1972. The Sox & Martin team was there in force as usual, but this was a tough crowd to beat. Qualifying rounds found Stuart McDade number one with a 9.59 at 144 mph by the end of Saturday in the Billy Stepp car. Next in line was Butch Leal with a 9.63 and 144.24 and then Ronnie Sox with 9.65 at 143.31 mph in his 1972 Hemi 'Cuda.

Round one of eliminations showed the top qualifiers winning consistently against the bottom of the field. Unfortunately, Bill Jenkins and his so-called Funny Car Vega took out top qualifier McDade with a 9.63 at 142 mph. Round two winners were Don Carlton, Butch Leal, Arlen Vanke, Don Grotheer, and Ronnie Sox. In round three, Carlton took out Sox on a holeshot in the *Motown Missile* Challenger with a 9.68 at 142.40 to Ronnie's quicker 9.64 at 142.18. The semi-final round saw Jenkins take out *Missile* and he then went on to beat Grotheer in the final for the win, ending two years of Mopar Pro Stock domination.

This win for Jenkins was significant in several ways. One was that he brought this small-block Vega to the show with an innovative, and in some eyes, questionable, tube-frame structure incorporated into the rear suspension, tying the 360-degree roll cage into the lightly acid-dipped body sills. The rear axle was an acid-dipped Dana 60 with 5.57:1 gears. The front subframe was stock but incorporated a Ford Pinto steering gear. It was not a total tube-frame as some believed.

Although unconventional and controversial, the *Grumpy's Toy IX* Vega passed NHRA tech inspection, with the sole exception of fenderwell headers that had to be redesigned and replaced by Hooker before qualifying and competing.

> "The semi-final round saw Jenkins take out *Missile* and he then went on to beat Grotheer in the final for the win, ending two years of Mopar Pro Stock domination."

Sox & Martin found out quickly that the new engine and weight restrictions "leveled" the playing field at the 1972 Winternationals. (Steve Reyes Photo)

Beeline Dragway

The AHRA winter meet at Beeline, near Phoenix, Arizona, was another hit with an overflowing crowd of entries that required an adjustment of operations to keep things moving without a hitch. Every top Mopar was there fighting for a top spot, but qualifying was led by Don Nicholson in his Maverick, now using a new 5-speed transmission.

Nicholson put down a best time of 9.60 at 143.08 mph. The Mopar entries followed with times of 9.62 to 10.02. Ronnie Sox was third with a 9.63, just behind Butch Leal. Sox red-lighted in the second round and the race ended up with a win by second qualifier Butch Leal over Bill Bagshaw's *Red Light Bandit*. Butch ran a 9.66 at 143 mph to Bagshaw's losing 9.75 at 141.

Aquasco Speedway

In March, at Aquasco in Maryland, Herb McCandless showed up with the Sox & Martin 1972 Pro Stock Hemi 'Cuda for some match racing. In the first round, after a huge smokey burnout, Herb beat Roy Hill, from High Point, North Carolina, in his Pro Stock Barracuda with a 9.75 and 141 mph over Hill's losing 9.87 at 140.16. In the next round the story was repeated but Hill had transmission troubles which gave the 9.71, 140 mph win to McCandless.

Herb was next matched with Virginia's Rick Holiday and a Hemi 'Cuda. The start was almost even, with Herb having a slight lead, which he held to the win at 9.65 at 139 mph.

NHRA Gatornationals

The NHRA Gatornationals were held on March 18 and 19, again at Gainesville, Florida. The Pro Stock field seemed to be getting faster and quicker with every meet but this one had some upsets and surprises. Carlton was only able to manage a 12th spot in qualifying with a relatively "slow" 9.701 at 141.28 mph. The cut-off was 9.72 in the 16-car field so they barely made the show in *Motown Missile*. Jenkins led qualifying again in his Vega and ran a 9.44 at 144.69 mph.

Jenkins beat McCandless in the number two Sox & Martin 'Cuda with a run of 9.62 to Herb's 9.75 in the first round. Sox was put away quickly by Carlton with a 9.58 when Sox uncharacteristically missed a gear. In the final, Melvin Yow red-lighted against Carlton, who won the event with a solid 9.55 ET. Ronnie Sox had to make a big push to match his winning year of 1971.

News from the Sox & Martin shop was the loss of Bird Shoffner and Joe Fisher. They left to join Sox & Martin Pro Stock customer Reid Whisnant to open a new drag racing car preparation facility in Atlanta, Georgia. The new business operated under the name of Atlanta Race Cars, Inc. and also offered accessories and parts for sale. (Bird Shoffner passed away in May 2013 at the age of 73.)

A new member joined the Sox & Martin team in 1972. Randy Dorton, from Charlotte, performed a variety of jobs including engine work. While working in Burlington, Randy stayed with Chick DeNinno. Randy later worked for Ron Lyles and moved to Hendrick Motorsports after leaving Sox & Martin.

IHRA Pro-Am Championship

The third annual IHRA Pro-Am Championship race was held at Rockingham, North Carolina, on April 29 and 30. In the first round of Pro Stock, Ronnie Sox opened with an IHRA top speed record-setting 9.68 at 145.63 mph. In round two, Sox beat Bob Lambeck with

David Sox rolls past the lights in the white Sox & Martin F/Stock 1972 340 Duster. He ran as quick as 11.70 at 113.70 mph in this car, built from a 1970 clinic car. (Steve Reyes Photo)

Chapter 4

a 9.45 against Lambeck's 9.56 challenge. In the final, Sox put away Don Carlton in the *Missile* with a 9.42 at 142.23 mph to Carlton's 9.54 and 144.46. Pro Stock times and speeds seemed to be getting better with each event.

The IHRA Pro-Am race was also the debut of Ronnie's 17-year-old brother David at a national event. David drove the white "Sox & Martin Test Car" 340 Duster in F/Stock 2 class. David and engine builder Mark Graves had already tested the car prior to this race at the fifth-mile Sportsman track at Farmington, near Winston-Salem. After some adjustments, they were ready for the big time. The team was unfamiliar with the small-block configuration so it took some time to work out the kinks.

IHRA Longhorn Nationals

The IHRA moved to Dallas International Motor Speedway in early June for its first annual Longhorn Nationals. Pro Stock qualifying found Don Carlton and *Motown Missile* on top with a 9.43, followed by Ronnie Sox in the red, white, and blue Barracuda with a far-behind 9.58.

Carlton dominated the entire event and in the final, beat Ronnie Sox with the low ET and top speed of the meet at 9.42 and 146.57 mph to Ronnie's 9.63 at 143.31. This was Ronnie's first loss at Dallas.

NHRA Springnationals

The NHRA Springnationals was held June 10 and 11 at National Trail Raceway near Columbus, Ohio, the first time at this track. The venue was smaller than the previous tracks and the track surface was not up to par, but its central location made for a big crowd of spectators. Again, Bill Jenkins and Don Carlton were top qualifiers with 9.52 and 9.66, respectively.

This race saw an increase in tire experimentation both in brand and size. Jenkins' crew changed tires on almost every run. In their attempts to increase traction, some racers ran slicks that looked almost as wide as Funny Car tires.

Sox & Martin planned to be ready for this big race with their new team-built 1972 Hemi Duster, but they arrived too late and missed the tech inspection by two hours. They had to run the already inspected Barracuda and qualified third with a 9.72 ET.

In the first of two matches against rivals, Sox beat former customer Reid Whisnant with a 9.71 to Reid's 9.78. Later, Sox beat West Coast rival Butch Leal with a holeshot win of 9.71 to Leal's 9.70.

In the semi-final Sox met his biggest rival, Bill Jenkins. The pair drew cheers and excitement from the crowd with their tire-smoking burnouts across the line, but when the lights on the tree went down, Sox red-lighted and lost to Jenkins' 9.63 at 143.31 mph. Sox's losing run of 9.66 was not up to the challenge anyway. In the final, Jenkins beat Don Grotheer for the win and the money.

National Challenge 72

Because Chrysler maintained its boycott of the 1972 NHRA Nationals, the big race was the National Challenge 72, held on Labor Day weekend at Tulsa. Interestingly, Buddy Martin and Don Garlits had to fly to Indianapolis on Friday afternoon in Jim Tice's private airplane to attend the *Car Craft* magazine All-Star Banquet to accept their awards for Crew Chief of the Year and Man of the Year, respectively.

Pro Stock qualifying at Tulsa was intense and the top spot changed quickly from one racer to another throughout the day, passing from Sox to Landy to Jenkins and back to Landy. When the resin and dust settled, Jenkins ended up with low qualifier at 9.395 and 146.57 mph followed closely by Dick Landy turning a 9.405 and 146.10. Unfortunately, both Landy and Jenkins suffered breakage during qualifying and had to spend a long, hard night repairing the damage. Ronnie Sox followed in third place with a still-quick 9.411 at 146.57 in the Duster.

One of the colorful badges that Sox & Martin used for promotional purposes during their career. These logos were also used for patches and decals that were sold to fans at events.

Sunday eliminations were a repeat of earlier 1972 races with Jenkins taking the marbles. By the end of round two, Sox was defeated in a holeshot by his rival Butch Leal with a 9.47 to Ronnie's quicker 9.45. On the other side of the elimination ladder, Sox & Martin team driver Herb McCandless, in his Dodge Demon, advanced to the final round, beating Nichols, Storbeck, and Whisnant along the way.

Herb was initially declared the loser in round four when his crew worked to readjust a wheelie bar following the burnout, causing him to miss the call. After his opponent, John Hagen, made his bye run, officials decided that Herb had not received his allotted 30 seconds to repair and make the start; the race should be rerun. Herb beat Hagen on the rerun with a 9.56 to Hagen's 9.78.

Professional Racers Association

By early 1972, professional drag racers, led by Top Fuel legend Don Garlits, began confronting NHRA President Wally Parks about the size of the purses for NHRA events. Garlits had learned during a recent Vietnam tour that racers in other professional categories were paid much higher for their wins. Garlits talked directly with Wally Parks at the January 15, 1972, Division 2 banquet, telling him that the only way drag racing would grow was to increase the purses for the winners.

By April 9, 1972, a group of professional drag racers signed a petition and told the NHRA that they would only appear at the NHRA Nationals if the race offered $25,000 in prize money to the winners of the three top pro categories, including Pro Stock. The petition also told the NHRA that the signers wanted to form a professional organization of the three pro categories.

On May 8, 1972, the Professional Racers Association (PRA) was formed. Don Garlits was the temporary president; temporary vice presidents for each class included Gene Snow for Funny Cars and Buddy Martin for Pro Stock. Mart Higgenbotham was the secretary and Steve Carbone was treasurer. Each member was required to pay a $100 fee per car, entitling them to a share of stock. The organization was incorporated in the state of Nevada on May 31, 1972. The primary purpose of the association was to guarantee the best 16 cars in each category at each event.

By May 12, the PRA announced plans to hold an event with a $25,000 non-contingent award to the winners of Top Fuel, Funny Car, and Pro Stock, with additional $2,000 awards to each runner-up and $500 to all qualifiers. They also planned to make an arrangement with the AHRA as sanctioning body of the event, eventually scheduled to be held at Tulsa. For this, the AHRA received 50 percent of any profits.

On June 1, the AHRA sent a letter to the PRA telling them that they would guarantee a $120,000 purse to be paid when the meet was conducted. Trouble began when the Top Fuel and Funny Car racers decided to lower the Pro Stock purse from $25,000 to $10,000. At about the same time, it was discovered that the AHRA did not actually have the cash to back up its contribution to the show and that Jim Tice of AHRA was backing the rest with his own personal note.

Meanwhile, Buddy Martin told Garlits that the Pro Stock drivers would not enter the race unless their purse was raised back to $25,000. Garlits agreed and the additional money was put up by six Top Fuel racers.

In late August, Bob Cahill, head of Chrysler racing, was on vacation. In his absence, Dick Maxwell told the NHRA that there would be no Chrysler Pro Stock entries at the Indianapolis NHRA Nationals in September in protest of the Pro Stock weight breaks. Maxwell also contacted Don Garlits and informed him that there would be no factory-supported Pro Stock drivers at the PRA Tulsa show unless the weight break difference between the small-block Chevy and the Chrysler Hemi were reduced from .5 lb/ci to .25 lb/ci. This decision amounted to a boycott of both races.

Toward the end of August, Bob Cahill cut his vacation short and returned to Detroit. He met with Garlits and Tice. Together, they made an agreement to allow the Chrysler Pro Stock racers to run at Tulsa if they were allowed to use powdered resin on the starting line. They also agreed that at future races the weight difference would be no more than .25 lb/ci. With this agreement, Chrysler lifted its boycott of the Tulsa race.

Meanwhile, Herb McCandless in the Sox & Martin Demon was keeping the Pro Stock action alive. He was low qualifier and winner at Atco on July 19 with the United States Racing Team and on July 26 he was low qualifier and winner at New England Dragway. Herb was also low qualifier and won at Englishtown on August 2 and Union Grove August 12. No Chrysler Pro Stock beat Herb's Demon to the finish line during 1972. The team's busy schedule included match racing two or three days a week during 1972.

Chapter 4

This Sox & Martin Hemi Duster was built completely in their shop at the same time a Hemi Demon was being built for Herb McCandless. This car is now restored; it is owned and used by Fred Ristagno in New Jersey. (Fred Ristagno Photo)

In the final, it was all for nothing as Jenkins put away McCandless with a 9.46 and 145 mph to Herb's losing 9.51 and 145 mph on a close race for the win and the money.

Final Events and Happenings

The big NHRA and PRA meets were not the only events with Pro Stock competition. In late September, Ronnie Sox set a new unofficial Pro Stock record at York US 30 Drag-O-Way in Pennsylvania running his car with a 6.75 lbs/ci weight. He beat Bill Jenkins in runs of 9.16 and 9.17 in the new Duster.

Unfortunately, Ronnie broke his right wrist in a motorcycle accident a day or so after the race and was out of action until it healed. Herb McCandless had to take over the job of driving the Hemi Duster for a while and had to take a loss against Jenkins at Island Dragway. Jenkins put down a quick run of 9.29 at 148.06 mph in the process.

The Sox & Martin colors of red, white, and blue are so important to the fans that Herb's Demon had to be repainted in those colors because of pressure from race promoters. By the close of the 1972 racing season, Ronnie Sox had won the United States Racing Team Driver Championship by totaling 520 points, beating out teammate Herb McCandless by 55 points. Herb later moved to driving a Dodge Dart Sport for Brooklyn Heavy's team from New York.

In September 1972, the AHRA announced that it would place the weight at 6.75 lbs/ci for Hemi and SOHC engines and 6.5 for both canted and inline-valve engines for the 1973 season. The IHRA adopted the same weight breaks and rules for its events, which was a departure from its flat 7 pounds across the board for 1972. The NHRA planned to try 7 lbs/ci for the Hemi and SOHC engines and 6.5 for everything else.

Ronnie Sox smokes the tires during a burnout in the 1972 Hemi 'Cuda at Rockingham. The 1972 'Cuda is identified by its four round taillights. (Photo Courtesy Bob McClurg)

1970–1972 Pro Stock 4-Speed Era

The Sox & Martin 1972 Hemi 'Cuda was displayed at a Fred Engelhart show in Elkton, Minnesota, in 2006. This car still uses the familiar Keystone chrome spoke wheels that have become closely identified with Sox & Martin. (Mike Galewski Photo)

It was at this time that Ted Spehar's Chrysler skunk works in Detroit started work on a 426 Hemi-powered Dodge Colt. Unfortunately, problems came up when considering the Colt for Pro Stock, one of which was the import status of the car. The NHRA was not pleased with this possibility, especially if the destroked Hemi was capable of high-RPM operation. The idea of using the Colt was really just to create a big reaction from NHRA and the competition as happened with the 1965 AWB cars.

Hemi Duster Number Two

Although the Sox & Martin team had already raced a Pro Stock Plymouth Duster in 1970, it was destroyed at the end of the 1970 season. A new and improved version was in the works for the 1972 season.

By early 1972, Sox & Martin had completed a 70 x 120-foot addition to their already impressive facility in Burlington. This new structure was to be used for building customer cars, which would free up space in the existing area to work on the team-built racer. The new Duster, along with a similar Dodge Demon for Herb McCandless, had been under construction by Dave Christie for almost a year and was finally ready by the NHRA Springnationals in June.

Herb needed the Demon to run in the Dodge section with the newly formed United States Racing Team. He built the car along with the help of assistant Gale Mortimer, who was a new part of the Sox & Martin team. Gale was working for Dick Landy and Herb was driving Landy's car when they first met.

The New Duster Comes Together

The new car was based on a chemically lightened body-in-white sent to the team by Mopar. The basic A-Body was lighter than the E-Body cars from stock, but this extra bit of work made it even lighter.

The Sox & Martin Hemi Duster posed in front of the Ronnie Sox Memorial Grandstand at a dragstrip in North Carolina. The appearance of this Duster is very similar to the later 1973 Duster purchased from Don Grotheer. (Fred Ristagno Photo)

The restored Sox & Martin–built Pro Stock Hemi Duster owned by Fred Ristagno was one of more than 240 Hemi cars displayed at the 2008 All-Hemi Reunion at Quaker City Dragway in Ohio.

Chapter 4

Both cars featured lift-off lightweight fiberglass deck lids, held in place with chrome pins and clips. The hood was also fiberglass and equipped with a new-design scoop to match the car's more aerodynamic nose-down attitude. Two large batteries were mounted at the rear passenger's side of the trunk floor and the fuel filler was in the center. The body was finished in the standard Sox & Martin red, white, and blue. The silver leaf lettering on the doors now stated that the mechanics were Jake King and Dave Christie.

The 108-inch-wheelbase chassis design was still based on the original 1968 A-Body construction and used

The rear suspension of the Sox & Martin–built 1972 Duster featured lightened brake drums and chrome-plated components including the Dana 60 axle housing rear cover and ladder bars. (Photo Courtesy Dave Christie)

The attention to detail of cars built in the Sox & Martin shop is shown by the lightening holes drilled in the reinforcements of the Dana 60 rear axle assembly. The cleanliness and simplicity of the construction helped to make maintenance easier at the track. (Photo Courtesy Dave Christie)

The rear suspension components of the 1972 Hemi Duster were made fully adjustable with Heim joints and slotted attachment holes. Most of the parts were chrome-plated for appearance and durability. (Photo Courtesy Dave Christie)

The 426 Hemi in the 1972 'Cuda used twin distributors to fire the 16 spark plugs. The car is shown here in later years on display at a show. (Mike Galewski Photo)

Mopar factory Super Stock springs with a link-leaf construction. The springs were assisted by long, adjustable ladder bars with five front positions and three rear positions for different strip conditions. The chassis was further improved by the addition of long dual wheelie bars to keep the front end where it should be at the launch. The rear axle was the standard Dana 60 with 5.38:1 gears and Summers axles. Giant 12.2 x 31.25 x 15–inch Firestone 9 compound slicks were mounted on Keystone wheels and attached to Chrysler drum brakes. The body and chassis were strengthened by the installation of a full chrome-moly roll cage.

The front suspension was also extensively modified for light weight and strength. The lower control arms were lighted with drilled holes and mounted special lightweight Hurst/Airheart front disc brakes. Six-cylinder Duster torsion bars were used for better weight transfer. A Ford Pinto rack and pinion provided steering control; it was more precise and lighter than the stock configuration.

The 426 Hemi engine was, of course, built by Chief mechanic Jake King to his exacting specifications and installed in the chassis with special tubular mounts. It had a 13:1 compression ratio and was equipped with 16 plug heads supported by twin Mallory magnetos. A Crane cam with D&D pushrods and springs was used, along with TRW pistons, and NASCAR forged-steel connecting rods and crankshaft. The oiling system was Milodon and the dual Holley 4500 Series 4-barrel carburetors fed through a Weiand cast-aluminum tunnel-ram plenum-type intake manifold. Hooker headers handled the spent exhaust

> "Jake was almost never seen without some type of tool in his hand."

gases. The Hemi power was transmitted to the rear axle by a Chrysler A-833 Red Stripe 4-speed Slick Shift transmission with a cast-aluminum case and housing.

The interiors of both the Duster and the Demon were similar but personalized (just a little) according to the different needs of Herb and Ronnie. The cars featured a fabricated aluminum instrument panel with Stewart Warner gauges. A Stewart Warner tachometer was mounted on top of the instrument panel. It was fitted with black Solar racing seats and the steering wheel was a special aftermarket racing unit. A Hurst Competition Plus shifter and line lock were mounted in the center of the front floor and sealed with a pleated black rubber boot. Stock black vinyl Duster interior door and quarter panels were retained for appearance.

This Duster is now restored with Sox & Martin colors and lettering and owned by New Jersey nostalgia racer Fred Ristagno.

Ready to Race

The new Sox & Martin Hemi Duster made its racing debut at the eighth annual IHRA Springnationals at Bristol International Dragway in Bristol, Tennessee. Rain pushed qualifying for the event to an all-day fest on Sunday, which put the end of eliminations at 10 pm Sunday night. In the first round, number-one qualifier Ronnie Sox beat Bobby Yowell, of Dayton, Ohio, with a 9.84 and 141.35 mph. In the second round Ronnie put away Stuart McDade with a 9.80 ET. Ronnie drove the car to semi-finals where he was beaten by Butch Leal's Duster. Teammate Herb McCandless in the Hemi

A smiling Jake King (left) and Ronnie Sox (right) strike a pose with the beautiful S-K Tools model for a publicity photo at the track. Jake was almost never seen without some type of tool in his hand. (Photo Courtesy Jake King Collection)

Chapter 4

Buddy and Ronnie were always ready to talk to fans and friends at the track. Their colorful clothes and hair styles show this photo to be from the mid-1970s. (Photo Courtesy Buddy Martin)

Demon also lost in the semi-final round to Bill Jenkins' super Vega.

In July 1972, Herb McCandless received a set of the new heads and promptly installed them on his Dodge Demon. From July through September of that year Herb was never beaten to the finish line in a race. His only losses were from a red light at Nashville and a broken clutch at National Trail in Columbus, Ohio.

Ronnie's younger brother David Sox also competed at this event in a white "Sox & Martin Test Car," an F/Stock 340 1972 Duster built from a 1970 clinic car. David won his class with a 12.28 and 112.28 and went on to the Top Stock Eliminator race. He lost any chance for Top Stock when he red-lighted against Roy Johnson in his Dodge. David ran this car as quick as 11.70 at 113.70 mph during this event.

In mid-June, the United States Racing Team held the third of its mid-week Pro Stock events at the Minnesota Dragway. The race packed the stands with one of the largest crowds ever to see the action.

During qualifying, the existing track record was broken five times with Ronnie Sox and Mike Fons making identical 9.54 runs in their Mopars. Don Carlton pushed his *Missile* to top speed of the meet with a record run of 143.76 mph. An all-Chrysler match-up saw Carlton beat Don Grotheer, and Dick Landy put away Arlen Vanke. Don Carlton beat Landy for the closest race with a 9.604 to Landy's losing 9.605.

The fight for Top Eliminator pitted Sox against Dave Strickler's Camaro. Nursing a bad clutch from his smokey burnout, Strickler was the loser to Sox's 9.58 at 143.08. In the final, Sox beat Mike Fons in the Rod Shop Dodge with a 9.55 at 143.08 to a losing 9.59 and identical 143.08 speed.

This win regained the manufacturer's points for Plymouth and put Ronnie Sox in the lead for driver points.

Ronnie continued to race the Duster through the remainder of the 1972 season but in October the car was damaged in a wreck at St. Petersburg, Florida, while

Ronnie's younger brother David began his drag racing experiences in this 340 F/Stock Duster. The Duster was identified as a "Sox & Martin Test Car." (Steve Reyes Photo)

Ronnie sometimes lifted the front end of the Hemi 'Cuda too high when track conditions were sticky. The Firestone front tires have Ronnie's name on them.

1970–1972 Pro Stock 4-Speed Era

Sox & Martin's 1972 'Cuda match race car waits at the line for a competitor to pull up for another exciting race. The crowds always knew there would be a great show when Ronnie Sox was driving and stirring the gears of his 4-speed Hemi racer. (John Foster Jr. Photo)

It was not unusual for Ronnie to pull the front wheels off the ground during the spectacular launches in his 1972 Hemi 'Cuda. The yellow dust is from the resin used to improve traction during these unofficial match races. (John Foster Jr. Photo)

match racing Larry Lombardo in the Bill Jenkins Vega. The Jenkins car was totaled but Ronnie's car was repairable. The front tire and a lower steering arm were replaced on the Duster and only the rear panel was damaged on the body. The car was repaired and repainted for another match race the following weekend.

The regular Sox & Martin shop crew was one member short after December 1972, when public relations and publicity man Tom Richardson resigned from the operation to pursue other interests. Changes in business operations meant that Ronnie and Buddy could no longer afford his services. Tom went on to work for Cale Yarborough, Roy Hill, Ed McCullough, and others before finally moving back to his home state of Texas, where he still operates a successful real estate business.

Buddy Martin Steps Up

Toward the middle of the 1972 racing season, Buddy Martin used his own time and money to travel to California to discuss the Pro Stock rules and weight situation with NHRA Executive Vice President Charles E. "Jack" Hart. Buddy tried to explain the Mopar racers' viewpoint in his well-known quiet, intelligent, and reasonable way, but it was clear that the powers at the NHRA had made up its collective mind and nothing he said would change it.

Buddy said later in a 1974 interview that he felt that the NHRA overcompensated, and by doing so, brought too many factors and variables into play at once. By reducing the wheelbase from 110 to 108 inches and allowing smaller engines and smaller, lighter cars it increased speeds and the amount of changes that would have to be made to adjust weight in any car. The decision also proved to make the cars more dangerous, as confirmed by subsequent wrecks and deaths.

In a December 1974 interview in *Super Stock & Drag Illustrated* Buddy said, "The bad part of it is that even when I talked to Jack Hart about this, he told me, sitting right in his own office, that if he could get Fords and Chevrolets racing against each other, he couldn't care less about what happened to Chrysler. That really dug deep." He knew that most of the spectators owned and drove Fords and Chevys so that is the market they targeted. They were in the promotion business rather than the drag-race sanctioning business.

At the beginning of the 1973 season, Buddy met and talked with NHRA President Wally Parks at the Winternationals. Martin proposed that the NHRA should publish the 1974 Pro Stock rules so that racers had a whole year to prepare new cars. Buddy proposed the same idea to AHRA president Jim Tice and IHRA head Larry Carrier, recommending that the three groups meet and establish a type of standardized rules.

Buddy also proposed that the rules be reorganized so that they would more closely represent what Pro Stock was originally intended to be, a heads-up class. The standardized rules would allow racers to run any and all events by all sanctioning bodies wherever they wanted without having to change the car for each race. This move would also make Pro Stock rules easier to understand by the fans and the press.

Wally told Martin he would think about his proposal and get back to him, but Buddy said in his December 1974 interview that he had not yet done so.

1973–1975
Pro Stock Evolution

Ronnie is looking intently at the tachometer as he launches the Don Hardy–built 1973 Hemi Duster. The low angle of the wheelie bars was designed to prevent wheelstands, which in turn increased ETs. (Photo Courtesy Dave Christie)

The beginning of the 1973 Pro Stock racing season started as usual, with the NHRA and AHRA winter races in California. The previous year had witnessed many changes with the introduction of smaller displacement engines and higher RPM.

CHAPTER 5

Chrysler Engineering Innovation

Although Chrysler had boycotted much of the 1972 season, 1973 saw Chrysler showing the results of the lessons learned from the previous year. In addition, the company had pushed for technical development through the winter. The new year was an opportunity for Chrysler to try out the new rules.

Camshaft

One of the most significant developments by the Chrysler engineering work was the adoption of the new Crane R290 high-lift long-duration roller lifter camshaft. This cam brought higher-RPM operating characteristics to the Hemi and moved the power and torque range to make use of the higher numerical gears (5.57:1 and 5.87:1) in the rear axle in conjunction with the long third gear (2.66, 1.64, 1.19:1) red-stripe A833 4-speed transmission.

This combination was designed to work with the large-diameter (32 inches) and wide (14 to 15 inches) tires required to achieve the traction needed to handle the engine's power.

Cylinder Heads

The Hemi received new D-5 aluminum cylinder heads, based on modified versions of the cast-iron D-4 heads designed by Bob Mullen. Mullen was a former Chrysler engineer who now worked out of his own shop in California. The development work on the D-5 was performed by former Chrysler engineer (and chief engineer of the 1968 A-Body Hemi cars) Robert Tarozzi at Keith Black's South Gate shop in California.

These new heads increased high-RPM breathing capabilities. Don Carlton was the first to use the new D-5 head in *Mopar Missile* at the 1973 Winternationals. This head was not available at that time for the rest of the Chrysler teams.

Transmission

One of the latest changes for Chrysler was the adoption of the Lenco 4-speed transmission, which replaced the tried-and-true A833 New Process 4-speed. The $2,700 Lenco used a planetary gear setup and a clutch pack to apply torque, but it did not need a clutch between gear changes. This design also allowed for a wider selection of gear spreads and ratios, and they were easily changed as needed. ETs with this transmission came to 9.22 by *Missile*, 9.11 for Butch Leal, and even 8.90 for Billy Stepp in Florida, who was testing at match race weight.

Some teams, drivers, and owners, including Buddy Martin and Ronnie Sox, were against the Lencos because they reduced the skill required to shift and drive; they felt that this took away from the quality of competition that they knew was important to the fans, who thrilled to the sounds of exceptional drivers such as Ronnie Sox shifting that heavy 4-speed with a lever and a clutch. Although Don Nicholson gained .07 second in his Pinto, Ronnie actually slowed down compared to the A833 when he tried out the Lenco.

Sox & Martin tested the Lenco for the first time in an updated 1972 Duster at an Irwindale, California, test session for Chrysler early in 1973 prior to the winter meets. With some tuning and chassis modifications, they improved the times over the next month and eventually used the Lenco across the board. It was a great equalizer and tightened up the field to make for more competitive racing. It brought a lot of work to the Sox & Martin customer car shop because many racers wanted parts and cars modified.

Chassis and Suspension

Pro Stock cars had evolved significantly in rear chassis and suspension development due to interpretations of the new rules. Competitive cars now featured coil-over shock absorbers, ladder bars, and three- or four-link rear suspension designs instead of the previous parallel-leaf springs and pinion

Chapter 5

snubbers. Adjustable Watts linkages and Panhard bars held the narrowed Dana 60 axles in place. Intricate tubular roll cages were tied into the unibody and the rear suspension, increasing safety and chassis rigidity.

Popularity versus Cost

Team Chrysler racers including Sox & Martin, Herb McCandless, Bobby Yowell, and Bob Lambeck brought their 1972 cars up to date rather than build new cars for the beginning of the season, but some already had new equipment in the works. These new cars included Hemi-powered Dodge Colts and Don Grotheer's Don Hardy–built super slick lightweight 1973 Duster with a 396-ci Hemi. All of this progress in engineering development and the accompanying speed added to the classes' obvious connection to the fans' street-driven cars. It brought the popularity of Pro Stock to a new high level. These changes also brought about a significant increase in the cost of building and racing the cars for the teams.

Because of the cost and technological sophistication involved, most teams were now hiring professional chassis and car builders rather than assembling the cars in their own shops. One of these shops was that of Don Hardy, located in Floydada, Texas.

Hardy built Mopar A-Body cars by welding the roll cage into the customer-supplied lightweight body and tying everything together at important stress points. The stock stamped and welded steel front subframe was replaced with steel tubing and the torsion bars were replaced with Koni coil-over shock absorbers. A high-tech rear suspension setup was used that incorporated a four-link design with long ladder bars and coil-over shock absorbers.

All of these features were incorporated into Don Grotheer's 1973 Duster and into the Sox & Martin cus-

Ronnie does a smokey burnout during a race at Milan Dragway in Michigan in 1973. This is the Hemi Duster built in the Sox & Martin shop during 1971. The strap is holding the hood because the hood is lighter now and the scoop is attached to the engine. (Tom Kasch Photo)

tomer cars built by Hardy. The final construction cost in 1973 was generally more than $8,000.

1973 Racing Results

National wins were few again in 1973, which was called "The Year of the Ford," due to the success of Nicolson and Glidden. A new Duster onboard in the spring brought hope for the future.

AHRA Winter Nationals

The 1973 AHRA Winter Nationals at Beeline Dragway near Phoenix was scheduled for February 1–4. The Pro

The rear of the 1973 Duster is raised for service and the hood is removed for engine checks during a test session at Milan. The top of the hood scoop is wrapped with duct tape to seal it. (Dick Oldfield Photo)

1973–1975 Pro Stock Evolution

Stock class was filled with cars of all types, loaded with the new dragster-type 4-speed Lenco transmission with four levers poking out of the floor. Ronnie Sox's car was an exception and started out well as the low qualifier at 9.17-second ET using his conventional Chrysler 4-speed.

The rest of the race did not go well for Sox; Sunday morning found him heading back to Phoenix after a warm-up run to change engines after spinning a bearing. When it was time to race, Sox put Jenkins away with a holeshot and a quick 9.40 at 145.86 to Jenkins' losing 9.25 t 146.34 mph. This was to no avail as Sox, shutting down early in a slick lane, was beaten by Don Nicholson with a 9.27 ET. In the final, Nicholson beat Melvin Yow with a 9.50.

NHRA Winternationals

The rest of the usual season opening program was set back a bit by weather. The 1973 NHRA Winternationals at Pomona, California, was scheduled for the first weekend of February but rain caused a postponement after two days of qualifying; the event spread over two weeks before it was all over. This put a big damper on what was proposed to be the richest and classiest field of Pro Stock racers ever assembled.

The Mopar teams, including Sox & Martin, were ready for what was their first time in NHRA national competition since the summer of 1972. This race was the chance for Ronnie Sox to grab his 16th NHRA Championship event, a record for any driver. The opportunity passed by him when the team decided that the Duster was not competitive and headed back to North Carolina.

Carlton's *Mopar Missile* showed up in the Sox & Martin transporter, ready for battle with all of Chrysler's marbles, including the 366-ci Hemi with D-5 heads and Lenco transmission. Unfortunately, this turned out to be the race of the Fords. In the end when the dust settled, Don Nicholson and his Pinto took the win in the final over Don Carlton with a 9.33 at 145.16 mph, a new national record. Both cars were using the new Lenco transmission, paving the way for more Pro Stock evolution.

NHRA Gatornationals

The 1973 NHRA Gatornationals at Gainesville, Florida, on March 16–18 was viewed with predictions of at least a dozen new Pro Stock entries. The track was known for its excellent traction and occasional tailwind. It brought a good opportunity for teams to present their best new equipment and performance. The tailwind situation showed itself this year, which caused the NHRA to not allow some attempts at record runs that would have had the unfair advantage.

The year of the Fords continued at this event when Dyno Don Nicholson made a swift run through the pack of contenders with blistering, consistent runs of 9.01 to 9.05. The day ended with Nicholson beating Don Carlton's next fastest time of 9.06 to Nicholson's 9.01 and then taking out Wayne Gapp in the final with a holeshot win at 9.04 and 150.50 mph. Nicholson also took the national Pro Stock record at this meet.

Farmington Drag Strip

A short time after the Gatornationals, David Sox was racing his white Pro Stock Duster in North Carolina. He was in the right lane at an event at Farmington Drag Strip near Winston-Salem, North Carolina, when spun bearings caused an engine seizure, pushing the car out of control at the end of the track; it broke the transmission housing and bent the rear axle.

The car, which had apparently been a former customer car, was destroyed. Ronnie had just installed the new Braswell 7390 carburetors and new polished Cragar wheels from his own car that was not racing that day. David was not badly injured but the car was scrapped.

NHRA Springnationals

The NHRA Springnationals at Ohio's National Trail Raceway on June 8–10 was the first race of the season where the new Mopar Pro Stock cars finally made some headway against the Fords and brought some encouragement to the fans and the racers.

David Sox drove this Pro Stock Duster during the 1973 season. While racing at Farmington Drag Strip near Winston-Salem, North Carolina, he lost control and the car was destroyed in a wreck at the end of the track. David was unhurt but the car was subsequently scrapped.

Chapter 5

Don Carlton's *Mopar Missile* started off the fray with a low qualifying time of the meet with a 9.327, matched by Nicholson. Third and fourth qualifying spots were filled with the Mopars of Ken Van Cleave at 9.36 and Butch Leal in his new Duster entry, recording a 9.37 ET. Ronnie Sox, driving the new Sox & Martin Hardy–built Duster acquired from Don Grotheer, put down a 12th-place time of 9.489, shared with Irv Beringhaus' new Dodge Dart Sport.

The Pro Stock action opened with Butch "California Flash" Leal putting down a first round win over Ronnie Sox with a 9.48 to Sox's losing 9.51. In the second round,

> **Although the Sox & Martin team did not find success at the NHRA Summernationals in July or the AHRA Grand Nationals, they did well at match racing events around the country.**

Carlton beat Bill Jenkins with a 9.45 at 146.81 mph to Jenkins' 9.48. Leal beat the Rod Shop Dodge, driven by Bob Riffle with a 9.52 at 144.92. The semi-finals saw the Fords and Chevrolets out for good as Leal beat Gapp with a 9.42 and Carlton stopped Melvin Yow with a 9.38 at 147.78. In the first all-Chrysler final since November 1971, Leal tried a little too hard and lost by a red light to Carlton's winning 9.40 at 147.78.

Capitol Raceway

Although the Sox & Martin team did not find success at the NHRA Summernationals in July or the AHRA Grand Nationals, they did well at match racing events around the country. At Capitol Raceway in Maryland, a four-way competition found Ronnie Sox facing Bill Jenkins, Roy Hill, and Don Nicholson in a classic rivalry, stirring up the rosin dust.

Nicholson's Pinto had problems with the header pipe falling off in the second round. With a Boss 302 head on one bank and a high-port head on the other, things did not match up well. The Pinto still won against Jenkins with a 9.13 at 149 mph to Jenkins' early start and 8.99 on the instant green start.

In the final race of the three-round show, Ronnie Sox put down Nicholson's head-start with a quick 8.91 at 151.17 to Nicholson's losing 9.04 at 151.13. Sox was the overall winner with three out of three round wins.

NHRA/U.S. Nationals

The 19th annual NHRA Nationals was held at Indianapolis Raceway Park on Labor Day weekend from August 30 to September 3. Attendees were treated to great weather with no rain.

A big difference for 1973 was the change of the name of the event to the U.S. Nationals, which it carries today. The name change was because of a declaration by the Automobile Competition Committee of the United States (ACCUS), the American branch of FIA (Federation Internationale de l'Automobile), the world automobile racing sanctioning body. ACCUS declared the Indy event to be the official United States Drag Racing Championship. The NHRA reported that the 1973 event attracted the largest crowd in U.S. Nationals history.

The 1973 Pro Stock battle began with a very wide-spread qualifying session. The Fords and Chevys were putting down the quickest times with Bob Glidden's Glidden & Allen 1972 Ford Pinto in the first spot with times of 9.03 to 9.11. Wayne Gapp was next with a 9.051 followed by Bill Jenkins in third at 9.06. The fastest Mopar was Butch Leal at a slightly slower 9.14 at 150.50 mph. Ronnie Sox showed a bit slower 9.193 at 149.25, his best in a while. *Mopar Missile* was surprisingly down with a 9.24 and Herb McCandless was behind it with 9.28.

When Pro Stock eliminations opened on Sunday Ronnie Sox made it through the first round by beating Carmen Rotonda and his newly finished Vega, 9.23 to 9.33. Unfortunately, Sox was put out by Bob Glidden in the second round with a losing 9.21 to Glidden's 9.05. At the end of the day it was Glidden for the win at 9.085 at 151.26 beating Wayne Gapp's 9.092.

Hemi Duster Number Three

The Don Hardy–built 1973 Duster created for Oklahoma racer and Chrysler Supercar Performance Clinic presenter Don Grotheer was an example of Chrysler's third generation of Pro Stock chassis development. This technologically advanced race car was an example of

1973–1975 Pro Stock Evolution

This Sox & Martin 1973 Hemi Duster was purchased from Don Grotheer. It was a state-of-the-art lightweight built by Don Hardy in Texas. However, Grotheer no longer needed it when his arrangement with Chrysler was dropped. (Dan Williams Photo)

The front fender modifications are evident as Ronnie launches the Don Hardy–built 1973 Duster during testing. All testing was done for the benefit of Chrysler, which used the information to improve the other teams' cars in addition to using it for product development. (Dick Oldfield Photo)

what happens when every nuance and interpretation of NHRA Pro Stock rules are utilized. Don Grotheer worked closely with Hardy to be certain that every opportunity was taken to make this one of the most competitive cars of the 1973 season.

The Chassis

Hardy began with a chassis that used basic Chrysler design but replaced the front subframe with fabricated chrome-moly square main tubes mounting Koni

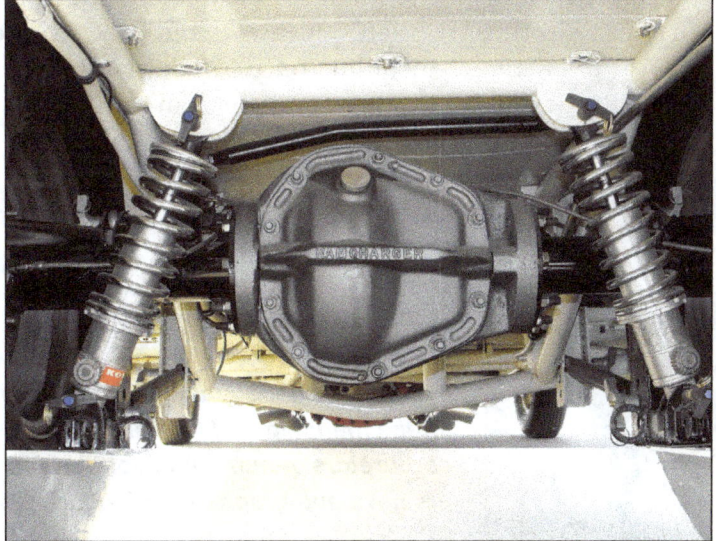

The sophisticated rear suspension of the Don Hardy–built Hemi Duster features dual adjustable coil-over shock absorbers and a lightweight cast rear axle center section provided by the Ramchargers.

tube shock absorbers. The upper and lower control arms were significantly lightened and held spindles that were switched side to side, placing the steering arms in front. They were operated by a Ford Pinto rack and pinion steering unit. This assembly further lightened the front end of the car. Lightweight disc front brakes were used.

The rear end of the Duster was designed with an easily portable rear axle, suspension, springs, and ladder bars that could be taken out as a unit by removing quick disconnect pins. The Dana 60 with 5.38:1 gears drove Summers axles mounted with Strange disc brakes. The big Firestone slicks were mounted on Rocket wheels. The rear of the Duster was set up to ride high for great aerodynamic efficiency at speed. Long wheelie bars were integrated into the suspension system.

The Interior

The body was a chemically lightened Duster with fiberglass front end and lift-off deck lid. The interior was bare bones with metal door panels (later trimmed with upholstery). The modern high-strength chrome-moly roll cage was designed as the ultimate in driver safety and featured double cross bracing in the rear compartment. The roll cage was welded integrally with the body subframe members and cowl.

Other interior parts were made of magnesium, steel, and titanium with rectangular boxes in the rear floor for any needed ballast. The driver sat on black vinyl Solar racing bucket seats; instruments were mounted in a fiberglass instrument panel. The car was built with a

Chapter 5

The interior of the trunk shows the recessed passenger-side battery mounting and the rear of the roll cage. The entire body was lightened so the sides of the quarter panels were filled with Styrofoam to stiffen them without adding weight.

The interior of the restored 1972 Sox & Martin Hemi Duster includes special racing seats, a racing steering wheel and a Hurst competition Plus 4-speed shifter and reverse Loc-Out.

Chrysler 4-speed and remote-mounted Hurst Performance Plus shifter and reverse Loc-Out handle.

The Engine

The engine, originally built for Don Grotheer, was a destroked 396-ci Hemi equipped with NASCAR connecting rods and TRW pistons providing a 13:1 compression ratio. Mullen cylinder heads were ported with 16 spark plugs that were fired by twin Mallory magnetos. A cast-aluminum Weiand intake manifold mounted two Holley 4500 Series carburetors. Oiling was handled by a Milodon system and exhaust gases were taken out with Hooker headers. A Crane roller lifter camshaft moved the stock valves.

The engine was mounted to a chassis plate and was moved to the rear and up against the steel firewall, as allowed by the new 1973 setback rules. The 2,700-pound Duster ran 9.20 at 150 mph at its initial testing at Baton Rouge. This engine was not included when Grotheer sold the car to Sox & Martin.

A Quick Sale

Don Grotheer planned to campaign this car aggressively for the 1973 season but when Chrysler announced a deep reduction in the number of supported teams for the year, Grotheer was left out in the cold. He did race the car a few times, including once in Louisiana and at an AHRA Grand American event at Tulsa in April.

The 426 Hemi engine was originally built by Jake King with the latest state-of-the-art components and included a cast-aluminum tunnel-ram intake manifold and two large Holley carburetors. A number of veteran racers have autographed the fenderwells.

1973–1975 Pro Stock Evolution

Buddy Martin takes a break for a drink as he talks with the crew during testing of the 1973 Hemi Duster at Milan, Michigan. The big truck was a great improvement over the previous open trailers and ramp trucks. (Dick Oldfield Photo)

The front wheels are up as Ronnie launches the 1973 Hemi Duster during testing. The front-end body structure has been noticeably lowered for aerodynamic benefits. (Dick Oldfield Photo)

Don moved to Ford and ran a Pinto, so the new Duster, minus its engine, was quickly sold to Buddy Martin. When it arrived at the Sox & Martin shop in Burlington, Dave Christie went through the chassis and Jake King put his own personal touches on the new engine being built. The body was repainted and lettered in the familiar Sox & Martin red, white, and blue.

The car's first appearance in Sox & Martin trim was at a May 3 NHRA Division 2 points race at Suffolk, Virginia. The next time Ronnie drove it was the NHRA Springnationals on June 10.

Soon after the Grotheer Duster was finished and put into service, the team-built 1971–1972 Duster (updated to 1973 trim) was sold to Will Smallwood in New York. It was heavier than the Grotheer car and, according to mechanic Dave Christie, there was not enough racing at the time to

The restored Don Hardy Hemi Duster appears exactly as it did when raced by Sox & Martin in 1973 and 1974. The red, white, and blue colors of the later Sox & Martin cars were based on Chrysler factory colors.

This is the restored 1973 Don Hardy–built Hemi Duster as it appears today. It is currently in the Greg and Kathy Mosley collection in Moline, Illinois.

Chapter 5

Jake King, Engine Builder

Jake wrote an article published in the July 1973 issue of *Hi-Performance Cars* magazine that explained all of the details of his methods and philosophy for building the engines for Sox & Martin race cars. Probably the most important point was that Jake only built the engines for the team race cars. He did not build customer engines, although he stressed at the time that the same quality parts and work went into the customer engines. He felt that Ronnie's driving and Dave Christie's chassis tuning made the difference. Of course, Jake's tuning at the track was also a factor.

Jake started with the same Chrysler Hemi block that anyone could purchase from the manufacturer. After checking a new block to be sure there are no irregularities or defects, Jake ground considerable material from the outside of the block to reduce weight and remove casting slag, burrs, and any contamination from the lifter galley. The galley area was then polished to assure smooth oil flow back to the oil pan.

Jake's choices for rotating parts were not difficult to make. Contrary to what most believed, Chrysler parts were almost always the best available so they went into a Sox & Martin racing engine. The crankshaft, pistons, rings, and connecting rods were all factory pieces, specially massaged by Jake King. The factory-issue NASCAR 13:1 pistons equipped with Dykes rings were the most dependable.

Special 7.061-inch-long forged-steel NASCAR connecting rods with floating piston pins were used, along with special bolts. Jake polished them to improve oil drainage and to help prevent stress cracks. Side clearance was set loose at .014 to .016 inch. The crankshaft was a Magnafluxed and balanced standard forged-steel Chrysler Hemi shaft with polished journals and radiused fillets. Main and rod bearing clearances were set at .0025 to .003 inch to stand up to Ronnie's 7,500- to 8,000-rpm launches and 8,000-rpm shifts.

The factory oil pan (as well as those used on most customer engines) was replaced with a special 10-quart aluminum unit built to Jake's specifications by Mac McCarter at a local welding shop. When Mac could no longer keep up with the demand, some were sourced from Charlie Gilbertson in Ohio. Sox & Martin sponsor, Milodon, built the custom pickup and oil pump. Jake installed his own special baffle plates to control oil movement during Ronnie's hard charges. Aircraft-quality braided aluminum external oil lines with aluminum fittings were used. Of course, the pan was always filled with 40-weight Valvoline Racing oil.

The engine's power was partly attributed to the then-new Crane R-290-446-4 roller lifter camshaft, designed expressly for Pro Stock applications. It was good for 8,800 rpm before the power began to fall off. This camshaft's lift at the valves was .700 inch for the intake and .678 inch for the exhaust with clearances set at .024 inch on the intake and .028 inch on the exhaust. Standard Hemi 1.52:1 and 1.57:1 ratio rocker arms were used, as were standard-size Chrysler valves and springs. The valves operated with special D&D steel pushrods to prevent bending. A Donovan gear drive setup turned the camshaft for accurate timing and precise adjustment.

Buddy helps Jake hook up everything after the 426 Hemi was installed in the Duster. The engine compartment and chassis were usually painted white to make servicing easier. (Dick Oldfield Photo)

1973–1975 Pro Stock Evolution

Jake worked on the Hemi as it was being re-installed into the Duster chassis at Pomona in 1972. The Hemi block was painted Ford blue because that was Jake's way of identifying his work. Also, the blue was a reminder of his Ford racing days. (Dick Oldfield Photo)

Buddy helps to attach the headers to the Hemi after it was installed in the chassis of the Duster. The engine still uses the brick-red spark plug wires from 1968. (Dick Oldfield Photo)

Cylinder heads were Chrysler cast-aluminum dual plug units with Mullen port jobs. All Sox & Martin engines, including those built for customers, received valve work and assembly in the shop by Levi Hester, a longtime employee. When the Mullen and D4 heads came into service in 1973, all assembly was done by Levi, who managed and oversaw all machine shop services, including piston machining and balancing.

Everything that Jake touched, he inspected closely, but he trusted Levi's work and judgment. The 16 spark plugs and dual magnetos not only ensured complete fuel combustion but greatly improved low-end response and kept the plugs from fouling.

Hooker 2¼ x 24– or 2¼ x 28–inch headers completed the system.

The intake manifold was a cast-magnesium Weiand tunnel ram based on development by fuel system expert John Bauman of Chrysler. Jake modified the unit by completely gutting the material between the runners to reduce weight and unshroud the runners to keep them cool. Jake then port matched everything to the heads, removing every possible restriction. The manifold mounted two Holley 4500 4-barrel carburetors fed by 1/2-inch fuel lines from the tank to the carburetors. Jake used the original jetting performed by Bauman, making changes only when needed at the track for maximum power output.

justify two Dusters. Moreover, the new Hemi Colt was on the horizon. This car went through a few owners and is today restored and owned by Fred Ristagno in New Jersey.

Big Changes for 1974

Chrysler began the 1974 racing season with an announcement that they would not be competing in Pro Stock at any NHRA national events. The continuing problem with weight breaks causing the Mopars to be less than competitive prompted them to make the decision to direct their most important factory teams and drivers to compete in Super Stock.

Butch Leal entered the fray with a new Ron Butler–built 1965 SS/B Hemi Plymouth. Sox & Martin fielded a 4-speed SS/A 1968 Hemi Barracuda, an original factory BO29 purchased from street racers in New Jersey. This car was updated with a new link-leaf rear suspension setup designed by Chrysler engineers.

Herb McCandless moved away from the Sox & Martin team at about this time and raced a 3,850-pound Super Stock 4-speed 1970 Hemi 'Cuda convertible sponsored by Rufus Lee "Brooklyn Heavy" Boyd. The mechanic on the 'Cuda was Vaughn Currie.

Herb's former Pro Stock Demon had already been sold to a racer in Puerto Rico, but it was later returned

Chapter 5

to the United States and is now restored and in the Todd Werner collection in Florida.

Other factory-supported drivers such as Arlen Vanke followed suit as quickly as they could locate and acquire a proper race car and get it set up.

In an interview with NHRA's *National Dragster* in early February 1974, Buddy Martin said, "It's business as usual" for all aspects of their operations, including match race bookings and customer car preparations. Buddy told *National Dragster* that they received a new batch of bookings and their schedule was as busy as ever. He said they would try to schedule races closer together to enable them to run more races during a busy week. Their work was slowed a bit when a tornado swept through Burlington and damaged the Sox & Martin shop building in February 1974.

Preparation work was started on the 1968 Barracuda in September 1973, just after the team began work on a new Hemi Dodge Colt. The new SS/A Barracuda was first run at Phoenix at the AHRA Winter Nationals and won its class at 10.26.

Ronnie raced the Barracuda at the NHRA Winternationals at Pomona and the Gatornationals at Gainesville before eventually selling the car to Eddie Smith in West Virginia. Smith re-lettered the car, calling it *West Virginia Hemi*. "Plymouth by Sox & Martin" was noted on the rear quarters. It is currently owned by collector Todd Werner in Florida and known to historians and enthusiasts as the "Boycott Car." It has been painted and lettered in Sox & Martin livery.

Logghe Brothers built the custom tubular-steel chassis for one of the two Sox & Martin Hemi Colts. The 426 Hemi is being mounted while the Colt body shell waits in the background. (Photo Courtesy Dave Christie)

The rear suspension links and roll cage were tied into the Logghe-built Hemi Colt chassis. The Hemi engine was mounted in the chassis with an aluminum engine plate at the front and rear. (Photo Courtesy Dave Christie)

The Dodge Hemi Colt

Ronnie and Buddy and the rest of the team were not merely resting on their laurels. By March of 1974, the new Pro-Stock/Match Race car, still painted white all-over, was being tested at Piedmont Dragway near Burlington. The new car was a radical Logghe-built 1973 Dodge Colt. This 96-inch-wheelbase monster was part of the continuing evolution of Pro-Stock racing at the time. The production Dodge Colt was based on the popular Mitsubishi Gallant GT coupe, normally equipped with a 96-hp four-cylinder engine. The Colt was considered a "Captive Import" by Chrysler and marketed to compete with other similar Japanese imported cars rather than American compacts.

The Hemi Colt was based on a chassis fabricated by the Logghe Brothers, Ron and Gene, in Michigan. Their business began as the Logghe Stamping Company in 1947. Founded by their father, Morris Logghe, the company started out building stamped original equipment parts for the big three automobile manufacturers. By 1965, the business had grown; it was now the premier design shop and builder of tube-frame Factory Experimental chassis for people including Dyno Don Nicholson, Fast Eddie Schartman, and Jack Chrisman.

Component Details

The 96-inch-wheelbase Hemi Colt chassis was built from 4130 moly tubing and used modern front and rear suspension with coil-over tube shock absorber design with Koni shocks. The rear suspension included supplemental traction bars that supported a Dana 60/Ramcharger setup narrowed to 38 inches. The Dana housing was equipped with Summers Brothers axles and a Chrysler 5.57:1 Sure Grip limited slip assembly. Front suspension used Logghe spindles, hubs, and anti-sway bars and Ford Pinto rack and pinion steering with Apollo titanium ends. All four brakes were Hurst/Airheart disc units. The front tires were 6.50 x 15 and the rear was capped off with 14 x 32 x 15 Firestone Drag 500 slicks on Cragar Super Trick wheels.

> "The Colt was considered a "Captive Import" by Chrysler and marketed to compete with other similar Japanese imported cars rather than American compacts."

Ronnie's office in the Hemi Colt was tight but safety was the priority. A minimum of instruments, a racing steering wheel, shifter levers, and racing seats were all that was needed.

The new Lenco transmission required three separate levers to operate. The levers used long heavy-duty rods to move the two-speed planetary gear sets. The Lenco brought the ability to shift quickly without the skill required for the 4-speed and Hurst shifter.

Chapter 5

The trunk of the Hemi Colt was filled with dual batteries, a fuel cell, and pumps needed to feed the powerful Hemi engine. The roll cage tubing was mounted in the trunk to stiffen the chassis and also served to protect the fuel cell.

The driver's compartment and rear wheel tubs were finished in black carpeted aluminum paneling fabricated by Al Bergler. Lightweight racing bucket seats were used and controls consisted of lightweight pedals and steering along with sticks for the Lenco transmission. Stewart Warner gauges and switches were used, including the tachometer, voltmeter, and selector controls for the dual batteries. The simulated instrument panel was painted.

The heart of the Colt was the Hemi engine, built and tuned by Jake King. As usual, Jake milled and polished the entire outside of the block for weight reduction and all interior surfaces were painted to aid oil flow to the pan. The Hemi was destroked to 3.48 inches, creating a 396-ci displacement with a stock 4.25-inch bore. TRW pistons were used and installed with a .0075-inch piston-to-wall clearance. The 7.061-inch-long connecting rods were Chrysler forged-steel NASCAR parts and 1/2-inch SPS bolts held the caps held in place.

The brain of the Hemi was the General Kinetics 328R-4721L camshaft used with Crane roller lifters and D&D pushrods. The cam had a lift of .731 inch at the valves using stock Hemi rocker arms. The valves were stock Hemi with a 2.23-inch intake and 1.94-inch exhaust head diameters held in place by stock Mopar valvesprings. Bob Mullen, in California, ported the dual–spark plug aluminum cylinder heads. Jake King, in the

The 1973 Don Hardy–built Pro Stock Duster had every state-of-the-art feature available at the time. The 426 Hemi engine was set back as far as possible for weight transfer. (Dick Oldfield Photo)

The Don Hardy–built Colt is backed out of the truck to prepare it for a day of racing. This Hemi Colt was acquired from East Coast racer Ronnie Lyles in 1974 when he had to drop out of racing for a while.

1973–1975 Pro Stock Evolution

The Hemi engine in the Colt had dual distributors and a fabricated aluminum intake manifold with two Holley 4-barrel carburetors. The Colt has the iconic blue-tinted headlights familiar to Sox & Martin fans.

Sox & Martin shop, surfaced and checked for proper chamber volume.

A dry sump system with an Ed Pink oil pan, Ron Butler pickups, a three-stage Weaver Brothers scavenge pump and a Milodon main oil pump lubricated the Hemi. A C.T.I. crank trigger system sending the fire to the 16 Champion spark plugs provided the ignition. Hooker provided the equal-length exhaust headers and a Lakewood Steel flywheel shield confined the Schiefer flywheel and clutch assembly. A Weiand cast-magnesium tunnel ram–type intake manifold mounted two Holley 4500 series 6214 carburetors fed by dual Stewart Warner electric fuel pumps.

Racing Exploits

One of the first match races for the new Colt was at York US 30 Drag-O-Way in Pennsylvania for the NHRA National Invitational event in May 1974. Although there was a continuing chance of rain over the weekend, the event was considered one of the wilder and most exciting races ever staged there. Of course, some of this excitement was thanks to the fast and furious Pro Stock competition and the much anticipated appearance of the Sox & Martin Hemi Colt.

The big race consisted of the Sox & Martin Colt against the Bill Jenkins' *Grumpy's Toy IX* Vega, driven by newly acquired team driver Ken Dondero. The first race

Ronnie Sox holds the Hemi Colt steady as he makes a burnout across the starting line. He was one of the few drivers who could handle the power and short wheelbase of the Hemi Colt. (Dan Williams Photo)

Ronnie Sox talks with his track crew during a testing session at Milan, Michigan. The car is the Don Hardy–built Duster that they purchased earlier from Don Grotheer. (Dick Oldfield Photo)

Chapter 5

The 1973 Duster sets up for a burnout at Milan Dragway in Michigan. Crew member Darrell Sweet holds the car to keep it in the water on the track while Ronnie drives. (Dick Oldfield Photo)

Ronnie Sox lines up for one of his many match races against Bill Jenkins. This one is at night and is taking place at Pittsburgh International Dragway near Pittsburgh, Pennsylvania. (William Truby Photo)

Ronnie Sox in his Hemi Colt and Bill Jenkins in his Chevrolet Vega are just launching off the line at York US 30 Drag-O-Way in Pennsylvania. Jenkins already has his left front tire off the track in this match race event. (William Truby Photo)

The Hemi Dodge Colt was equipped with a Parachute to stabilize and stop the small car at the end of the track. The Hemi Colts were hard to handle for most drivers but Ronnie Sox had them under control.

LeRoy Roeder of Oak Creek, Wisconsin, purchased the Pro Stock Hemi Colt from Sox & Martin when the team decided to cease operations in 1974. The Colt was quickly repainted and renamed Mini Hemi. (Mike Sopko Photo)

was over almost before it started because over-anxious Dondero red-lighted against Sox, who drove to an 8.87 at 153.06 mph win. The second race ended the same way with Sox finishing at 8.71 at 157 to Dondero's foul.

Another spring event was the southern-style match race presented at Thunder Valley Dragway in Marion, South Dakota. World Champion Wayne Gapp in the Gapp & Roush Ford Pinto faced Ronnie Sox in the Sox & Martin Hemi Colt. In the first race, Gapp launched off the line for a quick lead over Sox and held on to the end with a 9.184 at 148.51 win to Sox's losing 9.189 and 151 mph. Sox beat Gapp in the second race out of the hole with a decisive 9.005 at 152.28 win to Gapp's 9.04 and 147.78. Ronnie and Buddy ran five match races that weekend, making their schedule only by using their leased plane, flown by pilot Jack Armstrong.

The Logghe-built Colt was also raced at Xenia, Ohio, in June 1974 where Ronnie ran an 8.78 at 155 mph. He followed that with a trip to Union Grove Dragway in Wisconsin the next day, where he put down a run of 8.69 at 157 mph.

Sox & Martin and others hoped that the Colt would be a winner for 1974. However, after a number of races and tests by Billy Stepp and Don Carlton as well as serious wrecks by Bill Flynn and others in 1973, Chrysler decided to concentrate its support and efforts on the Plymouth Duster and Dodge Dart Sport. No Plymouth equivalent existed for the Colt so that put the brakes on any further development for the team.

The Move Rationale

In a half-page article in the June 4, 1974, edition of the Burlington *Daily Times-News*, Ronnie Sox talked at great length about the break with Chrysler and move to the Dodge Colt. In the lead to the article, racing reporter Elbert Marshall explained that Ronnie Sox made his debut in the new Dodge Colt two weeks earlier and had already won 12 straight match races. He pointed out that although the Colt was legal in the AHRA, it was not legal in the NHRA and IHRA so match races were the money game for Sox & Martin.

Ronnie explained, "The small cars are a lot more competitive than the large cars. They have a short wheelbase and more traction; they are far narrower across the front and shorter, thus having less frontal area; and so a small car pushes less wind than a big car."

Sox continued, "We haven't had much luck with the larger car since the sanctioning bodies began allowing the smaller ones to race. We've had this car built for several months, but Chrysler didn't want us to run it.

"We just decided to pull out from Chrysler and did this on our own. They cut us back this year and wanted us to campaign a Super Stock car, but we just couldn't make enough money on a Super Stock car. With this car, we can stay busy by match racing. This car is also legal for the big PRA meet at New York National."

The Don Hardy–built Colt purchased from Ron Lyles is now restored and safely in the Greg and Kathy Mosley collection in Moline, Illinois. The Colt is finished as it appeared when Ronnie Sox drove it.

Chapter 5

The colorful Sox & Marin Dodge D700 hauler was state of the art for its time. Professional drag racing teams had not yet moved to the large tractor-trailer rigs common later. Clyde Hodges was the team mechanic at this time. (Dick Oldfield Photo)

When Jake King left the Sox & Martin team in 1974, he went back to Burlington and opened this Gulf service station. This is what he had wanted to do for years and he looked forward to the opportunity. (John Mahoney Photo)

The Split

It was mid-1974 when the drag racing empire called Sox & Martin decided to split and Ronnie and Buddy took their interests somewhere else. The Logghe-built Hemi Colt, along with a spare engine, was sold to LeRoy

> **Ronnie and Buddy remained friends and business partners but not in drag racing, at least for now.**

Roeder in Milwaukee for $39,000. It was later sold to Stewart Pomeroy who raced it in the northern Midwest. The Don Hardy–built Hemi had already been sold and the big shop in Burlington was listed for sale.

Dave Christie left on July 30, 1974, and moved to Pennsylvania to work with Jenkins Competition in Malvern. He later went to work for Hendricks Motor- sports. Jake King also went out on his own. He went back to his original plan to open his own automotive repair shop. He opened up a two-bay Gulf Service Center at 1341 North Church Street in Burlington and spent the next several years taking care of business and spending time with his wife, Virginia, and their three children.

The Reasons

A number of reasons existed for the breakup of what had been a very successful operation for years. None of them involved any personality or other conflicts between the two principals, Ronnie Sox and Buddy Martin. They remained friends and business partners but not in drag racing, at least for now. Buddy and Ronnie had plans to go into the Firestone tire business together and Ronnie was working on developing his motel business on the North Carolina shore. Buddy and Ronnie's relationship with Chrysler was never a factor in their decision to retire from the business. As Buddy Martin said in a December 1974 interview with *Super Stock and Drag illustrated*, "Our relationship with Chrysler has been good. Chrysler has been a good company to work for."

1973–1975 Pro Stock Evolution

This 1968 Barracuda was built in 1974 expressly to compete in NHRA Super Stock after Chrysler decided to drop out of Pro Stock. It was protesting the NHRA rules that put a disadvantage on the Dodge and Plymouth Hemi racers. This car is currently in the Todd Werner collection.

The team's move back to Super Stock in 1974 was not a decision dictated by Chrysler. Various Mopar racers met with Chrysler and decided that it was better to run Super Stock and win than to continue in Pro Stock where they had little or no chance to win. The idea was to represent the sponsor and winning was the only way to do that. The NHRA rule changes and negative results for Chrysler products also affected Sox & Martin's engine building business because they had to be building and selling products that were winning. The most important reasons for the end of the operation were economic. The costs of racing had increased dramatically over the past few years, sponsors were dropping out, and parts became more expensive. It was going to cost almost twice as much to operate a race team for the year so, economically, it was just not a good choice.

To Race Again?

To Buddy, the decision to disband the operation was a business move, but Ronnie was hurt and upset by it in the beginning. At one point he told Buddy that he had no desire to get back into another car. Once the pair was out of the business, they both knew their only choice was to find other things to do.

Ronnie was interested in golf and pursued that sport throughout his life. Buddy wanted to spend more time

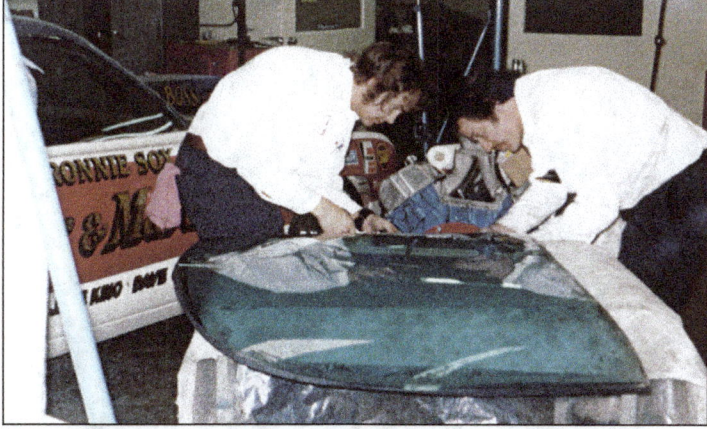

Sox & Martin team members Darrell Sweet and Dave Christie work to install the special lightweight glass in the newly built 1968 Hemi Super Stock Barracuda. This was an original BO29 Chrysler-built Hemi car that was acquired to compete in NHRA Super Stock for 1974.

This Brooklyn Heavy Hemi Duster was one of two Sox & Martin–built race cars that were bought in the late 1970s and ended up in the United Kingdom. The second car was a Challenger called London Heavy. (Alan Currans Photo)

at home with his family. Buddy's wife Carolyn and eight-year-old son Chris were also interested in golf so Buddy took up the game, although he never claimed to be an avid golfer. Buddy also decided to enter the retail furniture business.

At the time, Buddy said that although their racing days were over, he and Ronnie would never forget their experiences in drag racing and the people they had met and the good friends they had made. He said that their relationship with companies including Chrysler, Valvoline, Firestone, and others had been very good and that would never be forgotten. The racing business had been good to them.

It soon became evident that Ronnie Sox could not be held back from driving a race car for long. It took only a short time before Ronnie was looking for another ride to put him back in the seat at the dragstrip. He apparently acquired the former Herb McCandless/Brooklyn Heavy Hemi-powered Dodge Dart Sport and was already busy sanding down the paint to put his name on it. He traded some land to Buddy for a hauler truck and was on his way back to drag racing.

Enter Ronnie Lyles

In August 1974, at the PRO National Challenge on Long Island, Ronnie made some Pro Stock runs in the Don Hardy–built Dodge Colt that had been assembled and finished by Sox & Martin for New York racer Ronnie Lyles. Hardy built only one or two other Hemi Colts; they went to the Rod Shop team.

Ronnie Lyles came from a far different background than most Pro Stock racers. Much of his racing experience came from street racing in Brooklyn, New York, with a group known as the Mutt Brothers. He was well-known for purchasing ex-professional race cars for that purpose. Lyles was a competent driver, but most often, the driver was Ronnie Sox, whom Lyles first met in 1973.

The first round of Pro Stock competition at National Challenge 74 saw ex–Sox & Martin driver Herb McCandless in the Jack Roush *Hauler* Mustang II take out Mark Herrington with an 8.77 and 152.08 mph. Nelson DesChamps' former Sox & Martin Logghe Colt won when opponent Joe Verde red-lighted.

Ronnie Sox in the Ronnie Lyles–owned Hardy-built Hemi Colt grabbed an automatic win with a 9.06 and

A Company Biography

The importance of the Sox & Martin racing operation was illustrated clearly when, in 1974, Peterson Publishing, in conjunction with the Henry Regnery Company in Chicago, published *The Sox & Martin Book of Drag Racing*. This 228-page book had the bylines of Ronnie Sox and Buddy Martin as authors, but it was obviously produced with significant input from co-author Bill Neely and the editors of *Hot Rod*.

Although the first 26 pages were a condensed history of the Sox & Martin racing accomplishments plus some general black and white drag as well as color racing photos, the remainder of the book was an overall history and explanation of drag racing. The book also contained 15 appendices listing the records and wins of Sox & Martin, along with lists of national drag racing events and records through the years.

The book is still available online, but it is difficult to find.

The Sox & Martin Book of Drag Racing *was published in 1974 by the Henry Regnery Company and featured material from Bill Neely and the editors of* Hot Rod. *The jacket of this copy was signed by Ronnie Sox.*

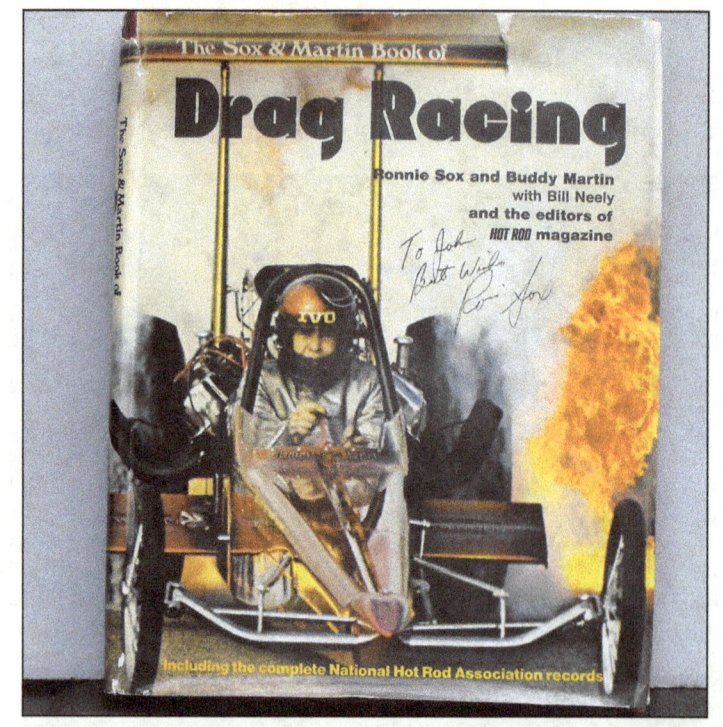

148.51 when Brian Gillis red-lighted. This was for naught when Sox red-lighted against Bill Jenkins in the second round. At the end of the day, Jenkins won the event with an 8.80 run at 155 mph in his Vega against Mike Fons in the *Motown Missile* Duster. This event was the first since the name of the organization was changed from the Professional Racers Association (PRA) to the Professional Racer's Organization (PRO).

Toward the end of 1974, Ronnie Lyles had to drop out of racing for a while and sold the Colt, along with three Jake King–built Hemi engines, to Ronnie Sox. Sox repainted the Colt in the familiar red, white, and blue Sox & Martin colors, painted Ronnie Sox on the doors in silver leaf, and ran the car in IHRA events for the rest of the 1974 season. Sox raced the car in a few match races and IHRA events through 1975.

In August 1974, Ronnie Sox was seen driving the ex-Herb McCandless–driven Brooklyn Heavy 1973 Dodge Dart Sport, converted to look like a 1975 Plymouth Duster, in the Pro American Championship event. The car was painted the familiar red, white, and blue but had only the name "Ronnie Sox" in big letters across the doors. Sox qualified sixth with a 9.18 behind McCandless in fifth with a 9.15. Ronnie was quickly out of the running when he lost to Wayne Gapp in round one.

1975 Racing Highlights

Early 1975 started off badly for Ronnie when a bad pre-dawn fire destroyed the Sox & Martin shop on the Tucker Street Extension in Burlington on Saturday, March 22. A neighbor called the E. M. Holt Volunteer Fire Department of Burlington at about 4:30 am but the 200 x 125–foot structure already had fire coming through the roof and front windows when they arrived. Soon after the fire equipment arrived, there was an explosion and the intensity of the blaze increased. Eventually, 60 firemen from four area departments were trying to contain the blaze that extensively damaged the facility, according to the Burlington *Daily Times-News*. It was said that Alamance County fire and rescue equipment was lined up for a quarter of a mile.

Because of the suspicious nature of the conflagration, the North Carolina State Bureau of Investigation mobile crime laboratory was called in to investigate the damage. An initial inspection by Ronnie and Buddy determined that a great deal of theft occurred before the fire began. In an interview with the newspaper reporters Ronnie said, "Whoever did it knew what they were looking for. They left one thing aside that was obsolete and took the latest piece that was sitting next to it." The pair estimated that there was more than $300,000 in damage and theft, but they did not think that their insurance would cover it all.

> **An initial inspection by Ronnie and Buddy determined that a great deal of theft occurred before the fire began.**

The damage was somewhat less in the garage so Ronnie gathered what he could and was back in service in April when he drove the Don Hardy–built, former Ronnie Lyles Hemi Colt to an 8.72 at 157 mph at Person Dragway (now known as Roxboro Motorsports) in Roxboro, North Carolina. Ronnie beat long-time rival Don Nicholson three-straight in a match race.

On Easter Monday, Sox established a new track record of 8.59 and 159.93 mph in his second race against Nicholson, repeating that time on his third and final race. Ronnie followed up this race with a best-of-three match race against Bill Jenkins at Atco, New Jersey, on April 6. Then, it was on to an eight-car event at National Trail Raceway in Columbus, Ohio, the following Sunday.

Later, in August 1975, Ronnie booked a special Pro Stock match race at US 30 Drag-O-Way in York, Pennsylvania, against the Jenkins Camaro, driven by Jenkins Competition team driver Larry Lombardo. Ronnie was driving the ex-Lyles Hemi Colt and put down an unreal 8.67 at 157.06 mph to Lombardo's losing 8.80 at 153.32 in round one. In the second round, Lombardo beat Sox with a 9.01 and 150.50 when Ronnie red-lighted. In the third and final round, Ronnie Sox took the event with an 8.68 at 158.45 to Lombardo's losing 8.83 at 154.10.

It was shortly after this that Ronnie Sox dropped out of racing for the remainder of 1975. He spent the rest of 1975 and part of 1976 taking it easy and working and playing with other projects and ideas, including golf and his oceanside motel operation in eastern North Carolina.

1976–1998
Changes in Relationships

Ronnie stands by the passenger's side of the Challenger while Buddy checks the fuel system. The front end has been removed for easier service. (Dan Williams Photo)

It was sometime during 1979 that the 22-year marriage of Ronnie and his wife, Pat, was dissolved, due probably more than anything else to the difficulties caused by Ronnie's long hours and many days and weeks gone on the road heading to and from drag racing events. Ronnie said in a 1990 interview for *Mopar Muscle* magazine that, "Seems like we got along good when I was traveling all the time, but when I stayed home we didn't."

CHAPTER 6

Ronnie Goes It Alone

From mid-1976 through 1991, Ronnie Sox was involved in several racing enterprises. By mid-1976, he worked out a deal with Ohio racer Billy Stepp and the ex–Lyles/Sox Colt was soon repainted and lettered as a *Billy the Kid* racer with Ronnie Sox as driver. Stepp's original Colt was wrecked when driver Bobby Yowell flipped it on a qualifying run at Bristol in June.

Gil Kirk of the Rod Shop bought the damaged Colt from Stepp. Kirk later purchased the former Roger Denney Hardy-built Colt; he painted and lettered it to Rod Shop livery using parts from the damaged Stepp Colt. Bob Riffle took over for former driver Gene Dunlap and drove it for the rest of the 1976 season.

The Colts generally ran in the NHRA Altered classes in Competition Eliminator and were not legal for Pro Stock. At the 1976 NHRA Nationals, both Ronnie Sox and Bob Riffle were out before the semi-finals, although both cars ran fast and straight. Sox was beaten by Wayne Jesel's D/Altered Camaro from New Jersey in the first round of eliminations.

By this time the Hemi Colts were running and gaining positive attention in IHRA Pro Stock competition where the rules favored the small cars in the professional class. When the 1977 NHRA rules were announced, the wheelbase requirements had changed; 92 inches was now allowed as the minimum. Billy Stepp, and a few other Mopar racers, went to the shorter and lighter Plymouth Arrow to compete in Pro Stock for the 1977 season. By June, a new car was ready and Ronnie Sox was the driver. The Arrow was built at Don Hardy's Texas shop. The tubular chassis was built to the normal Hardy standards of engineering and construction and had lightweight glass and body components for match racing.

Ronnie teamed with Gil Kirk and Clyde Hodges to drive this Rod Shop Hemi Colt at the 1977 NHRA U.S. Nationals as a fund raiser to benefit Don Carlton's wife. The Colt was entered in Competition Eliminator and ran 8.50s. (Dan Williams Photo)

Chapter 6

Ronnie and Buddy pose for a publicity photo in front of the newly finished 1978 Dodge Challenger prepared for NHRA Factory Experimental action. The Challenger was built by Clyde Hodges on a 99-inch wheelbase to Pro Stock specifications with a 408-ci Hemi. (Photo Courtesy Buddy Martin)

The 1,900-pound car was powered by a Paul Frost–built Hemi. Initial runs with Sox at the wheel brought times of 8.20s and a speed of almost 170 mph without using nitrous oxide. The Arrow was painted white with red side panels and a wide blue stripe across the roof, reminiscent of Sox & Martin days, but only the Ronnie Sox name was on the door as the driver above *Billy the Kid*.

Testing was ongoing with the Hemi Colts. It was a hot day at Milan, Michigan, on July 5, 1977, when Pro Stock driver Don Carlton was running tests for Chrysler with a stretched 117-inch-wheelbase version of the Hemi Colt. After making a number of runs, Carlton came back to the pits to drain and refill the Colt's radiator and refresh himself with a cold drink of water. He got back into the car for another run but somehow, possibly due to a blackout from heat exhaustion, Carlton crossed the line after the eighth-mile and ran into the grass, barrel rolling the car. He sustained fatal injuries from that crash and one of the most respected drivers and innovators was gone.

At the 1977 U.S. Nationals on Labor Day weekend, Ronnie Sox teamed with Gil Kirk and tuner Clyde Hodges to drive the Rod Shop Hemi Colt in Competition Eliminator to keep Don Carlton's name alive. Don's name was on the doors, Ronnie's name was on the window as driver, and American flag images were on the rear half of the Colt. The car went 8.50s running in A/FX class. This day's run was also a fund raiser for Carlton's wife, Jonnie, and their children.

The plans at that time were for Ronnie to drive a new Sox/Clyde Hodges car for 1978.

Ronnie climbed into the driver's seat of the new 1978 Challenger as Buddy kneeled by the door for a publicity photo. This car was equipped with a Lenco transmission to take advantage of the small-displacement Hemi. (Photo Courtesy Buddy Martin)

1976–1998 Changes in Relationships

Ronnie Sox decided to sport a full beard for the beginning of the 1978 season. Here, he waits inside the truck on a cold morning for race action to begin. (Dick Oldfield Photo)

The 1978 Sox & Martin Dodge Challenger waits next to the hauler for a race. Although built with a small-displacement Hemi, a larger engine could be installed for match racing. (Chick DeNinno Photo)

Together Again in Dodges

At the beginning of the 1978 drag racing season, Ronnie Sox found himself driving a new race car; this time it was a Dodge, not a Plymouth. Buddy Martin and Ronnie Sox had joined forces in early 1978 and a 1978 Dodge Challenger was built for Ronnie to drive in the NHRA A/Factory Experimental class and for match racing. The race car was based on the stock Dodge Challenger and Plymouth Sapporo, which were basically the Mitsubishi Gallant Lambda compact imports.

1978 Challenger

The Challenger race car was built by the new Sox & Martin crew chief Clyde Hodges. Although the car was intended for AF/X racing, under its skin, it was actually a Pro Stock car. The Challenger chassis had a 99-inch wheelbase and was fabricated by Hodges from steel tubing; the front suspension was based on a McPherson strut design.

The rear suspension was a four-link design with Koni shock absorbers that carried a narrowed (32½-inch) Dana 60 design rear axle with 4.57:1 Schiefer gears for quarter-mile competition and 4.86:1 for the eighth-mile. The rear axle used a Ramcharger magnesium center section that weighed only 40 pounds.

The hood was removed on the 1978 Challenger so the engine could be serviced during a race event. The lettering on the door told you that the mechanic was Clyde Hodges, who also built the car. (Tommy Erwin Photo)

Chapter 6

When a trip was long and required both cars, one was loaded inside the truck body and the other was carried on a double-stacker trailer pulled behind the Sox & Martin hauler. A skilled and careful driver was always needed to steer this rig down the road. (Chick DeNinno Photo)

The total car weight in race-ready condition was 2,233 pounds, just right for the 408-ci Hemi.

The engine used for A/FX work was a Hemi with a 4.310-inch bore and 2.48-inch stroke, displacing 408 ci. Factory-supplied pistons were mounted on standard 7.06-inch-long forged steel rods. Cylinder heads were Chrysler cast-aluminum versions reworked by Bob Mullen and carrying 2.38-inch intake valves and 1.87 exhaust valves. The camshaft used roller lifters and had .750-inch lift and 320 degrees of duration. The intake was a Weiand tunnel ram with two Holley 4500 carburetors. Headers were 2¼-inch-diameter tubes from Hooker. A Hemi with larger displacement was installed for match racing.

The Hemi was connected to the rear axle by way of a Lenco equipped with a 2.88:1 first gear and a Hays single-disc clutch. The body was fabricated by Clyde Hodges and it was painted red, white, and blue by Walter Thornberry. Of course, polished Cragar Super Trick wheels were used on all four corners.

The car was identified by NHRA Competition Number 265. It was raced on a limited schedule in 1978 and initial runs posted times of 8.80 at 155 mph.

1979 Omni

By the end of 1978 Ronnie and Buddy switched rides again and had a 1979 Dodge Omni built to run in NHRA Pro Stock. Chrysler decided to get back into the Pro Stock fray now that smaller engines and reasonable wheelbase rules were in place. By 1978 the market wanted small cars with tiny fuel-efficient engines so that is what the

Sometimes, the Sox & Martin D700 hauler was included as part of a display of their race cars. The Omni Pro Stock together with the red, white, and blue truck made for an interesting display. (Chick DeNinno Photo)

For 1979, Sox & Martin built a small-block Dodge Omni for Pro Stock and match racing. Here, the body is fitted and painted but not yet finished and lettered. The car was wrecked and later, after being sold, it was cut up. (Chick DeNinno Photo)

1976–1998 Changes in Relationships

A look at the rear of the Omni clearly shows the large slicks, parachute, and long wheelie bars, all needed to keep this little but powerful small-block-powered car firmly on the track. This car was later sold to Jerry Hurley and driven by Dempsey Hardy. (Chick DeNinno Photo)

manufacturers based their drag race program efforts on. The newest entry for 1979 was the Dodge Omni.

Ronnie, Buddy, and Chrysler wanted to have a new car ready for the 1979 season and the winter races on the West Coast. The Omni 024 was introduced late in 1978 so when the team was ready to build the new race car, Chrysler provided a pre-production standard car.

According to *Hot Rod* writer Al Kirschenbaum in an article about the car, this Omni was a stock 90,000-mile example that had been used for advertising and proving ground service. The silver and black sport model used in the paper and TV media was the same car seen in January but with the familiar red, white, and blue finish and with "Sox & Martin" painted on the side.

The Omni Pro Stock car was built in short order with a Don Hardy chassis finished in the Sox & Martin shop by crew chief Chick DeNinno. The chassis was fabricated from the same Clyde Hodges–designed suspension components used in the previous Challenger. It had a four-link and cast-magnesium Dana 60 rear axle center section, but this time it carried 5.86:1 gears to support the new high-RPM engine and 3.10:1 low-gear Lenco transmission configuration. New Firestone W-Series tires took up the torque of the small-block V-8.

The Omni body was constructed from a fiberglass component acquired from Harry Glass in Florida. Chick DeNinno oversaw the entire build operation then took the car to Hammerly Auto Body in Allentown, Pennsylvania, to have it painted.

The engine was based on an A-Series small-block V-8, similar to the 360-ci engine used in standard Chrysler passenger vehicles and trucks. This one made power from 337 ci and was built by Diamond Racing Engines. The valve system was based on standard Mopar Performance off-the-shelf parts, but oiling was handled with dry-sump components from Moroso and Paul Gentilozzi. A special aluminum tunnel ram intake manifold with a plenum mounted a pair of Holley 770-cfm carburetors. The engine developed its power all the way to 9,400 rpm.

Omni number two was later restored to 1979 race condition and is now owned by collector and dealer Reed Koeppe in Nebraska. Both Omnis have a Jet X logo on the sides. (Chick DeNinno Photo)

The 1979 Sox & Martin Omni Pro Stock hood scoop angled downward compared to those used on previous cars. The iconic red, white, and metallic blue finish was maintained. (Chick DeNinno Photo)

Chapter 6

The Omni Pro Stock was wrecked during a match race with Don Nicholson at Dragway 42 near West Salem, Ohio, on the way to the 1979 U.S. Nationals. A crash had become almost expected at this race but this time the Omni was totaled. (Chick DeNinno Photo)

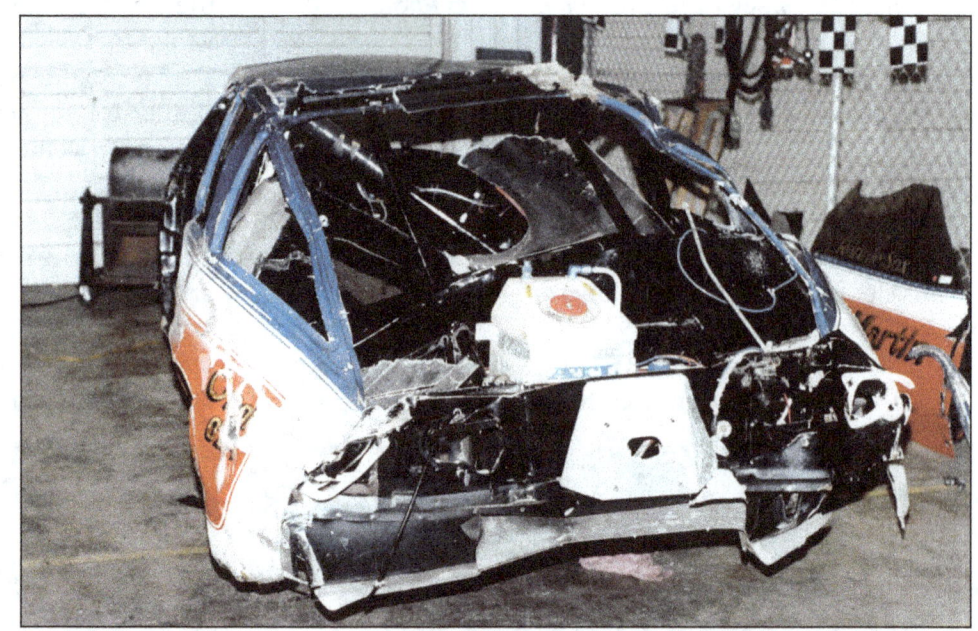

After the Omni crashed at Dragway 42, Chick loaded it back on the truck and drove back to Burlington to pick up the other car. He prepared the second Omni and hauled it back to Indianapolis for the event. (Chick DeNinno Photo)

Soon after the small-block Dodge-powered Omni Pro Stock was completed, Chick and the Sox & Martin team began working on a similar Don Hardy–built Omni, but this one was powered by a Hemi and was intended for match racing. Both cars were identified by the familiar "Jet X" logo on the doors.

1979 Racing Highlights

After joining up again in 1978, Ronnie and Buddy has a rocky season in 1979. One of the two Omnis was destroyed, and by the end of the year, wins were few.

NHRA Gatornationals

One of the first major events of 1979 was the NHRA Gatornationals at Gainesville, Florida. As usual, weather was a factor; it was cool and windy for the 10th annual event, held in late March. By the second round of Pro Stock, Don Camponello in his Chevrolet Monza beat Jim Kinnett in his Don Hardy–built Plymouth Volare with an 8.68 at 156 mph. In the same round, Ronnie Sox in the Sox & Martin Dodge Omni put away Larry Lombardo in the Jenkins Competition Camaro with an 8.61 at 155. Bob Glidden also came out of the second round a winner, running 8.55 at 149 driving a Plymouth Arrow.

1976–1998 Changes in Relationships

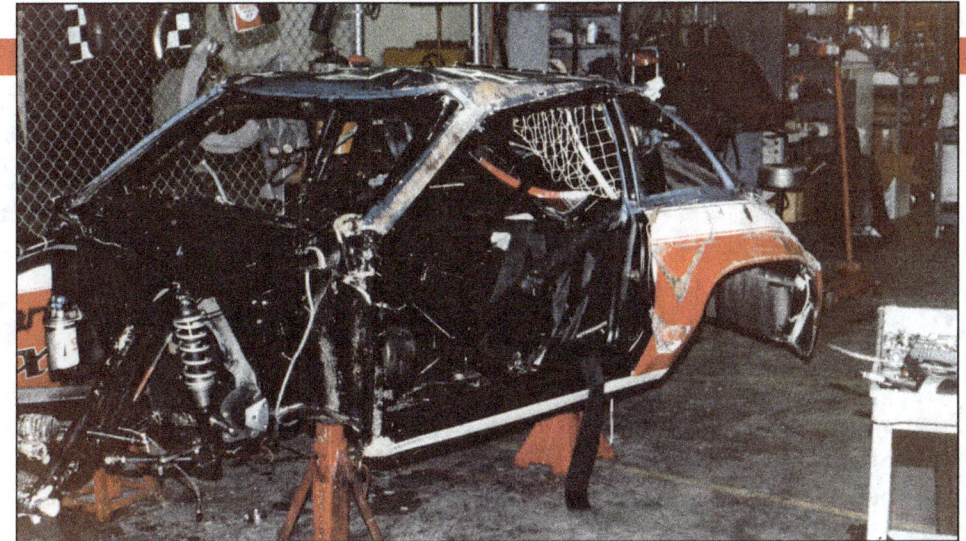

The car had been rolled at this year's "annual crash" so there was not much left that could be salvaged. The crew removed any useable parts and disposed of the rest. (Chick DeNinno Photo)

In the semi-final round, Sox put down Camponello for the win with an 8.65 at 155 mph and Glidden won over Brad Yuill with a record-breaking ET of 8.48 at 150. In the final round, it was side-by-side Mopars with Sox against Glidden. Ronnie knew he had a tough way to go against Glidden so he tried cutting a close light. He tried a little too hard on his screaming high-RPM start and lost the race with a big red-light jump to Glidden's 8.53 at 147 mph.

Dragway 42

It was standard procedure over the past few years for the team to stop at Dragway 42 near West Salem, Ohio, on the way to the NHRA U.S. Nationals to compete in a match race with Don Nicholson. This year was no different. The race was already set up and arranged for Ronnie, Chick, and the Hemi-powered Pro Stock Omni to be there. The small-block Pro Stock car was left in Burlington so the NHRA-legal car was ready to run.

It was also common procedure for Nicholson to somehow wreck Ronnie and his car in the last two of these races. In 1978, Ronnie was run into the guard rail by Nicholson. This year, the incident was significantly worse and the Omni was totally demolished.

Because the Indy race was important, Chick loaded up the car and hauled it back to Burlington. He unloaded Omni number one, prepared the second Omni, loaded it onto the trailer, and headed back to Indianapolis in time for the race. The car was not the one they had originally chosen but at least Ronnie was there for the competition. It was a long, hard trip for Chick as crew chief and truck driver.

IHRA Mountain Motor Nationals

By the fall of 1979, the IHRA ran its second annual Mountain Motor Nationals Pro Stock event at Maryland International Raceway. This event was conceived by announcer and promoter Ted Jones, who was Competition Vice President of the IHRA in 1976. Jones presented the idea to President Larry Carrier and by August 1978 the first race was announced.

The concept was to set a standard weight for Pro Stock cars and allow any engine size, thus eliminating a lot of the problems arising with other systems, such as that used by the NHRA. The Mountain Motor race became sort of a "Run What Ya Brung" Pro Stock class with few rules. The race was put together by Maryland track owner Tod Mack and partner Larry Clayton.

This time, the Mountain Motor concept was the motivation so the Sox & Martin Omni in its familiar red, white, and blue colors was entered in the 1979 race. Ronnie and Buddy were running two cars for the 1979 season; they brought their IHRA and match race Plymouth Arrow to this event.

In the last race of round one, Ronnie was up against Billy "Crash" Craddock's Mustang, driven by Alfred Williams. At the lights, Ronnie beat Williams with an unbelievable 8.09 at 170 mph to the Mustang's losing 8.78 and 128. The 7-second edge was getting close to being broken but it was a hot weekend so power was down a bit.

In the semi-final round, Sox was up against Minnesota-based Warren Johnson in a Camaro. Johnson must have felt pushed to be against the "Boss" because he left when Ronnie's last stage light lit and threw the 8.12 at 155 run-away to Ronnie's winning 8.14 and 168.50.

Chapter 6

Throughout the tour with the Omni, Ronnie sold T-shirts emblazoned with the legend "The Boss is Back!" along with a picture of the car. Sox & Martin never failed to present themselves as a class act in every way. (Photo Courtesy Diane Sox)

Sox went up against Lee Edwards in the final round. Just as Ronnie finished his burnout, lights began to flicker in the Arrow and smoke came out from under the instrument panel. Crew Chief Chick DeNinno made it to the line to lift off the deck lid and disconnect the battery.

Ronnie checked under the panel, looking for the problem, but the smoke stopped so he drove forward for the burnout. He staged, but the line lock didn't hold and he lit the red light in his lane. Edwards sat waiting for Ronnie to get right while DeNinno tried to solve the problem. When the race was finally run, Edwards beat Sox with an 8.10 to Ronnie's losing 8.13.

> **By the end of the 1980 season, Ronnie and Buddy split up again with Buddy heading back to the furniture business. Ronnie, as always, was unsure and out of sponsors, but looking for another race.**

It looked as if 1980 was going to be a promising year with back-to-back wins at Darlington and Rockingham to start the IHRA season. However, it wasn't meant to be. Times dove down into the 7.80s with Warren Johnson taking the championship. (David McGee Photo)

1980 Results

The 1980 season started strong with two IHRA wins, but further success was not in the cards. The team split again at the end of the year.

IHRA Winternationals

The 1980 season started with the IHRA Winternationals held at Darlington International Raceway on March 21–23. Ronnie found himself back in the winner's circle after finishing off Sam Carroll with an 8.13, capturing his first championship since 1972.

Rockingham

With the season off to a great start, team Sox & Martin carried the momentum to Rockingham where, again, Sox devoured the competition and posted his second straight victory in the finals, this time over John Brumley.

Mountain Motor Nationals

In August 1980, the Mountain Motor Nationals event was again held at Maryland International Raceway, but cooler weather than the previous year predicted more power and faster times. Track owner Tod Mack had the dream of establishing the largest independent Pro Stock race in the country and the success of the first two events was making his dream a reality. The low qualifying times of the 1980 race were a reason for more success and the top names in Pro Stock were lining up to compete.

Warren Johnson's Camaro was first and posted a flat 8-second pass. His lead was quickly busted when Pat Musi made a 7.99-second run. Dyno Don Nicholson's new Mustang barely made it into the 16-car field so it was clear that competition was going to be tough.

The top drivers in the country were winners after the first round of competition on Sunday. The names included Bill Jenkins, Rickie Smith, Warren Johnson, and Sox & Martin. Alfred Williams took a win in the first round over Nicholson. Pat Musi posted low ET of the round with an amazing 7.95 at 168 mph over Bill Clayton.

In the second round, seventh-place qualifier Rickie Smith ran an 8.15 and 170, but lost to Jenkins' holeshot run with an 8.24 at 165. In the semi-final round, Warren Johnson's Camaro put away Jenkins with a blistering 7.82 at 175 mph to Jenkins' losing 8.18. Ronnie Sox had already put down two 8.13 passes in a row, but he was beaten by Pat Musi running a 7.91 against Sox's 8.13 and 167.

By the end of the 1980 season, Ronnie and Buddy split up again with Buddy heading back to the furniture business. Ronnie, as always, was unsure and out of sponsors, but looking for another race.

1981 Season in a Mustang

The original Sox & Martin team again had adjustments. In 1981 crew chief and builder Chick DeNinno moved back to Maryland and started working for NASCAR driver and owner Harry Hyde. By early 1981, Ronnie found a new ride and a new car when he teamed up with a long-time racer and former Sox & Martin race-ready engine customer Dean Thompson from Louisiana.

Dean was the owner of a successful oil pipeline company and had been involved in drag racing since the late 1960s. He originally used Sox & Martin–built Hemi engines but, by 1971, had switched to Ford products and met Jack Roush, who provided him with power.

Roush and Thompson won the NHRA Division 2 Competition Eliminator title for four years and grabbed a Comp World Championship in 1976 with Wayne Gapp driving a 351 Cleveland powered B/Dragster.

In 1980, Thompson decided that Pro Stock was the next step up so he contracted Don Hardy to build a chassis and had Jack Roush Performance in Livonia, Michigan, build a car based on the Mustang and a Boss 429 Ford engine. Because Thompson was already

The Dean Thompson Jack Roush–built 1981 Mustang had a chassis built by Don Hardy. It used a 488-ci Boss 429 based engine with 1,024 hp and 731 ft-lbs of torque. The finished car weighed about 2,000 pounds. (David McGee Photo)

Chapter 6

Ironically, Ronnie Sox began his drag racing career in a Ford in the 1950s on the streets of Burlington. More than 30 years later he piloted a Ford Mustang. (David McGee Photo)

aware of Ronnie's driving skills and winning records from their previous connection, he contacted Ronnie to drive the car.

Sox even visited the shop in Michigan to witness the engine capabilities on Roush's dynamometer and helped Roush's body and paint man, Ed Nowakowski, finish the car. A beautiful black paint with gold and red striping made the car stand out at the track.

The Mustang was based on a Hardy-designed and built tubular chassis with four-link rear suspension and Koni shock absorbers holding up the rear. The rear axle was a dependable 9-inch unit carrying 4.56:1 gears. The car was powered by an IHRA-size 588-ci Boss 429 Shotgun with a cast-iron block. That big displacement was accomplished with a bore and stroke of 4.440 and 4.750 inches, respectively.

This engine went through a lot of testing over the winter and the final output was pegged at 1,024 hp and 731 ft-lbs of torque at 7,000 rpm. The engine was connected to the driveline by a 4-speed Lenco transmission. Initial testing of the 2,000-pound car showed a best pass of 7.86 at 174.90 mph at Rockingham.

IHRA Octane Plus Winternationals

The 1981 IHRA season opener as always was the Octane Plus Winternationals at Darlington, South Carolina. Rain drowned out the scheduled first weekend so the race was rescheduled for the following week. The timing of the competition was set back even more by the South Carolina law that prevented any racing before 2 pm on Sunday so it helped that some qualifying had been accomplished on the previous Saturday before the rain arrived.

Don Nicholson set the low qualifying time of 7.88 at 176 mph, making him the favorite and the one that the rest of the field had to beat. This was the quickest time ever run at an IHRA national event.

Nicholson followed through in the first round with a 7.81 at 176, beating Keith Allbritton's 8.25. Ronnie Sox and the Thompson Mustang made it to the third round but were beaten by fifth qualifier Rickie Smith with a 7.96 at 173 mph over Sox's losing 8.04 at 173.

IHRA World Nationals

Ronnie Sox and Dean Thompson's next important effort was at the first IHRA World Nationals held at

Norwalk Raceway Park in Ohio during the summer of 1981. Again, heavy rain affected Saturday qualifying but the rest of the race went on as planned. Ronnie put the Thompson Mustang in its first qualifying position with a 7.92, just a bit faster than the other two cars out of the eight-car field that placed below the 8-second bracket.

During the final round, Sox advanced through the field beating 18-year-old Chuck Sneed and Keith Allbritton, while opponent Warren Johnson put away Virginia's Harold Robinson and Rickie Smith. At the lights, Ronnie had the advantage off the line and held that lead to best Johnson with a 7.91 and 175 mph to the losing Chevy Monte Carlo's 7.99 and 167 for the win.

Wins and a Bonus

Maybe the "Boss" was finally back on track. He ended the year as IHRA Pro Stock World Champion. Ronnie won four races in 1981, including the Winston World Nationals, the Northern Nationals, the Summer Nationals and the U.S. Open Nationals. This was his last drag racing championship. An added bonus was the fact that Ronnie's son, Ronald Dean Sox, served on his crew for this championship year.

Forced Retirement in 1982

The 1982 season found a new emphasis on NHRA Pro Stock action with some equipment changes to meet the new 500-ci displacement limit. At the beginning of the year, Ronnie Sox and the Dean Thompson Mustang were seen as the best bet for winning the gold. Although Sox continued his match race and IHRA competition, he and the three other major contenders, Warren Johnson in an Oldsmobile; Rickie Smith, now in a Don Hardy–built 1982 Mustang; and Harrold Denton, in the former Don Nicholson Ford Mustang II, were the leaders of the pack. Ford power expert John Kaase took care of the engine building and tuning for both Denton and Smith.

Ronnie Sox started the year out strong by winning the IHRA Winter Nationals at Darlington, making that his 13th IHRA career win and second national title for the year and the all-time career winner in IHRA Pro Stock racing. Later in the summer of 1982, Ronnie put down another season win at the IHRA Northern Nationals at Milan, Michigan, beating Warren Johnson in the final round.

It was not long after this apparent run of success that Ronnie Sox was put back out to pasture when team and car owner Dean Thompson decided to get out of the drag racing business. His Louisiana oil pipeline laying business was going downhill and Dean had to pull out for financial reasons. Ronnie was hopeful that Dean's business would turn around and he would be back in racing, but by the end of 1982 there was no sign of that happening.

This change left Ronnie Sox with little to do but look for another ride and work on his golf game. He still had income from the sale of the building in Burlington but that would be running out soon if he didn't find a car to drive.

> **It was not long after this apparent run of success that Ronnie Sox was put back out to pasture when team and car owner Dean Thompson decided to get out of the drag racing business.**

Ronnie also had his own reason for leaving racing; it was around that time that he suffered some painful health problems. The first diagnosis was that he needed a hernia operation. The pain returned a short few weeks after that painful procedure, so he went back for more tests and X-rays. This time, he was told he had tumors in his intestinal system, but further X-rays indicated that this was not the problem.

It wasn't until Ronnie had more tests at Duke Medical Center that the real problem was identified. Ronnie reported that it turned out to be relatively minor and was quickly corrected with medicine.

Jump to a Camaro

Ronnie's opportunity for a new ride finally came when he connected with Gary Duckworth from Maryville, Illinois, just east of St. Louis, Missouri. Gary had started his racing engine building business in 1980 and was looking for a winning race car combination to bring publicity and recognition to his work.

Chapter 6

In 1983 alone, Duckworth garnered six new track records, four top qualifiers, and five wins. He was considered one of the most successful independent racers and was one of the most respected drivers in the business. Duckworth had successfully raced the Pro Stock Camaro; noted Mopar driver Darrell Alderman drove it in 1984. Gary drove the car to a new AHRA record of 7.53 seconds at 183.29 mph; it also held ADRA speed and ET records.

Gary also took the Camaro to a UDRA Eastern Pro Stock Championship. The UDRA awarded Gary the Best Appearing Car Award and third place for highest point earners in Pro Stock for 1984.

Sometime late in the 1984 season, Darrell Alderman split with Duckworth and moved to a 630-ci Jerry Haas–built car. Gary Duckworth and Ronnie Sox had already met so when the arrangement with Alderman broke up, Gary called to offer him a job driving his new Pro Stock Camaro.

Car Specs

The red, white, and blue striped Gary and Donna Duckworth Camaro was based on a chassis that Duckworth built himself. A 9-inch Ford rear axle held up the rear of the car and was equipped with Weld wheels and Goodyear slicks.

The power came from a Duckworth-built 634-ci cast-iron Bow-Tie block 454 Chevrolet-based engine with a .035-inch overbore and a 4.75-inch HTC crankshaft and with 14:1 compression ratio VIN pistons on C&A connecting rods. A Comp camshaft and roller lifters actuated the 2.35-inch Manley intake valves, along with Jesel rocker arms, pushrods, and stud girdles. Dart provided the aluminum cylinder heads.

Two Holley 4500 series 4-barrel carburetors were mounted on a fabricated aluminum tunnel-ram intake manifold. The engine connected to the rear axle by way of a Lenco 4-speed transmission.

Racing Summary

Ronnie had been out of the sport for three seasons so he did not have to think too long to accept. Ronnie posted a career best time of 7.56 at 183 mph at the 1984 IHRA Fall Nationals at Bristol.

That was not Ronnie's first run with the Camaro. He won the first round with a 7.63 and 182.18 against Jerry

This 1985 Camaro Pro Stock, owned by Gary Duckworth in Illinois, offered Ronnie Sox more opportunities to show his continuing success capabilities. Gary was a great driver himself but wanted Ronnie to drive his car at national events. (Gary Duckworth Photo)

1976–1998 Changes in Relationships

The 1985 Gary Duckworth Camaro may have been the only race car Ronnie Sox drove since 1962 with a completely red roof. Ronnie kept hints of his red, white, and blue colors but Gary did not allow him to put "The Boss" on the hood scoop. (Photo Courtesy Diane Sox)

Ronnie was given this IHRA trophy for winning Champion Pro Stock at the 1985 IHRA Pro Am Nationals at Rockingham, North Carolina, in the Duckworth Camaro. Gary Duckworth has the trophy in his collection.

Yeoman and then beat Charlie Pepper's Thunderbird in the second round with a 7.58 and 182.92 run. Unfortunately, Sox red-lighted in the third round against Bob Glidden, shutting off early with a 7.68 and 167 mph.

Sox also took third place at the IHRA U.S. Open Nationals at Rockingham in late 1984, running a blistering 7.54 at 183.67. Gary's Camaro, with Ronnie driving, also took first place at the Blaney, South Carolina, Drag Strip Pro Stock Bash with a win over Jim Ruth's *Party Time* Pontiac Trans Am with a 7.58 ET.

Ronnie drove the Camaro at several races in 1985, including the 15th annual IHRA Motorcraft Pro Am Nationals at Rockingham Dragway in North Carolina on May 3–5 where he qualified eighth. He upset Bruce Allen in the David Reher–Buddy Morrison–tuned Camaro in the final with a 7.724 second run at 180.72 mph and a .0596 reaction time, taking first place in Pro Stock at the race and receiving an IHRA trophy for his efforts.

After the win Ronnie said, "I think I'll just fly to Vegas. I feel hot." This race was Ronnie's fourth win in this event at the Rock. The trophy actually went home with Gary Duckworth, who still displays it at his engine building shop in Maryville.

One Request Denied

Like many other professional race drivers, Ronnie needed nothing more than a car to drive and races to run. Duckworth said that Ronnie booked all of his own match races around the country and showed up at the track to drive only. Ronnie was not paid to drive so car owner Gary Duckworth kept whatever was won at the events. When the day was over, Ronnie went to his next race or back to North Carolina depending on what plans he had made.

Gary did his best to support Ronnie's habit except for one request. Duckworth refused to paint "The Boss" on the scoop as Ronnie wanted but gave in to his insistence of a thin blue stripe on the white and red Camaro body. The Camaro was later sold to Paul Weatherford.

Chapter 6

Two timeless adversaries square off in a match race at Great Lakes Dragway. Ronnie Sox and Arnie "Farmer" Beswick were quick to capitalize on the revival of match racing by building historic drag cars. (Photo Courtesy Mark and Laura Bruederle)

Nostalgia Takes Over

By 1988 Ronnie's efforts at continuing and reviving his racing career had slowed down. However, fans and promoters were beginning to recognize the interest in the good old days of drag racing. One of the first people to take advantage of this interest was collector, car show promoter, and former drag racer Frank Spittle of Davidson, North Carolina.

The First Event

Frank decided to present his first nostalgia event at Charlotte Motor Speedway's modern eighth-mile dragstrip. Because 1963 was considered the beginning of what became the great Super Stock and Factory Experimental era, Frank chose 1988 as the 25th anniversary of the cars and drivers that made the sport what it was for more than two decades.

Frank began to contact everyone he could think of who might have been involved in racing during that era and found that almost everyone was excited and enthused about the idea. With such important personalities as Bill Jenkins, Malcolm Durham, Hayden Proffitt, Arnie Beswick, and Pat Minick promising to attend, the event had to be special. Of course, no event of this type would be complete without the attendance and support of the legendary Ronnie Sox and Buddy Martin, who looked forward to it with great enthusiasm.

Although spectator attendance was low, probably because of not enough publicity about the event, the racers wholeheartedly enjoyed the reunion and the opportunity to see, and sometimes drive, their old race cars on the dragstrip. The event included real drag racing and match racing in addition to the attendance of the drivers and owners from the past. Buddy said, "If there is anybody here who is enjoying this more than me, I would like to know who it is and what they are doing!"

Ronnie also commented, "I think it's great seeing these guys. I didn't know if some of them were still living, and knowing they are gives me a great feeling. I think very positively about events like this!"

Pontiac racer Arnie Beswick was very impressed and commented, "The finest event that any individual has ever put together! I just can't thank Frank Spittle enough."

Barracuda Match Racing

During 1988 Ronnie decided to get into the driver's seat of another 1968 Hemi Barracuda. The car Ronnie drove was one originally owned by Bill Vanwey in Dayton, Ohio. It was an original BO29 Hemi Barracuda.

In late 1969, Vanwey needed money more than a race car so he sold the all-red-painted Barracuda to Billy Stepp. Stepp did not keep the car long and traded it for a 4-speed version already in their stock vehicle. Stepp eventually sold the car and it passed through a couple more owners before falling out of sight for a while. Ronnie bought the car from Larry Zane and finished it in Sox & Martin livery for his match racing and nostalgia activities.

Ronnie toured the country, finding lucrative match racing everywhere. Incredibly, Ronnie actually drove this Hemi Barracuda longer than any other Hemi-powered car. It was later sold and restored and is identified by its SS/B class identification and 784 Competition Number on the windshield and quarter windows.

This car had a wide blue stripe down the center of the hood. It also had much larger and wider rear tires than appeared on earlier versions. This Barracuda later went to collector Phil Painter but is currently part of the fabulous Rick Hendrick collection and museum in Concord, North Carolina.

1992 Carlisle Productions

One of the more interesting events featuring Ronnie Sox, who was still driving his Tim Richards–built Hemi-powered 1968 Hemi Barracuda, was at a 1992 Carlisle Productions show. With the help of promoters Bill and Chip Miller and collectors and enthusiasts including Jim Kramer, Mike Guffey, Dick Towers, and others, it was decided that this would be a recognition of the 25th anniversary of the 1968 A-Body Hemi Super Stock cars. In addition to a number of original 1968 Hemi Darts and Barracudas, original drivers were present including Ken Montgomery, Bill Stiles, Jack Werst, and of course, Dick Landy and Ronnie Sox.

The highlight of the event was a match race between Landy and Sox, just like in the old days. A day at nearby South Mountain Dragway was the venue for this historic race and it was all done just like it was in the past. Both Dick and Ronnie went through the important operation of sweeping the resin onto the track.

Buddy Martin did not make this event, but Ronnie's son Dean was there to watch the bout. Being more of an exhibition event than an actual race made the winner unimportant, and Ronnie even worked in the grass pit area to fix a clutch to keep the show going.

Racing the Comet Replica

That first nostalgia event must have stirred up old feelings in Ronnie because by mid-1989, he was already putting the finishing touches on a specially-built modified fiberglass replica of his 1964 Mercury Comet Cyclone.

The car, built with help from partner Travers Webb, was powered by a 707-ci Sonny Leonard–built Ford Shotgun engine that he purchased from Rickie Smith. The power to the rear axle was controlled by a 3-speed Lenco transmission. The already-powerful Ford was

> *The highlight of the 1992 Carlisle Productions show was a match race between Landy and Sox, just like in the old days.*

enhanced by the generous and timely application of nitrous oxide from the twin bottles in the trunk. A large aerodynamic Pro Stock style scoop was mounted in the center of the hood, feeding the two Holley 4500 series carburetors.

The engine had fuel injectors added to it by the 1992 season. Sox reported that the car's build cost was between $90,000 and $100,000 and was state of the art. Tommy Mauney built the chassis.

The fiberglass body was custom built by C. D. Simmons; it was a rather impressionistic chopped and lowered, sculpted version of a 1964 Comet Cyclone. The additional downforce needed for its 200-mph runs was provided by a wide, flat spoiler mounted to the rear deck. The original paint finish was similar to earlier Sox & Martin cars: a white body with red side panels and a blue roof. However, the paint scheme was changed two more times and the body was later modified for more tire clearance.

Ronnie ran the Comet at a Ford Funday event at Atlanta Dragway in August 1990 and posted a 7.06 and 200.51 mph match race win against Norm Wizner's losing 7.25 at 192.

The new sportsman car was scheduled for its official debut at the Bristol race in the fall of 1989.

Chapter 6

Ronnie's Pro Mod 1964 Comet replica continued racing successfully in the Southeast for three years. This photo shows the grille painted on the fiberglass body to resemble an original 1964 Comet grille. The body has been modified with a hump over the rear tires. (Joe Marsingill Photo)

Even after more than 23 years of professional drag racing, Ronnie Sox still had a big smile and warm welcome for his fans wherever he went. This is Ronnie at Darlington in September 1991. (Joe Marsingill Photo)

The first version of Ronnie's 1964 Comet Pro Mod was painted similar to his older cars with a blue roof and red and white on the body. The car launches hard after a burnout from the line at Darlington in 1990. (Joe Marsingill Photo)

1976–1998 Changes in Relationships

Later, the Comet Pro Mod had another new paint finish that featured a lot more white but kept the large red hood scoop emblazoned with "The Boss." Here, the Comet lifts the front wheels at Darlington. (Joe Marsingill Photo)

IHRA Winternationals

It was actually the spring of 1990 before Ronnie's new Comet was introduced to the general public. The season opener was the IHRA Winternationals at Darlington, South Carolina, during the second week of March. The big news for 1990 was the introduction of the new heads-up Pro Modified, Eliminator modified from the old Quick Eight Eliminator class.

The first 25 entries in the class included Mike Ashley from New York, who qualified number one with a 7.07 and 198.36; Bill Kuhlman from St. Louis was second with a 7.127 at 197.84; and barely making the field at number 16 was Ronnie Sox with a 7.61 at 182.36 mph in his new replica 1964 Comet. Ronnie made it to the semi-final round of Pro Mod as the crowd rose to their feet for the battle, but Sox only made a 7.41 and 157.22 losing run against winner Tim McAmis with the low ET of the meet at 7.01 at 200.68.

IHRA Wolverine Blue Racer Fall Nationals

The last major IHRA event in the 1990 racing season was the Wolverine Blue Racer Fall Nationals held at Bristol, Tennessee. A number of veteran racers were present including Gene Snow, Bill Kuhlman, Rickie Smith, and of course, 51-year-old Ronnie Sox in his Pro Mod 1964 Comet.

In addition to the regular competition, some special shootout events were scheduled throughout the season.

This Jim Bralley shot shows Ronnie and his 1964 Comet Pro Mod after winning the IHRA Tosti Asti Spumante Gateway Nationals at St. Louis in 1990. The trophy and bottle of bubbly were some of his prizes for the triumph. (Photo Courtesy Diane Sox)

Ronnie poses with his replica 1964 Comet Pro Mod between rounds at Darlington. Always the professional, his racing suit matches the color scheme of the car. Here, the scoop is blocked to keep debris out of the engine. (Photo Courtesy J. C. Childress)

Chapter 6

Friends Helping Friends

It was not unusual for competitive Pro Modified racers to help one another when the need arose. One such example occurred during the 1991 IHRA Tosti Gateway Nitrous Nationals at East St. Louis.

On the way to the track Ronnie stopped and worked out of Pro Mod champion Bill Kuhlmann's shop in Wentzville, Missouri, for a couple of days doing basic maintenance on the Pro Mod Comet. Ronnie pulled into Wentzville in his cabover big rig and white trailer with "Ronnie Sox Race Team" and "World's Fastest Ford" in big blue letters on the sides and back.

Ronnie and Bill were great friends and had raced together and talked many times; Ronnie knew that Kuhlmann, number six

Racers Ronnie Sox (left) and Bill Kuhlmann (right) became very good friends over the years and were close until Ronnie's passing in 2006. Here they pose in front of Bill's Pro Mod Camaro. (Bill Kuhlmann Photo)

In 1991 Ronnie stopped at the garage of his friend and champion Pro Mod racer Bill Kuhlmann in Wentzville, Missouri, to do some repairs on his Pro Mod Comet. The fit was tight as Ronnie backed the Comet out of his big trailer. (Bill Kuhlmann Photo)

Ronnie had a large truck and trailer by this time and used it for his race and show events. The flyer on the door lists the prices of his promotional items for sale. (Bill Kuhlmann Photo)

By this time, the Ronnie Sox Race Team traveled in a large truck and trailer, equaling anything used at that time. Ronnie used the trailer for storing and hauling his race car plus selling merchandise from the side. (Bill Kuhlmann Photo)

On this particular trip out West, Ronnie brought his dad "Nub" along for help and company. He is posing here alongside Ronnie's red, white, and blue Comet. (Bill Kuhlmann Photo)

Ronnie knew that Kuhlmann's shop had all of the tools, equipment, and skilled helpers he might need to work on his big Ford engine. Here, the Comet is already torn down and work has been started. (Bill Kuhlmann Photo)

on the Competition Plus top-20 Pro Mod drivers of all time list and first door slammer driver to surpass the 200-mph mark with his Camaro in 1987, would be a good working companion and have everything Ronnie needed.

Ronnie's father, Willard M. Sox, was traveling with him on this trip and sat in the shop watching patiently as Ronnie and the Kuhlmann crew worked on the Comet's big Ford engine. Ronnie's father enjoyed the day because he had a good conversation with Bill's father.

Kuhlmann's son Barry said that he still remembers the race. Qualifying was cut short because of rain and Ronnie didn't get into the show. Ronnie was not happy and said that he had never failed to qualify before. It was a bad break especially considering that he had been the winner of that race the previous year.

Ronnie Sox and Bill Kuhlmann remained good friends until Ronnie's passing. When Bill had a really bad day in 2000 at Virginia Motorsports, Ronnie was quick to his side.

Kuhlmann had taken his Pro Mod Chevy on a run to try to be the first door slammer in the 5-second bracket. But, at some point, the engine exploded and broke the crankshaft, pushing it out through the bottom of the block and separating the block from the rest of the drivetrain. The engine and car burst into flames and crashed.

Kuhlmann was trapped in the car and the fire was so bad that the safety crew did not want to get too close; they let it burn, thinking Bill was dead. He was taken to the hospital at Richmond and was in an induced coma for 12 days. Ronnie visited Bill in the hospital, although Bill was unaware of it at the time.

Bill Kuhlmann related one of his memories of Ronnie Sox. "There is something that will stick in my mind forever when it comes to Ronnie Sox.

"When you're a guy who started racing at 16 years old and you worked your butt off just to be able to race on the same track as some of the people who you only saw on film or in books and now you're standing in the staging lanes, qualified number one with a guy named Sox standing next to you, and he says, 'Hey Bill,' you listen!

Ronnie's dad looks on intently as the technicians from Bill Kuhlmann's shop tear into the Ford engine. The problem seems to have been something related to the huge pistons. (Bill Kuhlmann Photo)

Chapter 6

Friends Helping Friends CONTINUED

Ronnie works on a piston but needs his glasses for the close work. He's installing the rings on the giant buckets used in the big Ford engine. Kuhlmann's shop was fully equipped for any type of repairs or maintenance. (Bill Kuhlmann Photo)

"You don't expect his words to be something that you will take to your grave but that's how those little things happen. On one early occasion he said, 'You know that there are over 400 guys here who think that they are professional racers and/or drivers, but you and I know that there are only two here.'

Ronnie and the rest of the crew at Kuhlmann's work underneath the Comet while Ronnie's dad watches patiently. Of course, Ronnie's dad had a service station himself so he knew what was going on. (Bill Kuhlmann Photo)

"I knew exactly what he meant and was honored that he felt that way about me.

"A lot of people don't know that heroes are just regular guys who go about things a little differently than others. Ronnie was one of my heroes who became a good friend and despite the fame, he remained a really good person."

These were sponsored by Summit Racing, Weld, Lunati Cams, and others. Sox did not fare well in the Summit Quick 8 Pro Mod Shootout and lost to Blake Wiggins 6.93 at 200.61 when Ronnie shut off early.

Ronnie was obviously ready for racing this time, qualifying fifth with a 6.96 and 203.19 mph effort. Although his racing experience over the last few years had been sporadic, he made it clear that he was still serious about his work and had not lost anything to time. In round one, Sox beat Bob Lasardo with a 7.00-second ET and 200 mph even. He followed up by putting away "Killer" Brooks' Camaro with a broken starter with another 7-second-flat and 200-mph pass.

In the semi-final round Sox, with lane choice, faced number-one qualifier Scotty Cannon and his 1940 Willys. Ronnie showed his talent and experience with a holeshot win over Cannon with a winning 7.02 to beat Cannon's quicker 6.93 run. In the final round against Mike Ashley, Sox won his second race of the season by way of Ashley's red light foul.

The IHRA Pro Modified World Championship went to Tim McAmis.

Ronnie Sox continued to successfully race the Pro Mod Comet well into 1994. The IHRA gave a 100-pound weight advantage to all cars based on a pre-1969 model so Sox and other racers, such as Scotty Cannon from South Carolina, continued to take advantage of those bodies. By then Ronnie was sponsored by Patrick Ford in Fayetteville and also by Winnebago. The Comet had a new white and red paint job and the rear of the body was redesigned for more tire clearance and to lower the body. A round hump can easily be seen just beneath the sail panel of the roof.

Carolina Dragway

Sox and Cannon faced each other for a season opener contest at Carolina Dragway in Jackson, South Carolina,

Ronnie was a competitor always and never ran a race without checking his time and speed after a run. Ronnie's Comet and championship were noted on his cap. (Photo Courtesy Diane Sox)

By 1992, Ronnie's Pro Mod Comet had a new paint design with a lot more blue on the top and the bottom. The body maintained the hump over the rear tires for clearance. (Joe Marsingill Photo)

This is a group of attendees at a 1995 Super Stock Reunion. Buddy Martin and Ronnie Sox are seated at left in the front row. The back row includes Don Nicholson (far left), Phil Bonner (second from left), Dave Christie (light-colored jacket), Arnie Beswick (fifth from right), and Malcolm Durham (far right). (Photo Courtesy Dave Christie)

early in 1994. The Sox team changed back to a single-stage nitrous system for 1994, replacing the troublesome three-stage setup used in 1993.

Ronnie's son Dean came along to help with maintenance. The team had clutch problems that caused a couple of red lights before and during the match races with Scotty Cannon and his 526-ci Chevy-powered 1941 Willys coupe. After a red-light foul in round one, Sox put more counterweights in the clutch to try again. In the second round, Cannon beat him out of the hole and maintained that lead to the finish with a 4.32 and 162 mph for the 1/8-mile track, beating Ronnie's 4.49 and 153.24.

In round three, Sox had the clutch working properly and put a .444 to .465 holeshot on Cannon but still lost to Cannon's blown Chevy with another 4.32 and 166 for the win to Sox's losing 4.49 and 158.85 mph.

Ronnie and the Comet did well but could not put themselves ahead of the supercharged cars for the rest of the event. Ronnie actually drove this Pro Modified Comet longer than any other race car in his career.

Another Reunion in 1995

At the end of 1994, planning for the 1995 drag racing season, Ronnie again teamed with his old partner Buddy Martin for a new charge at the IHRA Pro Stock class. The reunion was initiated by long-time Ford racing sponsor Patrick Purvis of Patrick Ford in Fayetteville, North

Chapter 6

Carolina. Purvis had already sponsored a number of NASCAR drivers including Ronnie's 1994 Pro Mod racer. He thought it would be a great idea for some old-timers to show the young folks how it is done. Buddy was supportive of the idea and wanted to see Ronnie back in a first-class ride that was capable of winning.

Thunderbird Out, Probe In

Both Buddy and Ronnie had been contemplating a return to IHRA and NHRA Pro Stock and even had plans of building two new cars and making it to the 1995 NHRA U.S. Nationals. Purvis offered them a chance to get back into the action. The new Ford was based on

Racing greats (from left to right) Ronnie Sox, Richard Petty, and Buddy Martin got together for a photo session during their induction into the racing Hall of Fame in Virginia. (Photo Courtesy Diane Sox)

From left to right, Ronnie Sox, "Big Daddy" Don Garlits, and Buddy Martin display the painting of their race cars presented at their induction to the International Drag Racing Hall of fame in Ocala, Florida. (Photo Courtesy Diane Sox)

Buddy Martin waits behind the short-lived 1994 Ford Thunderbird Pro Stock. Their primary sponsor was Patrick Ford in Fayetteville, North Carolina. The Thunderbird was later replaced with a Ford Probe. (Geoff Stunkard Photo)

Ronnie stands next to his Ford Probe in the staging lanes. Sox & Martin campaigned Fords toward the end of the duo's run together in the mid-1990s. (David McGee Photo)

a 1995 Thunderbird mounted on a Tommy Mauney–built chassis.

The Shotgun Ford engine was a Jon Kaase–built 810-ci monster with two Holley Dominators mounted on a tunnel ram with plenum manifold. The new white and red Thunderbird made some shakedown runs of 6.90 at 202 mph with Ronnie at the controls so the potential was there. The new car was featured in the August 1995 issue of *Super Stock & Drag Illustrated* with a full-color center spread.

Partway through the 1995 season, Sox & Martin, like a few other Ford teams, decided that the Thunderbird was not working as well as they would have liked, although at the IHRA Empire Nationals in New York in late June, Ronnie qualified number one with a 7.02 ET.

The new choice was the shorter-wheelbase Ford Probe so the Thunderbird was set aside. It eventually went back to Patrick Ford's stable.

The new Probe was built entirely by Sox & Martin mechanic and builder Chick DeNinno in Chick's race

The 1995 Ford Probe Pro Stock entry was built entirely in the Sox & Martin shop by Chick DeNinno, who had been with the team for years. DeNinno operated his own chassis fabrication business in Maryland prior to joining Sox & Martin. (Chick DeNinno Photo)

Ronnie had the new Ford Probe Pro Stock available to attend the Super Stock Magazine Nationals Reunion at Virginia Motorsports Park. Initial runs with the Probe looked very promising. (Photo Courtesy Diane Sox)

The big John Kaase Ford engine in the Probe was equipped with aluminum Hemi-type cylinder heads, a fabricated aluminum tunnel-ram intake manifold, and two large Holley 4-barrel carburetors. (Chick DeNinno Photo)

The body of the Ford Probe was constructed from steel panels, fiberglass, and composite materials fitted to a full tubular chassis on a chassis plate in the shop. (Chick DeNinno Photo)

Chapter 6

car shop, Fabrication, Inc., in Maryland because most of the Sox & Martin facility in Burlington was empty and the equipment had been sold. The engine was an 814-ci Shotgun-based Pro Stock, similar to the engine in the Thunderbird.

The Crash

The Probe was finished by mid-season and was run once at the Virginia Motorsports Park dragstrip in Dinwiddie. That white and red Ford Probe almost caused the end of Ronnie Sox. Ronnie, Buddy, Chick DeNinno, and Ronnie's 33-year-old son Dean took the Probe to the IHRA Parts Pro 16th annual Summernationals held on July 7–9 at U.S. 41 Dragway in Morocco, Indiana. Roy Hill led the field in qualifying by posting a .0400-second effort so he was considered the best choice to win. Hill's hopes were crushed when a crankshaft broke early in the event.

Ronnie qualified ninth and made it to the quarter finals where he was lined up in the left lane against sixth qualifier Jerry Yeoman in his 1994 Oldsmobile Cutlass. Ronnie was first at the lights with a 7.008 ET at 197.02 mph. His .534 reaction time was not as good as he would have liked but he was still getting used to the new car.

Ronnie faced Mike Bell from Sophia, North Carolina, in his 1995 Thunderbird in the semi-final round. With

The Probe roll cage was considered a "funny car" type of design and offered the greatest possible protection for the driver. The wheel opening modifications are shown clearly here. (Chick DeNinno Photo)

Chick DeNinno pushes the Ford Probe Pro Stock to the staging lanes at one of its first outings. The silver-leaf lettering was not yet painted on the doors or scoop. (Chick DeNinno Photo)

Some of the Sox & Martin Probe's maiden runs were at Virginia Motorsports Park in early 1995. Even in a Ford, Ronnie Sox maintained his "Boss" moniker. (Photo Courtesy Diane Sox)

The Probe was hauled back to the pit area after Ronnie's crash and it caught everyone's attention. Chick DeNinno and the other crew members had to determine the cause and extent of the damage. (Chick DeNinno Photo)

Once the Probe was loaded on the truck to be hauled away, it became clear how important the properly designed and built roll cage had been. Chick's quality work and attention to detail helped save Ronnie's life. (Chick DeNinno Photo)

Buddy guiding at the front and son Dean in the rear with radio contact, Ronnie backed the Probe into the right lane. Mike was slightly ahead at the start. Just a short way into the race, Ronnie's Probe poured smoke out of the back of the car, pointed sharply right, and then swung back left. It crossed into the left lane and barely missed the rear of Bell's car.

After almost hitting the left side barrier, the Probe rolled over onto its right side, and then barrel-rolled and bounced 13 times down the track, losing parts and momentum along the way. The car finally came to rest on its wheels, facing the starting line, minus the front end and doors, when a fire erupted in the engine compartment.

Buddy watched in awe and concern at the line while Dean rushed to the scene in his golf cart. The track medical personnel were already attending to Ronnie, who was unconscious at first. The emergency team had to use Hurst's Jaws of Life equipment to extract Ronnie from the car. Emergency personnel first led Dean away from the car, but he was soon back, holding Ronnie's right hand and talking to him as Ronnie was placed in the ambulance.

Announcer Bret Kepner interviewed Chick after the crash, asking him about the accident and what could have caused it. Chick said a large AN oil line–fitting had vibrated loose, dumping engine oil underneath the tires causing it to get out of shape.

Chick said later that Dick Landy called right after the crash and asked him what happened. Chick told him and Landy replied that he experienced the same problem with the Earl's oil line he used on his engines, which vibrated loose on a dyno engine.

The car had been built to every safety standard and that saved Ronnie from any further serious injuries. It was later determined that Ronnie suffered some eye inju-

> **After almost hitting the left side barrier, Ronnie's Probe rolled over onto its right side, and then barrel-rolled and bounced 13 times down the track, losing parts and momentum along the way.**

ries that affected his vision for a few months but was otherwise all right.

It was one of the worst crashes in a long time and most thought this could be the end of Sox's drag racing career. However, those who knew him remembered that extra unused Pro Stock Thunderbird still waiting in Patrick's garage.

Chapter 6

The Sox & Martin crew members button up the Dakota as Buddy looks on intently. Unfortunately, factory backing funds were cut back for 1999 and the Pro Stock truck turned into a one-year wonder for the team. (Photo Courtesy Mark and Laura Bruederle)

The Team Goes Truckin'

Ronnie Sox took some time to recuperate after his horrendous wreck in July 1995. During this time, the NHRA added a new Pro Stock Truck class to its professional drag racing categories. Pickup trucks had become very popular and the NHRA saw this as a great opportunity to increase its fan base. It seemed that almost everyone had a pickup truck, so racing on the dragstrip looked like a natural direction to go. NASCAR had already added a truck series to its racing schedule so it was an easy decision.

While Ronnie was still in the hospital recovering from his eye injuries, he got the itch to race again. Later on, he called Buddy and said that he wanted to go NHRA truck racing. He thought the class had a lot of sponsorship potential and would be fun. In 1997, Ronnie made a couple of laps in one of Roy Hill's Pro Stock trucks and enjoyed the experience. After discussing the idea with Buddy, they decided to put a team together. A call to former Sox & Martin mechanic and race car builder Chick DeNinno and crew member Jim Hayter turned the concept into reality.

The first job, of course, was finding a sponsor. As it happened, the sponsor found them. Former Top Fuel sponsor Monte Bailey called Buddy and expressed his interest in backing them for a Pro Stock Truck effort. Bailey was the owner of Bailey Trucking in Brownsburg, Indiana, and knew the advertising value of racing. A race shop was soon set up near the Bailey headquarters in Indianapolis. They also received some support from Mopar Performance, but according to Buddy, he turned down a full support deal because Mopar would have wanted the truck painted black, which was their current theme. Ronnie and Buddy knew that the familiar red, white, and blue colors were important for them and it's what Sox & Martin fans expected.

Ronnie had these two colored sketches to choose from to determine the paint and lettering scheme for his Pro Stock Dakota truck. Appearance was always important with Sox & Martin. (Photo Courtesy J. C. Childress)

The 1998 Dodge Dakota Pro Stock truck was the last vehicle raced by the team of Sox & Martin. It was sponsored by Bailey Trucking in Indianapolis, Indiana. (Photo Courtesy J. C. Childress)

1976–1998 Changes in Relationships

Buddy backs Ronnie up at the Fram Route 66 Nationals. Ronnie qualified the Dodge in 13th place but was eliminated in round one by Scott Tidwell. In an interview, Ronnie admitted that the team was about two to three months behind and was trying to catch up on the fly. (Photo Courtesy Mark and Laura Bruederle)

1998 Dodge Dakota

The truck was built entirely by top race car chassis builder Jerry Haas at his shop in Fenton, Missouri, near St. Louis. Sox & Martin mechanic Chick DeNinno traveled to Fenton to supervise and stayed with the build operation until its completion. Its full steel-tube chassis supported a Jerry Haas 9-inch rear axle filled with Mark Williams parts. Lamb carbon-fiber disc brakes provided the stopping power. The adjustable four-link setup and electrically controlled shock absorbers held the suspension and axle in place.

The attention to detail of the build was shown by the metallic blue finish on the entire tubular frame structure that matched the color scheme of the truck. The special Dart/Chrysler racing engine was shipped to Fenton and installed while the truck was being built at the Jerry Haas shop.

The front suspension and steering was the same as that used on any standard Pro Stock race car. The front stopping power was fabricated completely with Mark Williams brakes and Lamb carbon-fiber discs, as in the rear. The front shock absorbers were electrically controlled, as were the rear units.

The body was based on a standard club cab Dakota with fiberglass front fenders, hood with large cowl induction hood scoop, and full rear deck cover. Of course, the truck was painted in a modernized version of the iconic red, white, and metallic blue of Sox & Martin and featured the Sox & Martin name in gold-leaf lettering on the doors. The body colors and design were created from drawings by Ronnie and featured the colors in three horizontal levels.

The driver's compartment featured all fabricated aluminum panels with a fiberglass replica Dakota instrument panel housing an aluminum AutoMeter four-gauge cluster in front of the driver. Black racing seats placed Ronnie in the right position to perform his shifts on the Long shifter hooked to either a Liberty or Jerico 5-speed transmission. The transmission was connected to the engine with the same type of clutch used on the big-block Pro Stock engines.

The 358-ci 900-plus-hp engine was built by Richard Maskin and his Pro Stock engine team of Dart Machinery in Troy, Michigan. It was based on a small-block Mopar

> **The attention to detail of the build was shown by the metallic blue finish on the entire tubular frame structure that matched the color scheme of the truck.**

Performance Magnum block and cylinder heads that Dart was contracted by Chrysler to build.

The heads referenced as the R3 design by Chrysler were essentially copies of the 18-degree GM small-block head of the day. The block, however, wasn't adequate for the task at hand. Having a good cylinder head but no Chrysler block available, Maskin made the decision to use a block that he had designed for General Motors. It was the Oldsmobile Rocket block from years prior.

Chapter 6

Team Recruitment Methods

J. C. Childress, the youngest and newest member of the team, recounts how he connected with Ronnie Sox. "In 1997, I ended my enlistment in the U.S. Marine Corps. I had always been a big fan of Sox & Martin. I had seen Ronnie race several times while I was in the Marines. I always loved the red, white, and blue Mopars so one day, while working on my race car, I thought I might want to paint it like one of their cars.

"I called information and asked for the number of Ronnie Sox in Graham, North Carolina, and I was shocked when she gave it to me. To my surprise, when I called, Mr. Four Speed himself answered.

"We talked for a long time and Ronnie began to ask me a lot of questions. Then he told me about plans for the new Pro Stock Truck class and offered me a job!

"I drove down and met Buddy at his dealership and then I drove to Ronnie's house and we went out to eat Mexican food.

"That was the beginning of a special friendship."

The Rocket block was based on the small-block Chevy. However, it featured a raised camshaft and wider oil pan rails for better windage and the ability to put a bigger core cam in it.

While these first engines were being built, Dart and Chrysler worked on a new block for Mopar Performance but there was a difference of opinion regarding how the block should turn out. Chrysler felt that it should be able to retrofit this new engine block into older models and lead the performance of the engine into the future.

Maskin knew that this was impossible because the differences between the features of an aftermarket versus a racing block couldn't be interchanged. Therefore, he returned the project to Chrysler rather than perpetuate what he felt was the inevitable. The Olds blocks were reconfigured and machined to fit the Chrysler heads. Eventually, they looked like Chrysler engines and ran as they should have.

The new Chrysler heads performed well using the flatter 18-degree valve angles. That design allowed for more efficient combustion chamber design and better combustion. The valvecovers on the Pro Stock engine were standard black-finned aluminum Mopar Performance items. A fabricated aluminum tunnel-ram intake manifold was topped with a pair of Holley Dominator 4500 series 4-barrel carburetors.

Only three of these engines were built; the last one went to Mexico where it dominated and won every race it entered.

The finished truck was transported to Indianapolis and prepared for competition. Sox & Martin raced the Pro Stock Dakota through the 1998 racing season with Jim Hayter, Chick DeNinno, and J. C. Childress as mechanic and crew.

First Race and Testing

In April 1998, Ronnie and J. C. loaded up the minivan and headed off to their first race in Commerce, Georgia. J. C. experienced another of Ronnie's passions when the engine broke a valve on a dyno test run and their trip

By this time the team was called Sox & Martin Motorsports and with the support of Bailey Trucking and Mopar Performance, sported a modern rig as big and impressive as any at the track. Buddy Martin's EZ Auto business was also advertised on the trailer sides. (Photo Courtesy J. C. Childress)

Ronnie Sox blasts off the line at Virginia Motorsports Park as the Dakota performs a smokey burnout for the crowd. The truck was capable of 181-mph speeds at the lights. (Photo Courtesy J. C. Childress)

was postponed for a while. The two of them spent some of their waiting time at the movies where Ronnie showed his love for popcorn. J. C. said Ronnie could put away a lot of it and enjoyed it immensely.

They were finally underway and met Buddy and Chick with the Dakota in Tennessee. There was no big rig this time. The big truck was not ready yet so they took off with the truck in a small enclosed trailer pulled by a one-ton dually pickup.

At this first race in the truck, Ronnie had to learn about the new equipment, including hooking up the cam-lock safety belt system. This pressure didn't bother him and his first pass in competition with no testing resulted in a .001 reaction time at the line.

Testing finally came when the team drove from Georgia to Darlington Dragway for a few days.

The entrance to the office of Sox & Martin Motorsports near Indianapolis did not give away the true nature of the business operation inside. (Photo Courtesy J. C. Childress)

Crew member Chick DeNinno watches as the Sox & Martin Pro Stock Dakota launches level and straight. Buddy turned down a full Mopar deal because they would have had to paint the truck black at the time. (Photo Courtesy J. C. Childress)

Chapter 6

This is the second version of the Pro Stock Truck engine installed in the metallic blue tubular chassis of the Dakota. It is based on an LA Series block like those used in Dodge trucks. (Photo Courtesy J. C. Childress)

It was business as usual for Buddy as he walks from the staging area to the line in preparation for a pass at the 1998 U.S. Nationals. (Photo Courtesy Mark and Laura Bruederle)

Race Prep

After testing, the truck was delivered to Herb McCandless' house and shop because Bailey's new 10,000-square-foot Indianapolis facility was not completed yet. Ronnie and the crew worked on the truck every day to prepare for the next races, before taking it to the finished shop in Indianapolis. By this time, the new large red, white, and blue tractor-trailer rig was completed and it was of course, the nicest on the NHRA circuit.

While working with the Bailey facility in Indianapolis, J. C. and Chick lived in a nice rented house in Lebanon, Indiana, and drove about 30 minutes each way to work. The only member of the Pro Stock truck crew not living in Indiana was crew chief Jim Hayter, who flew in from Oklahoma for each race and stayed in Lebanon with Chick and J. C. while the truck was being prepared.

The chemistry among the crew was not very good. Ronnie would not deal with Hayter. Chick did not like Hayter's cigarette smoking. Apparently, Jim Hayter did no work on the truck at the shop, but merely directed operations for each race preparation session. Some, including Ronnie, felt that too much emphasis and money was spent on polishing and appearance instead of horsepower.

At the track, Chick and J. C. set up the awning, laid down the pit flooring, and roped off the pit space. After

1976–1998 Changes in Relationships

Veteran Super Stocker Bob Reed built this 1968 Hemi Barracuda for Ronnie so he could continue his racing and personal appearance activities in a proper Mopar. The car was not built from an original BO29 Hemi Barracuda. (Photo Courtesy Diane Sox)

every pass, they towed the truck back to the pits and removed the doors and front end. Then they removed the rear tires, driveshaft, and interior, transmission, clutch housing, and clutch. Jim Hayter then cut the clutch discs and adjusted the valves. Chick and J. C. assisted anywhere possible, often while headers, carburetors, or rear axle gear ratios were changed.

Back at the shop after each race, the truck was raised, the interior removed, and all rubber cleaned from the underbody. J. C. cleaned everything on the truck and hauler rig and sprayed the underside with Lemon Pledge to prevent more tire rubber from accumulating on the car.

The Dart engine was only used for a few races. It did not produce the power the team needed to compete with the other Pro Stock Truck teams. After a discussion about the problem, Ronnie suggested changing to Fulton Competition power, but it was decided to lease engines from Nickens Brothers Racing. This improved the power output, but they were still behind other trucks in that regard.

Mopar Pulls Sponsorship

Ronnie even drove the truck at the 1998 NHRA U.S. Nationals in Indianapolis. At the end of the 1998 season, Team Mopar announced that they would support only two individual Pro Stock Truck teams for 1999. The factory-backed entries were Bo Nickens of Nickens Brothers Racing and Todd Patterson of Patterson Brothers Racing.

Mopar associate sponsorship was provided for Craig Eaton, Dale Eaton, Tom Yancer, Robert Freeman, Sondra Sikes, Ronnie Sox, and Chris DeSalvo. At the end of the 1998 season, the Sox & Martin team decided to call it quits and sold the truck and all of its equipment to veteran Chrysler Super Stock and Pro Stock racer Ed Miller in Virginia. The truck was never raced again and was put in long-term storage.

Ronnie on His Own Again

After the final dissolution of Sox & Martin racing, Buddy returned to his various other business activities in North Carolina but Ronnie never seemed to lose the drive and desire to continue drag racing. He still had the 1968 Hemi Barracuda that he acquired in 1989. Now, he confined his driving mostly to exhibitions and shows rather than actual racing.

> **The Dart engine was only used for a few races. It did not produce the power the team needed to compete with the other Pro Stock Truck teams.**

Enter Bob Reed

It was about this time that Ronnie met Super Stock builder and racer "Bullet Bob" Reed from Salisbury, North Carolina. By this time, Ronnie's 1968 Barracuda had been sold and Bob thought that Ronnie should have a proper fast and quick car to drive, so he built a 1968 Hemi Barracuda and finished it in Sox & Martin colors. Ronnie and Bob attended nostalgia events and raced each other in match races much like those from the peak of Sox & Martin racing.

Sometime in 1999 Reed contacted Ronnie Sox and proposed an opportunity for him to continue racing in

Chapter 6

Jim Childress (left), Ronnie Sox (center), and J. C. Childress (right) pose alongside the new 1968 Hemi Barracuda. It was built and tuned by "Bullet Bob" Reed to provide Ronnie Sox with a suitable Hemi-powered race car to entertain the fans and compete in match races. (Photo Courtesy J. C. Childress)

the style he most enjoyed, a 4-speed-shifted Super Stock car. Bob built and maintained a 1968 Hemi Barracuda for Super Stock/A class. He had already built and raced his own NHRA and IHRA multi–record holder 4-speed 1968 Hemi Barracuda so he knew very well how to create a winning car for Ronnie. Bob built the car with the latest Super Stock–legal technology and parts.

Along with winning races and meeting his fans at later races and reunions, Ronnie also had a number of opportunities to meet fellow Mopar racers and friends including "Akron Arlen" Vanke. Here Ronnie and Arlen talk between activities at a Super Stock and FX reunion. (Photo Courtesy Diane Sox)

The New Barracuda

The basic car was not an original BO29 Hurst-built Barracuda but a standard production car built and modified for Super Stock competition. Reed built the car in his own garage and used new fiberglass parts from Year One and WS Fiberglass. A full 12-point roll cage was installed to NHRA specifications and painted white to provide a lighter and brighter interior. The Barracuda even had the iconic blue-tinted headlights and parking lights that the Sox & Martin cars had since 1965.

Reed used Jaz racing seats, and Ronnie was safely secured with a five-point Simpson harness. VDO gauges kept Ronnie informed of what was happening under the hood. The familiar red, white, and blue Sox & Martin finish was accomplished by Jerry Cline. Of course, mechanic Bob Reed replaced the familiar Jake King name lettered on the doors. The entire underbody and front suspension components were also painted white to ease visibility for service.

Bob Reed built the engine starting with a new Mopar Performance cast-iron Hemi block with final machine work by Barnett Performance in Atlanta, Georgia. The Barnett Brothers were well known for producing winning Mopars since the 1960s. Bob prepared and installed a Crankshaft Specialties crankshaft hooked to Venolia pistons with Childs & Albert connecting rods. A Crane R296-4778-08 roller lifter camshaft operated the valvetrain.

The blueprinted cast-iron Hemi heads were provided by Indy Cylinder heads built to NHRA specifications.

Ronnie Sox poses with the 1968 Hemi Barracuda that Bob Reed built. Bob built this car so that Ronnie could have a proper race car to drive for reunions, exhibitions, and match races. (Geoff Stunkard Photo)

Dick Landy Industries built the custom fabricated cross ram, two 4-barrel intake manifold that mounted a pair of Holley 4160 List 4235/4236 4-barrel carburetors. Hooker Super Competition headers helped the exhaust gases exit the engine.

The drivetrain had a Bob Reed–built Dana 60 rear axle housing loaded with 5.57 gears and Mark Williams axles. The housing was narrowed to 46 inches to leave room for the wide Goodyear slicks and Weld wheels. The ultra-low gears were appropriate to deal with the many 1/8-mile tracks in the South. Major sponsorship was provided by Smith Stokes Chrysler Plymouth in Reidsville, North Carolina. Crew members on the team were Chief Engineer Steve Smith, Dave Gambrell, and Debbie Dunlap. One of the first events to feature Ronnie and the car was the 2000 Chryslers at Carlisle show in Pennsylvania.

In a 2001 interview, Sox said, "I'm certainly glad that I was able to race at the time that I did. Today's racing technology has diminished the role of the driver way too much. Back in the days of the 4-speeds, the driver had a lot more to do with the outcome of the race, and I couldn't imagine anything being more fun than that."

> **By 2003, the last vestige of the Sox & Martin story went away in Burlington. At a zoning meeting in Alamance County, change was approved for the former Sox & Martin racing facility.**

No More Tucker Street

By 2003, the last vestige of the Sox & Martin story went away in Burlington. At a zoning meeting in Alamance County, change was approved for the former Sox & Martin racing facility that had been 3167 Tucker Street. The location was rezoned C1 to allow new and used automobile sales and other uses. Later the building was again repurposed and used as a church.

The Continuing Legacy

Owner Clark Rand always wanted Ronnie to have the opportunity to drive his cars whenever they were displayed with him at any show or reunion. This event was the 2006 Holley NHRA National Hot Rod Reunion at Bowling Green, Kentucky, and was one of Ronnie's last events. (Geoff Stunkard Photo)

In 1999, Ronnie Sox toned down his exhibition racing, shows, and touring and spent time working at his home in North Carolina. His greatest passion after drag racing had always been golf and that was where he directed his time. In addition to being an avid golfer, he was known for working on and building custom golf clubs for others at his home shop. It was around this time that Ronnie's future second wife, Alecia Diane Price, called him to make a set of clubs for her.

Diane had first met Ronnie some years earlier and they even spent some time together and corresponded by phone, but they had not seen each other for about five years. Diane lived in Richmond, Virginia, so it was a bit of a trip to North Carolina. Diane says that he called every night and the pair was soon dating long distance; he asked her to move to North Carolina, which she did.

According to Diane, "We eventually parted ways because of the 17-year age difference. I wanted to get married and have babies and Ronnie had grown children almost my age. Ronnie didn't want to start over at 40. This appeared to be a May–September love affair headed for a downward spiral."

At their next meeting in 1999, the relationship started up again. Diane describes the meeting, "When I went there to pick up the clubs, I had not seen Ronnie in five years. When he opened the door, it was like time had stood still for me and all these emotions came flooding back to me. Needless to say, he, too, felt the same way. I spent the weekend to visit with his family and from that point on we were inseparable. Two years later, he proposed."

Ronnie and Diane were married on April 28, 2001, at Sandston Baptist Church in Sandston, Virginia, surrounded by family and friends.

A Devastating Diagnosis

It was only a short time after their marriage, on September 11, 2001, that Ronnie was diagnosed with advanced prostate cancer, which was devastating for both of them. At that time, Ronnie even selflessly suggested that the marriage be annulled because his condition and increasing needs were not fair to Diane. As Ronnie expected, Diane refused that offer.

Diane confessed about that time, "I told him that he had broken my heart years ago, and if he didn't mean those vows for better or worse, in sickness and in health, 'til death do us part, then he could annul the marriage, but I would never forgive him, to which he replied, 'I knew you would say that, but I had to give you an out.'"

At that time, Duke University Hospital gave Ronnie a year, but he fought it for almost five years with radiation and chemotherapy treatments, even going into remission during the first year.

Final Appearances

After his cancer diagnosis, Ronnie still visited car shows and racing events but began to dial back his schedule a bit. Some of the more interesting events were those attended by collector and enthusiast Clark Rand of Fair Grove, Missouri. Rand owned four restored original Sox & Martin race cars and enjoyed displaying them. He usually brought two of the cars to a show. These great cars included at various times the 1968 Hemi Barracuda, 1967 Hemi Plymouth RO23, 1973 Don Hardy–built Hemi Duster, and the Don Hardy–built Hemi Colt.

Diane and Phoebe, their Maltese, attended racetrack and show events with Ronnie when possible. Ronnie never stopped being the professional and always wore his Sox & Martin team shirts and hats. (Photo Courtesy Diane Sox)

Chapter 7

Ronnie always worked on his own cars when touring with exhibition and reunion events in later years. Here, at a track event, Ronnie removes the Dzus fittings that secure the hood on his 1968 Hemi Barracuda. (Photo Courtesy Diane Sox)

Announcer Dave McClelland interviews Ronnie Sox after he received the Wally Parks NHRA Motorsports Museum Board of Directors Award for Sox & Martin at the third annual Holley NHRA National Hot Rod Reunion, presented by DuPont Automotive Finishes. The award was the first such honor presented at the Reunion. (Clark Rand Photo)

Like Ronnie and Buddy, Clark was never afraid of allowing the fans close to the cars. More than anything else, Clark was interested in promoting and paying homage to Ronnie Sox as the great professional racer that he was. To have him there with the race cars was important. Clark made sure that, if at all possible, Ronnie was there so he could meet and talk with the fans. These events included the shows and reunions at Fred Engelhart's place in Minnesota as well as the big show every year at the annual NHRA Holley Drag Race Reunion at Bowling Green, Kentucky.

Ronnie and Diane attended the events and spent the weekend with Clark and his wife at the shows. These events were an opportunity for Ronnie to discover how much the fans admired and loved him for what he meant to them and to drag racing. He told Diane and Clark that he was never aware of how much his fans loved and admired him.

Ronnie and Diane both expressed their thanks to Clark and Colleen Rand for their efforts. It truly kept up Ronnie's spirits and the fight for his life. Diane said that Ronnie would not have smiled as much as he did those last few years if not for the efforts of Clark and Colleen Rand, making sure that Ronnie and Diane were there with his cars and that his fans were there to show their love and support.

In addition to the racetrack and car show appearances, Ronnie received hundreds of caring letters, cards, and calls from his incredible fans. The day Richard Petty called to see how he was doing really made his day. Ronnie and Diane were also able to spend some valuable time together with their friends Lloyd and Erma at Nags Head on the eastern coast of North Carolina, for some needed relaxation. Buddy Martin traveled to Ronnie and Diane's home in Richmond several times to spend time with him and these visits meant the world to Ronnie. Diane remembers one time when Buddy was getting ready to leave and Ronnie extended his hand to shake and Buddy grabbed Ronnie and hugged him.

Ronnie enjoyed himself while greeting friends and fans at the Holley NHRA National Hot Rod Reunion at Bowling Green in 2005. (Clark Rand Photo)

The Continuing Legacy

Ronnie Sox poses with his Don Hardy–built Hemi Colt at one of Fred Engelhart's events in Elkton, Minnesota, in 2005. At that time, the Colt was owned by Clark and Colleen Rand but is currently in the Greg and Kathy Mosley collection. (Clark Rand Photo)

The Last Days

Ronnie Sox spent the last days of his life at home with his wife, Diane, and their beloved little dog, Ms. Phoebe, at his side. Diane described that time, "Ronnie's last words to me before passing were to promise him that I would never forget how much he loved me and he thanked me for taking such good care of him and never leaving his side.

"Ronnie died peacefully at home with me, our faithful Maltese, and our best friends Erma and Lloyd at his side."

Ronnie made his last full quarter-mile pass on a dragstrip at Rockingham Dragway on April 16, 2006. His 8.81 ET at 155.625 mph in the Bob Reed–built Hemi 1968 Barracuda proved that he was a racer to the end. Prints of the color photo taken of Ronnie making this run titled "Ronnie's Last Ride" were sold and the proceeds were donated to the North Carolina Prostate Cancer Coalition.

Diane called Ronnie's family and Buddy a little after 8:00 pm on April 22, 2006, to inform everyone of his

> **After his cancer diagnosis, Ronnie still visited car shows and racing events but began to dial back his schedule a bit.**

Ronnie Sox and Arnie Beswick attended a reunion held in Elkton, Minnesota, in 2005. A number of restored Sox & Martin race cars were also in attendance. (Clark Rand Photo)

The determination and will of Ronnie Sox is shown in this Greg Burrow photo of Ronnie making his last full quarter-mile pass at Rockingham Dragway on April 16, 2006. He ran an 8.81 ET at 155.625 mph in the Bob Reed–built Hemi 1968 Barracuda. (Greg Burrow Photo)

SOX & MARTIN

Chapter 7

Clark and Colleen Rand's 1967 and 1968 Sox & Martin Hemi race cars, along with a number of others, prepare for a parade lap in front of fans at the NHRA U.S. Nationals in September 2006. This was a final tribute to Ronnie Sox after his passing on April 22. (Geoff Stunkard Photo)

passing. With Diane's guidance and encouragement, Ronnie became a Christian in 2003 so he was ready when God was ready for him and he was not afraid.

Two visitations were held for Ronnie. The first was April 26, 2006, at the Parham Funeral Home in Richmond, Virginia, and the second at Rich and Thompson Funeral Service in Graham, North Carolina, on April 27 and 28. A memorial service was held in Graham on Saturday, April 29, 2006. The published obituary notice stated that, "The Boss, as he was often referred to, was in the minds of many, the greatest drag racer in the history of the sport."

The Ronnie Sox Foundation

Because of a conversation with Ronnie prior to his passing, Diane Sox formed the Ronnie Sox Foundation (RonnieSox.org) in August 2006 in Ronnie's memory.

Ronnie was concerned at that time not with himself, but with the many children who would be diagnosed with some form of cancer at a young age and never have the opportunity he had to live a full life and enjoy the things that he wanted to do. Diane wanted to use this foundation as her way of honoring Ronnie, his legacy, and her love for him as a friend and spouse.

The Ronnie Sox Foundation chose St. Jude Children's Research Hospital in Memphis, Tennessee, because of Ronnie's sincere concern for the children whose lives are affected and cut short by cancer. This facility has treated children of all 50 states and 70 other countries.

Diane and Buddy raise funds for St. Jude from the sale of Sox & Martin promotional products such as die-cast model cars, posters, and giveaway drawing programs. Both have spent much of their own time and resources traveling to car shows and drag racing events to encourage contribution and participation in the foundation.

Because of the continued popularity of Ronnie Sox and Sox & Martin, products have been contributed and created by businesses such as Indy Cylinder Heads and Supercar Collectibles. One of these contributions was a complete new 426 Hemi engine with a cross-ram intake and two Holley carburetors. The idea came from *Mopar*

Online Adoration

The adoration of Ronnie's many friends and fans did not stop at his passing. An online Legacy.com guestbook was started at that time and continues to this day, supported in perpetuity by loyal fan Dante Delbasio. At the time of this writing, there are almost 450 heartfelt entries, each telling about their relationship and connection with Ronnie Sox and what his accomplishments and persona did to change their lives.

Some of these comments brought out what Ronnie and Sox & Martin meant to those who were there through all of those great years. Some convey what they meant to those who may have been too young, but still appreciate the impact of the greatest team in drag racing.

The Continuing Legacy

After Ronnie's passing, Diane Sox created the Ronnie Sox Foundation to donate to the St. Jude Children's Research Hospital in Memphis, Tennessee, to help fight children's cancer. This is one of the decals used to promote these efforts. (Photo Courtesy Diane Sox Collection)

A special-edition custom-built 2008 'Cuda was produced in conjunction with Mr. Norm's Garage in Chicago and given away in a drawing to benefit the Ronnie Sox Foundation. Robert Duclos of Waterloo, Illinois, was the lucky winner in the 2011 Las Vegas drawing.

An original 2008 Dodge Challenger SRT 8 was modified with new front and rear composite body panels to give it the iconic appearance of a 1970–1971 'Cuda. The paint and lettering were added to create a modern representation of a Sox & Martin race car.

The 2008 Sox & Martin 'Cuda was equipped with a modified version of the 6.1-liter Hemi V-8 with power enhanced by a Kenne Bell supercharger. The owner drives this car regularly and attends a number of shows and events with it.

Chapter 7

Muscle editor Randy Bolig and it was built with contributions from Indy Cylinder Heads, A&A Transmission, and others.

At the date of this writing, the foundation has raised $260,000 for St. Jude with the help of these businesses and numerous others, including the Rands, the Painters, and Shafi Kesler.

Appreciation of the Legacy

Even after the passing of Ronnie Sox, the appreciation and admiration of the history and the cars of Sox & Martin continued. A number of reunions, nostalgia races, and car shows feature the legacy of Sox & Martin in various ways. Most memorable were the events that Clark Rand and his wife, Colleen, continued to attend with the two restored Sox & Martin race cars remaining in their collection. Many of these events included the opportunity for fans to buy promotional items and contribute to the Ronnie Sox Foundation.

2006 NHRA U.S. Nationals

The first significant tribute event was at the NHRA U.S. Nationals at Indianapolis Raceway Park in September 2006, just four months after Ronnie's death. At 6:00 pm Friday of the Labor Day weekend show, with little advance notice, seven Sox & Martin Pro Stock and Super Stock race cars paraded down the sportsman spectator-side return road in tribute to Ronnie Sox. The cars included those owned by Clark and Colleen Rand, Todd Werner, Greg and Kathy Mosley, and others. The NHRA presented a video tribute to Ronnie and to Sox & Martin.

During qualifying for the race, Bob Panella Jr. drove a modern Pro Stock Hemi red, white, and blue Dodge Stratus painted and lettered in tribute to Sox & Martin. This event raised thousands of dollars for St. Jude cancer research.

2007 Nostalgia Super Stock

Another of these events was the Nostalgia Super Stock race held at Kansas City International Raceway in 2007. Clark and Colleen Rand brought their 1967 Belvedere RO23 and 1968 Hemi BO29 Barracuda to the event, which was also attended by Diane Sox and Buddy Martin. Although famous racers such as "Big Daddy" Don Garlits and his wife Pat and "Farmer" Arnie Beswick were also in attendance, the two Sox & Martin race cars were the highlight of the show.

Although Diane and Buddy were kept busy selling and signing promotional posters and die-cast model cars, Clark decided at some point to sweeten the pot by offering a ride down the dragstrip in the 1968 Hemi Barracuda, driven by Buddy, to a contributing fan winning a drawing.

2008 All-Hemi Reunion

The big event for performance Mopar fans came in August 2008. It was called the All-Hemi Reunion and it was presented by Jim Kramer, Dick Towers, and others at Quaker City Raceway in Ohio. Of the more than 240 Hemi cars in attendance, the Hemi-powered cars of the Sox & Martin team were some of the most important and popular.

All of the red, white, and blue Sox & Martin cars, from the 1965 and 1967 Belvederes to the 1968 and 1970 Barracudas, were stand-outs. Just when no one thought this display could be topped, Clark and Colleen Rand brought out their newly finished 1969 Dodge D700 ramp truck and open trailer.

The rig (although not an original Sox & Martin truck) was found in Kentucky and restored authentically by Fred Engelhart and his sons in Minnesota. It was presented to Clark as a surprise gift for his many years of business. The truck's first major showing was at Quaker City and it was clearly a crowd favorite.

The truck was painted and lettered exactly as a Sox

Pro Stock racer Bob Panella Jr. created this modern Dodge Pro Stock tribute to Ronnie Sox and Sox & Martin and then ran the car at the 2006 NHRA U.S. Nationals at Indianapolis. Additional support was provided by Mopar Performance and Direct Connection. (Geoff Stunkard Photo)

The Continuing Legacy

Bob Panella Jr. of Panella Trucking and Bailey Trucking created this poster commemorating the tribute Pro Stock Dodge debuted at the Ronnie Sox Tribute organized at the 2006 NHRA U.S. Nationals. (Photo Courtesy Buddy Martin)

At some of the reunions held in Minnesota and other venues, Sox & Martin crewmembers appeared along with Ronnie's wife, Diane. Here, Dave Christie, Chick DeNinno, Diane Sox, and Buddy Martin pose for a photo at a gathering. (Photo Courtesy Diane Sox)

A number of collectors of restored Sox & Martin race cars live around the country, but none are more devoted than Greg and Kathy Mosley of Moline, Illinois. The Don Hardy–built Hemi Colt and Hardy-built 1973 Hemi Duster are proudly featured in the Mosley collection.

& Martin "Big Boss" race rig would have been in 1968; it included a flat open trailer. The rig was displayed at the event with the 1968 Barracuda on the truck and the 1967 Belvedere on the open trailer.

2015 Jake King Auction

On July 15, 1995, the drag racing world lost Jake King at age 66. He is survived by his wife, Virginia (Neese) King, and their three children. Just prior to his untimely death, King was inducted into the *Super Stock* Magazine Hall of Fame. In 2006, he was posthumously inducted into the East Coast Drag Times Hall of Fame, and on February 21, 2015, Jake was also inducted into the North Carolina Drag Racing Hall of Fame.

A recent example of the continuing interest in the Sox & Martin team legacy was the spring 2015 auction of the personal items owned by the late Jake King. These items included Jake's tools, jackets, trophies, and even

At a Nostalgia Super Stock event at Kansas City International Raceway (KCIR) in 2007 Buddy Martin and Diane Sox appeared along with Clark Rand's 1967 and 1968 Sox & Martin cars. Here, a drawing winner waits for a ride down the track with Buddy Martin driving the 1968 Hemi Barracuda.

Chapter 7

This is the only time that both of the existing Sox & Martin 1967 Hemi Plymouths appeared together since 1968. John Mahoney (left), Buddy Martin, and Clark Rand (right) show off their cars for a reunion in Minnesota in 2006. (Geoff Stunkard Photo)

Buddy Martin prepares at the starting line for a quick drive down the track at KCIR in 2007, taking the winner of a prize drawing for his exciting ride in the Sox & Martin 1968 Hemi Barracuda.

It was always a pleasure at the Hot Rod, Super Stock, and Muscle Car nostalgia shows when Buddy and Diane had the opportunity to meet with other drag racing legends such as "Big Daddy" Don Garlits. Here, in 2007, Buddy and Don talk about old times at KCIR. (Clark Rand Photo)

I met with Buddy Martin and Diane Sox for the first time while purchasing a Sox & Martin poster at the Nostalgia Super Stock racing event at KCIR in 2007.

Fred Ristagno's restored 1972 Sox & Martin Hemi Duster was one of about 240 historic Hemi cars that appeared at the once-in-a-lifetime All Hemi Reunion at Quaker City Dragway in Ohio in 2008.

The Continuing Legacy

The debut of Clark Rand's newly built D700 Dodge hauler rig was at the 2008 All Hemi Reunion at Quaker City. Restorer Fred Engelhart had this authentic truck hauler and trailer built especially for Clark Rand in appreciation for his business.

The restored Dodge truck and open trailer loaded with Clark Rand's restored Sox & Martin 1967 and 1968 race cars was the hit of the show at Quaker City.

The restored Ronnie Sox Pro Mod Comet was displayed at a car show in Greensboro, North Carolina, along with the original trophy won by Sox & Martin at the 1964 NHRA Winternationals at Pomona, California. (Laverne Zachary Photo)

This wall clock was one of the many interesting items sold at the spring 2015 auction of the Jake King estate in North Carolina. John Mahoney was the lucky winning bidder of this clock from Jake King's garage in Burlington. (John Mahoney Photo)

a clock from Jake's Gulf Service garage. Personal items such as Sox & Martin racing jackets sold for as much as $2,400 each.

The Race Cars that Keep on Racing

It quickly became clear that Ronnie Sox and the Sox & Martin team would not be forgotten. Dozens of restored original and tribute replica cars continue to appear at races and shows.

Dean's Tribute

Ronnie's son Dean decided soon after Ronnie's passing to make his own tribute to his father by finishing the build started with Ronnie of a 1973 Hemi Duster in full red, white, and blue Sox & Martin livery. Ronnie commissioned the build of this exhibition car, equipped with a 950-hp 572-ci Hemi built by Indy Cylinder Heads. The car is equipped with an A-727 TorqueFlite transmission and a 4.56:1 rear axle. Dean displayed the Duster outside, along with Ronnie's driving suit and helmet, at Ronnie's funeral service.

Dean showed and raced the car at a number of nostalgia events in the Piedmont and eastern North Carolina area until finally selling the car at auction a few years later. In early 2006, Dean had the unique opportunity of racing against his father, who was driving the 1968 Hemi Barracuda, head to head at a dragstrip in North Carolina. Dean's replica Duster is identified by the Competition Number 23 Pro on the roof quarters.

Chapter 7

Ronnie's son Dean raced and exhibited this replica Sox & Martin Hemi Duster for a number of years in tribute to his father. Here Dean stands the car on its rear wheels in 2011. It was begun as a project with Ronnie before his passing. (Geoff Stunkard Photo)

Greg and Kathy Mosley decorated the wall of their beautiful museum with a neon-lighted replica Sox & Martin sign with the logo that Ronnie and Buddy used for their parts and racing business. The original version of this striped sign was designed by Public Relations Director Tom Richardson.

> **Photos of the Duster with its front wheels high in the air are popular with fans and enthusiasts around the world.**

The Team Hemi Duster

Fred Ristagno in New Jersey has the unusual honor of owning and racing the only Hemi Pro Stock Duster actually built completely in the Sox & Martin shop. The car is painted and lettered as it was when Ronnie and Herb drove it, and Fred continues to drive, race, and show the car at nostalgia events on the East Coast.

Photos of the Duster with its front wheels high in the air are popular with fans and enthusiasts around the world. This Duster is identified by the Competition Number Pro 200 on the roof quarters.

1970 Backup Hemi 'Cuda

Another interesting original Sox & Martin car that is still raced and driven is the 1970 'Cuda that was found and restored in Missouri by R&R Salvage owner Ron Slobe. This Hemi 'Cuda was actually delivered in late 1969 and was a Super Stock backup car that used a stock carburetor configuration.

Its restoration was completed in 1989 and included a Hemi built by Oregon, Illinois, builder Larry Pontnack. Former Super Stock and Pro Stock driver Larry Griffith drove the car and performed its first exhibition runs at the 1989 Mopar Nationals. The 'Cuda now has a Pro Stock–type engine and a TorqueFlite transmission; it ran a 9.90 on its first pass.

This car has no competition number. Ron Slobe died in 1993.

1967 Hemi Plymouth

One of the earliest efforts at finding, preserving, and restoring a genuine Sox & Martin was that of John Mahoney in Overland Park, Kansas. In the fall of 1985, John met a young man named Ronnie Jones at a local speed shop who said he owned an old Sox & Martin race car. He said that his uncle and father bought the car directly from Sox & Martin in 1968 and raced it under their names, Collins & Jones.

The Continuing Legacy

It was the spring of 1986 before John called the number the young man gave him. When he did call, it was answered not by Ronnie Jones but by Phil Collins, who said that he actually owned the car, which was a 1967 Belvedere GTX. He told the story to John about how the car had been purchased from Buddy Martin at the 1968 NHRA Nationals at Indy. After some discussion and a few weeks of thinking by both men, John arranged a deal to purchase the Plymouth for $2,000.

The car was now in Kansas City, so John wasted no time to see the car. The Plymouth had been repainted over time, but close inspection showed evidence that it was indeed a former Sox & Martin race car. Original Rangoon Red paint, accompanied by signs of the stripes on the cowl and deck lid, confirmed its history.

Over a few years, John Mahoney had the car restored and painted back to its 1968 appearance. He wanted Jake King to build the engine but he declined and instead, John had Herb McCandless build a suitable Hemi for it. Carl Clayton was hired to fly to Kansas City to apply the correct lettering.

The finished car, in addition to the documents John located, number plates received with the car, and numerous new parts, produced an entire complete package for historical authenticity. The car is seldom shown in public but it did appear in 2013 at the Mopar Reunion in Minneapolis alongside Clark Rand's 1967, placing both cars together for the first time since 1968.

It was a wonderful highlight for John to be with his car, and at the same time, be with Buddy Martin and Diane Sox and the rest of the team.

1968 Hemi Barracuda Replica

Racer and builder Dave Collette created a replica of the Sox & Martin 1968 Hemi Barracuda for shows and exhibitions. This car is identified by the competition number 720 and SS/B on the quarter windows but has no contingency decals on the front fenders. Dave and his wife, Kathy, made this car available for nostalgia events to help Diane raise money for the Ronnie Sox Foundation.

1964 Factory Experimental Comet Replica

At least two replicas of the Sox & Martin 1964 Factory Experimental Comet exist. Both are finished and lettered in the red, white, and blue livery. One of the Comets, owned by Ken Goodsey, is shown frequently and run in exhibition races at nostalgia events. It has the original 715 Competition Number from 1964 on the windows.

1965 AWB Belvedere Hardtop

Years before Ronnie's passing, Mopar enthusiast Pete Haldiman of Colorado built an authentic-appearing replica of the Sox & Martin 1965

John Mahoney's restored 1967 Hemi Plymouth is painted and lettered as closely as possible to the original design and colors. The Belvedere body trim was installed in 1967 to make the multiple racers appear identical. (John Mahoney Photo)

John Mahoney shows his restored 1967 Sox & Martin Hemi Plymouth at events around the Kansas City area when possible. The lettering was done by Carl Clayton, who did the original work for Sox & Martin. (John Mahoney Photo)

Chapter 7

The historical importance of Sox & Martin is the reason that a number of plastic model kits were produced in later years. They are still popular among collectors and model builders. This is the Revell Motorsports 1967 Plymouth Hemi GTX.

This is one of the versions of the 1/25-scale model of the Sox & Martin Hemi 'Cuda. This one was produced by Jo Han, known for its racing and high-performance car models. This box is unique in that it has pictures of Jake, Ronnie, and Buddy.

Plymouth AWB hardtop, painted and lettered as the original car appeared at the 1965 AHRA Winter Nationals at Beeline Dragway in Scottsdale, Arizona. Later, Pete built a 1960s Dodge ramp truck to haul the car.

On the East Coast, Petie Eavers built and raced a modernized replica of Ronnie's 1965 AWB Belvedere hardtop, and on at least one occasion in Virginia, allowed Ronnie to make a wheels-up pass in the car.

1970 440-Powered Superbird Replica

A replica of the 1970 440-powered Superbird built by John Pappas is in Birmingham, Michigan, because the original Hemi Superbird no longer exists. This car had a Six-Pack scoop grafted to the original hood and the car is painted red, white, and blue and lettered as a Sox & Martin car. It has no contingency decals or competition number.

Model Cars and Commemoratives

One of the first indications that anyone or anything has a large following is when die-cast and plastic model cars and kits are built and sold around the world. Sox & Martin has a long and positive list of such creations that continue to be valuable and popular among collectors and enthusiasts. Some of the earliest and most collectible plastic kits were produced while the team was still active and on top in the drag racing world.

Top model makers including Jo Han, Revell, and MPC wasted no time getting on the bandwagon to take advantage of the fame and marketing power of Sox & Martin. Various 1/25-scale kits were soon available of the 1970 'Cuda, the 1972 'Cuda, 1970 Duster, and 1970 Superbird. Some even had photos of Ronnie, Buddy, and Jake on the box art, something seldom seen in the model car world. Not many other racing teams' mechanics were known by name to the fans and public. The kits' instructions included full details of how to paint and finish the models authentically.

1/18 Scale

In recent years, the popularity of metal die-cast 1/18- and 1/24-scale models has grown immensely and, of course, some of these had to include some of the Sox & Martin race cars. Production and retail sales companies such as Supercar Collectibles and Highway 61 have pro-

MPC was another popular maker of plastic model kits. This one was a 1/25-scale model of the Sox & Martin 1972 Hemi Barracuda with three options for building.

The Continuing Legacy

MPC also produced a high-quality 1/25-scale model kit of the team-built 1972 Hemi Duster Pro Stock. This kit was part of the company's Pro Stock series. The box art featured an actual photo of the real car.

Supercar Collectibles produced and sold a limited number of metal die-cast 1/18-scale replicas of the 1965 Sox & Martin AWB sedan. A similar model of the 1965 AWB sedan was also available.

A very accurate 1/18-scale die-cast metal example of the Sox & Martin 1969 Plymouth Road Runner was custom finished and based on a stock Road Runner model. It was created about 20 years ago by an unknown builder and sold commercially in a very limited edition.

This 1/18-scale die-cast metal replica of the Sox & Martin 1968 Hemi Barracuda was produced and distributed by Supercar Collectibles in Minnesota. It is an accurate replica of the original car owned by Clark Rand.

duced very high-quality 1/18-scale models that represent the color and the history of Sox & Martin racing.

These cars include versions of the 1965 AWB hardtop, 1965 AWB sedan, 1967 RO23, and 1968 Hemi Barracuda, and 1968 Hemi Road Runner. Also available is a 1/18-scale die-cast version of the white 1963 Chevrolet Z11 that started Sox & Martin on the path to fame.

Recent new 1/18-scale models by Highway 61 and distributed by Supercar Collectibles of the daily driver cars used by Ronnie and Buddy in 1970 are also available.

1/25 Scale

One of the higher-quality plastic kits was the 1967 Plymouth Hemi GTX introduced in 1995. In 1992, Ed Sexton, of Revell-Monogram in Chicago, contacted John Mahoney about producing a 1/25-scale plastic model kit of John's 1967 Sox & Martin Belvedere GTX. Ed knew that John owned the only restored example of the 1967 car at the time. He asked John to assist them in creating the model.

John is sure that Ed knew about the existence of the car through conversations with Ronnie and Buddy. They had a local standard GTX to use for the dimensions but they wanted John to help with the race configuration and Sox & Martin appearance and equipment. John visited Chicago on two occasions and received the grand tour of the Revell facility while they were working on the car.

When the model kit was produced and released in 1994, John received 75 kits plus a 16 x 20–inch print of the original cover artwork by Tim Ryan (in Michigan) as payment. In addition, John's name was mentioned in the instruction sheet included with the models. The 1967 Sox & Martin Belvedere model was so successful that it was re-released in 2013 with some slight cover-art changes.

Chapter 7

John Mahoney's interest and devotion to the history of Sox & Martin and of his 1967 Hemi Plymouth motivated him to go to the extreme level of crafting not only a model of his car but a scale model of the model box in 1/25-scale to display with it. (John Mahoney Photo)

Of course, there are many skilled model builders who produced their own unique conversions of existing kits. One such builder is Laverne Zachary in North Carolina, who expertly built 1/25-scale plastic models of Ronnie's red 1962 Chevy 409, Jr. Clark's black 1962 Chevy 409, and Sox & Martin's white 1963 Chevy 427.

1/64 Scale

The interest in Sox & Martin was not limited to scale model kits. Toy manufacturers such as Johnny Lightning, Hot Wheels, and others also made much smaller 1/64-scale toys for younger children to play with and for collectors to desire. These small models were built of the Hemi Duster, Superbird, and the 1970 Hemi 'Cuda.

The Digital Universe

Even the most modern Internet web sites and social media pages have not lost touch with Sox & Martin and the team's contribution to drag racing history. An Internet search for Ronnie Sox brings up as many as 541,000 results and one directed at Sox & Martin finds more than 19 million.

Fans, friends, and enthusiasts support a number of websites including ronniesox.org, which links to the Ronnie Sox Memorial and the Ronnie Sox Foundation. Both Wikipedia and Moparwiki have sites telling the history and biography of Ronnie Sox.

Facebook has four separate pages on Ronnie Sox and Sox & Martin including "Sox & Martin: A Tribute to a Legend in Drag Racing," as well as sports team, athlete, and community pages about Ronnie Sox.

Of course, many former Sox & Martin team members and families have their own Facebook pages where you can talk with them and tell them how much this history means to you.

Amazingly, the history of Sox & Martin extends beyond the lives of those old enough to have been there. And many people who were either not yet born, or were too young to be a part of their adventure, are still fascinated by it.

This is the original box for the first version of the 1967 Plymouth Hemi GTX. John Mahoney built this 1/25-scale model of his own car and the scale replica of the box. John owns a print of the original box art. (John Mahoney Photo)

A special-edition 1/18-scale die-cast replica of the Sox & Martin 1967 Hemi Plymouth GTX was produced and distributed by Supercar Collectibles as a tribute to Ronnie Sox after his passing in 2006. (John Mahoney Photo)

The Continuing Legacy

Laverne Zachary in North Carolina built this 1/25-scale kit. It was painted and finished to be a replica of Ronnie's red 1962 Chevrolet 409 bubble top Mr. 409 I. (Laverne Zachary Photo)

This 1/25-scale plastic model was constructed skillfully by Laverne Zachary in North Carolina. He painted it and applied the decals to make a correct replica of Buddy Martin's 1963 Chevy Z-11. (Laverne Zachary Photo)

This is a 1/25-scale model of the black 1962 Chevy owned by Junior Clark and tuned and maintained by Ronnie Sox. It was called Mr. 409 II to Ronnie's Mr. 409 I car. The model was built by Laverne Zachary. (Laverne Zachary Photo)

In addition to the many scale models and kits of Sox & Martin race cars, many much smaller toy versions were produced over the years. This is one of the cars in the popular Johnny Lightning Dragsters U.S.A. Limited Edition Series.

SOX & MARTIN

Index

A
Adam, Allen, 75, 76
Alderman, Darrell, 136
All-Hemi Reunion, 99, 164
Allard, Sydney, 24
Allbritton, Keith, 134, 135
Amblewagon, 28
Andress, William, 33
Aquasco Speedway, 46, 95
Ashley, Jack, 11–13, 141, 144
Atkins, David, 80

B
Baccaruda, 37, 38, 39, 44
Bagshaw, Bill, 69, 95
Bailey, Monte, 150, 152, 154, 165
Banning, Bob, 82
Barnett, Warren, 87, 156
Bartel, Bob, 12, 34
Bauman, John, 113
Bee Line Dragway, 29
Bell, Mike, 148, 149
Bell, Wally, 25
Bergler, Al, 116
Beringhaus, Irv, 108
Beswick, Arnie, 12, 31, 138, 145, 161, 164
Billy the Kid, 125, 126
Black Arrow, 35
Black, Keith, 69, 105
Bolig, Randy, 164
Bonner, Phil, 19, 23, 30, 35, 145
Booth, Wally, 78, 79, 82, 86
Boyd, Rufus Lee, 98, 113, 121, 122, 123
Brannan, Dick, 19, 33
Branstner, Dick, 34, 39
Bristol International Dragway, 33, 45, 60, 79, 80, 82, 86, 87, 101, 125, 136, 139, 141
Brooks, Lorenzo, 144
Brown, Larry, 15
Brumley, John, 132
Buckel, Mike, 30
Buckeye & Vernon Racing Team, 36, 38, 39, 44
Butler, Ron, 113, 117

C
Cahill, Robert, 25, 41, 57, 79, 97
California Flash, 28, 30, 108
Camponello, Don, 130, 131
Canadian Grandnationals, 88
Cannon, Scotty, 144, 145
Capitol Raceway, 108
Carbone, Steve, 97
Carlsbad Drag Strip, 38
Carlton, Don, 69, 74, 75, 78, 81, 86–89, 94–96, 102, 105, 107, 108, 119, 125, 126
Carolina Dragway, 144
Carolina Thunder, 61
Carolina Thunder II, 61
Carrier, Larry, 87, 103, 131
Carroll, Sam, 132
Cars Magazine Super Stock Championships, 71
Cars Magazine Super Stock International, 64
Cecil County Dragway, 31, 45, 65
Charlotte Motor Speedway, 34, 65, 95, 138
Childress, J. C., 141, 150, 152, 153, 154, 156
Chrisman, Jack, 22, 115
Christie, Dave, 15, 39, 52, 66, 72, 75, 77, 83–86, 98, 99, 100, 104, 111, 112, 114, 120, 121, 145, 165
Chrysler Nationals, 68
Clark, Junior, 15, 47, 56, 61, 158–162, 164, 165, 166, 167, 169, 171, 172, 173
Clayton, Bill, 133
Clayton, Carl, 57, 63, 77, 84, 169
Clayton, Larry, 131
Cline, Jerry, 156
Cobbs, Tom, 19
Coddington, Tom, 75, 76
Coletti, Joe, 54
Collette, Dave, 169
Collins, Phil, 63, 168, 169
Color Me Gone, 24, 28, 29
Comp World Championship, 133
Cossey, Wiley, 49, 62, 63, 66
Couch, Buster, 71
Craddock, Billy, 131
Crowder, Freeman Lee, 91
Currie, Vaughn, 83, 113

D
Dallas International Motor Speedway, 67, 80, 96
Darlington Dragway, 153
Darlington International Raceway, 132, 134, 135, 140, 141
Daytona Speedweeks, 12, 39, 45
DeNinno, Chick, 39, 67, 74, 95, 127–133, 147–153, 165
Denton, Harrold, 135
DeSalvo, Chris, 155
DesChamps, Nelson, 122
Dondero, Ken, 117, 119
Dorton, Randy, 95
Drag Racing Championship, 64, 108, 135
Drag Strip Pro Stock Bash, 137
Dragway 42, 130, 131
Duckworth, Gary, 135–137
Dunlap, Debbie, 125, 157
Durham, Malcolm, 74, 138, 145

E
Eaton, Craig, 155
Eaton, Dale, 155
Eavers, Petie, 170
Eckstrand, Al, 24, 28, 29, 35
Edwards, Lee, 132
Engelhart, Fred, 99, 160, 161, 164, 167

F
Farmington Drag Strip, 96, 107
Faubel, Bud, 28, 29, 30, 33, 35
Fisher, Joe, 66, 67, 77, 78, 80, 81, 82, 95
Fodermaier, J. J., 28
Fons, Mike, 75, 78, 87, 89, 90, 94, 102, 123
Freeman, Robert, 91, 155
Frost, Paul, 126

G
Gambrell, Dave, 157
Gapp, Wayne, 107, 108, 119, 123, 133
Garlits, Don, 24, 25, 69, 92, 96, 97, 146, 164, 166
Gentilozzi, Paul, 129
Gibson, Red, 57, 77, 84
Gilbertson, Charlie, 112
Gillis, Brian, 123
Glass, Harry, 21, 32, 37, 59, 121, 125, 129
Glidden, Bob, 106, 108, 130, 131, 137
Golden Commandos, 15, 28, 29, 31, 33
Goodrich, Dave, 25
Goodsey, Ken, 169
Graves, Danny, 49
Graves, Mark, 49, 96
Great Lakes Championships, 71
Griffith, Larry, 65, 76, 88, 89, 168
Gross, Jerry, 46, 51
Grotheer, Don, 40, 49, 51, 61, 62, 67, 74, 80, 83, 88, 89, 90, 94, 96, 99, 102, 106, 108–111, 117
Grove, Tom, 28, 47, 54, 58, 74, 78, 92, 93, 97, 119, 159
Grumpy's Toy IX, 94, 117
Guffey, Mike, 139
Gurney, Dan, 83

H
Haas, Jerry, 7, 136, 151
Hagen, John, 88, 97
Haldiman, Pete, 169
Hallahan, Dick, 66
Hardy, Don, 104, 106, 108, 109, 111, 116, 117, 119, 120, 122, 123, 125, 130, 133, 135, 159, 161, 165
Hardy, Dempsey, 129
Harrop, Bob, 28, 29, 30, 33, 35, 36
Hart, Jack, 93, 103
Hauler, 48, 61, 62, 120, 122, 127, 128, 155, 167
Hayter, Jim, 150, 152–155
Hemi Honker, 28
Hendrick, Rick, 95, 139
Hernandez, Francisco, 19–25
Hester, Levi, 57, 113
Hielscher, Bill, 80
Higgenbotham, Mart, 97
Hill, Roy, 10, 65, 95, 103, 108, 148, 150
Hodges, Clyde, 120, 125–129
Holiday, Rick, 66, 95
Holyfield, Dave, 13
Hoover, Tom, 79
Hot Rod magazine Drag Championships, 24
Hurst, George, 19, 21, 22, 32, 41, 43, 50, 57–59, 66, 69, 71, 77, 81, 85, 101, 110, 115, 149
Hustlin' Hemi II, 28
Hyde, Harry, 133

I
Indianapolis Raceway Park, 13, 17, 23, 28, 35, 36, 47, 61, 63, 64, 68, 69, 71, 82, 88, 96, 97, 108, 130, 131, 150, 152–155, 156, 162, 164, 167, 169
Ingoll, Bill, 24
Irwindale Raceway, 57, 105
Island Dragway, 98
Ivo, Tommy, 24

J
Jarrett, Ned, 16
Jenkins, Bill, 15, 35, 45, 47, 67, 68, 70, 74, 78, 82, 86, 93–98, 102, 103, 107, 108, 117, 118, 120, 123, 130, 133, 138
Jesel, Wayne, 125, 136
Johnson, Roy, 102
Johnson, Warren, 88, 131–133, 135
Jones, Dale, 63
Jones, Jack, 74
Jones, Parnelli, 22, 23
Jones, Ronnie, 168, 169
Jones, Ted, 131
Joniec, Al, 69

K
Kaase, John, 135, 147
Kansas City International Raceway, 164, 165, 166
Kepner, Bret, 149
King, Jake, 23, 24, 29, 34, 37, 39, 54, 57, 60, 62–66, 71, 73, 75, 77, 79, 81, 83–85, 90, 93, 100, 101, 110–113, 116, 120, 123, 156, 165, 167, 169, 170
Kinnett, Jim, 130
Kirk, Gil, 125, 126
Kirschenbaum, Al, 129
Knudsen, Semon E., 14
Koeppe, Reed, 129
Koffel, Dave, 49, 62
Kuhlmann, Bill, 142-144

L
Lambeck, Bob, 86, 95, 96, 106
Landy, Dick, 28–30, 35, 40, 45, 46, 51, 55, 62, 66, 67, 69, 74–76, 79, 80, 82, 89, 90, 96, 99, 102, 139, 149, 157
Landy's Dodge, 28, 30, 79
Law, Bo, 11, 82, 134
Lawliss, Bob, 36
Leal, Butch, 19, 28–30, 35, 36, 46, 90, 94–97, 101, 105, 108, 113
Learner Plymouth, 30
Leong, Roland, 69
Lindamood, Roger, 24, 28, 30
Lions Drag Strip, 21, 55
Livingston, Gerald, 91
Livingston, John, 91, 92
Logghe Brothers, 114, 115, 119, 120, 122
Lombardo, Larry, 103, 123, 130
London Heavy, 121
Long Beach, 21, 23, 38, 55
Lyall, Dave, 78
Lyles, Ronnie, 95, 116, 119, 122, 123, 125

M

Mack, Tod, 131, 132
Madison Township Raceway, 15, 87
Mahoney, John, 6, 42, 47, 50, 51, 63, 91, 120, 166–169, 171, 172
Mancini, Ron, 45, 67
Maple Grove Dragway, 74, 78
Marshall, Elbert, 119
Maryland International Raceway, 16, 17, 18, 36, 39, 45, 65, 74, 95, 108, 131, 132, 133, 147–148
Maskin, Richard, 151, 152
Mauney, Tommy, 139, 147
Maxwell, Dick, 57, 79, 97
May, Jack, 17, 18,
McAmis, Tim, 141, 144
McCandless Jr., Herb, 61, 63, 67, 76, 79, 81, 82, 83, 87–90, 94, 95, 97, 98, 99, 101, 102, 106, 108, 113, 122, 123, 154, 169
McCarter, Mac, 112
McCullough, Ed, 103
McDade, Stuart, 88, 89, 94, 101
McDuell, Billy, 35
McFarland, Jim, 54
McNichol Jr., H. J., 28
Melrose Missile, 28, 29, 35
Mid-South Super Stock Championships, 71
Milan Dragway, 106, 111, 117, 118, 126, 135
Miller, Bill, 139
Miller, Chip, 139
Miller, Ed, 40, 49, 62, 155
Millwee, John, 90
Minick, Pat, 138
Minnesota Dragways, 43
Montgomery, George, 24, 139
Mopar Muscle, 124, 162
Mopar Reunion, 169
Mortimer, Gale, 99
Mosley, Greg and Kathy, 111, 119, 161, 164, 165, 168
Motown Missile, 76, 86–89, 92, 94, 95, 96, 123
Mr. 409 1, 13
Mr. 409 II, 15, 61, 173
Mr. 427, 15, 18
Mr. 427 II, 18
Mr. Bardahl, 80
Mr. Norm's Garage, 163
Mullen, Bob, 105, 110, 113, 116, 128

N

Nancy, Tony, 24
NASCAR Winter Drag Championships, 16, 27, 31, 36, 38, 39, 44, 45, 73, 101, 110, 112, 116, 133, 146, 150
National Association of Drag Strips, 42
National Trail Raceway, 96, 107, 123
Neely, Bill, 122
New England Dragway, 97
Nichels, Ray, 12, 13
Nichols, Larry, 24, 97
Nicholson, Don, 13, 20, 22, 23, 24, 30, 33, 34, 69, 87, 88, 90, 95, 105, 107, 108, 115, 123, 130, 131, 133, 134, 135, 145
Nickens Brothers Racing, 155
Norwalk Raceway Park, 135
Nowakowski, Ed, 134

O

O'Conner, Jim, 35
Old Dominion Dragway, 34
Oldfield, Richard, 76, 106, 109, 111, 112, 113, 116, 117, 118, 120, 127
Olympics of Drag Racing, 64, 71
Ontario International Speedway, 82, 83, 89, 90
Ostrich, Gary, 47
Otto, Ed, 34
Outlaw, 31

P

Painter, Phil, 63, 84, 139
Paper Tiger, 28–30, 32–35, 37
Paper Tiger Too, 32, 34
Pappas, John, 170
Parks, Wally, 24, 74, 97, 103, 160
Party Time, 137
Passino, Jacque, 19
Patterson Brothers Racing, 155
Pepper, Charlie, 137
Perry, Patricia, 11
Person Dragway, 6, 123, 144
Petrie, John, 40, 62
Petty, Richard, 31, 72, 73, 92, 146, 160
Phillips, Buckeye, 36, 89, 90
Piedmont Dragstrip, 9–12, 15, 16, 31, 115, 167
Pitcock, Forrest, 28–31
Pittman, K. S., 24
Platt, Hubert, 39, 47, 61, 69
Pomeroy, Stewart, 120
Pomona, 21, 22, 30, 54, 62, 66, 74, 79, 85, 92, 94, 107, 113, 114, 167
Pontnack, Larry, 168
Poole, Barrie, 67
Professional Racers Association, 97, 98, 119, 123
Proffitt, Hayden, 15, 24, 138
Purvis, Patrick, 145, 146

Q

Quaker City Raceway, 99, 164, 166, 167

R

Rand, Clark and Colleen, 47, 56, 158–162, 164–167, 169, 171
Ray Nichels Engineering, 12
Red Light Bandit, 90
Redd, Geno, 95
Reed, Bob, 129, 155, 156, 157, 161
Reeker, Dale, 25
Regnery, Henry, 122
Richardson, Tom, 70, 54, 73, 77, 92, 103, 168
Richie, Les, 19
Riffle, Bob, 108, 125
Ristagno, Fred, 98, 99, 101, 113, 166, 168
Robinson, Willie, 89, 135
Rockingham International Dragway, 69, 72, 83, 95, 98, 132, 134, 137, 161
Roeder, LeRoy, 119, 120
Ronda, Gas, 19
Ronnie Sox Foundation, 162, 163, 164, 169, 172
Ronnie Sox Memorial Award, 12
Roush, Jack, 119, 122, 133, 134
Rowley, Vernon, 36
Ruth, Jim, 137
Ryan, Tim, 171

S

75-80 Dragway, 16, 17
Sanair Facility, 88
Satmary, Joe, 87
Schartman, Eddie, 24, 80, 115
Sexton, Ed, 171
Shepard, Larry, 80
Shoffner, James Leonard, 15, 61, 77, 95
Sikes, Sondra, 155
Simmons, C. D., 139
Skelton, Ed, 69
Slobe, Ron, 168
Smith, Dick,
Smith, Eddie, 114
Smith, Lee, 28, 29, 30, 31, 33, 34, 35, 39, 46
Smith, Rickie, 133, 134, 135, 139, 141
Sneed, Chuck, 135
Snow, Gene, 38, 97, 141
Sox, David, 9, 10, 102
Sox, Diane, 159, 160, 161–166, 169
Sox, Jeffrey Brandon, 16
Sox, Rhonda Jo, 16
Sox, Ronald Dean, 135, 139, 145, 148, 149, 167, 168
Sox, Tommy, 9, 10
Sox, Willard M., 9, 10, 143
Spittle, Frank, 138
Stahl, Jere, 23, 25, 45, 88
Stepp, Billy, 86, 88, 89, 94, 105, 119, 125, 139
Stiles, Bill, 44, 139
Strader, Jack, 12
Strickler, Dave, 24, 25, 28, 29, 33, 35, 36, 78, 102
Stroppe, Bill, 19, 21–23
Super Stock Magazine Nationals, 6, 30, 31, 34, 64, 78, 147
Sweet, Darrell, 88, 118, 121

T

Tanner, Bill, 40, 62, 80
Tarozzi, Robert, 57, 105
Tennessee Thunder, 92
The Boss, 36, 45, 86, 132, 137, 141, 162
The Flying Carpet, 28
The Ramchargers, 15, 23, 24, 28–31, 109
The Sox & Martin Book of Drag Racing, 122
Thompson, Dean, 133, 134, 135, 162
Thornberry, Walter, 128
Thornton, Jim, 24, 28
Thunder in Carolina, 13
Thunder Valley Dragway, 33, 87, 119
Thunderball, 25
Tice, Jim, 96, 97, 103
Tidwell, Scott, 151
Tosti Gateway Nitrous Nationals, 142
Towers, Dick, 139, 164
Tri-State Dragway, 68, 69
Turner, Al, 19

U

U.S. 41 Dragway, 148
Ugly Duckling, 24
Union Grove Dragway, 54, 58, 92, 93, 97, 119
United Drag Racers' Association, 42
United States Drag Racing Championship, 108
United States Drag Racing Team, 24, 25
United States Racing Team, 97–99, 102
Untouchable, 12

V

Van Cleave, Ken, 108
Vanke, Arlen, 43, 44, 45, 49, 61, 67, 69, 76, 79, 82, 83, 86, 87, 94, 102, 114, 156
Vanwey, Bill, 139
Vaughn, Linda, 40, 66, 71, 83, 113
Verde, Joe, 122
Virginia Motorsports Park, 147, 148, 153

W

Wallace, Pee Wee, 62
We Haul, 87
Webb, Travers, 139
Werner, Todd, 114, 121, 164
Werst, Jack, 81, 139
West Virginia Hemi, 114
Whisnant, Reid, 87, 88, 89, 95, 96, 97
White, Glen, 66
Wiggins, Blake, 144
Wiggins, Fred, 76
Wilcom, Bill, 16
Williams, Alfred, 131, 133
Williams, Mark, 151, 157
Wilson, Larry, 15, 17, 18, 61
Wynn's Jammer, 25

X

Xenia, Ohio, 119

Y

Yancer, Tom, 155
Yarborough, Cale, 103
Yeoman, Jerry, 137, 148
York US 30 Drag-O-Way, 17, 30, 31, 34, 35, 64, 67, 70, 78, 82, 98, 117, 118
Yother, Cecil, 35
Yow, Melvin, 87, 95, 107, 108
Yowell, Bobby, 101, 106, 125
Yuill, Brad, 131

Z

Zachary, Laverne, 13, 167, 172, 173
Zane, Larry, 139

Additional books that may interest you...

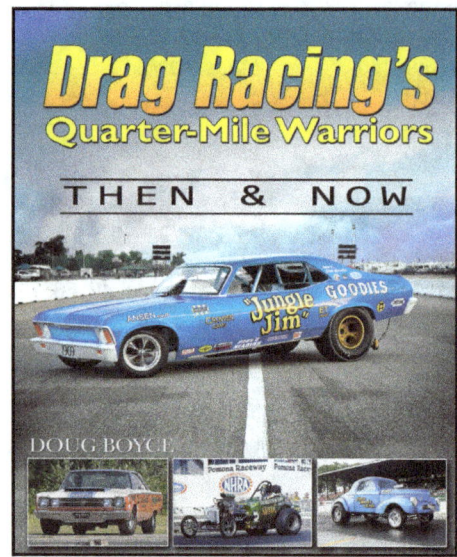

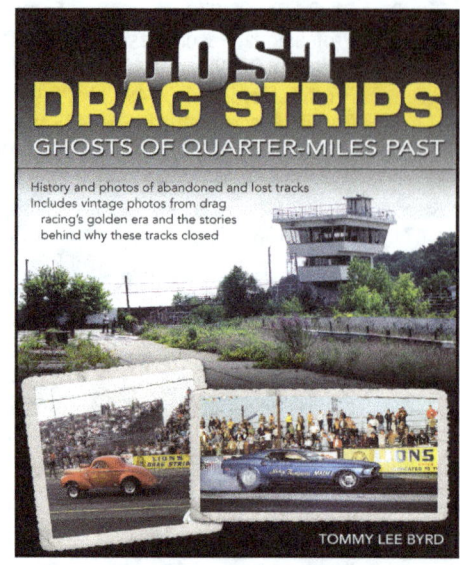

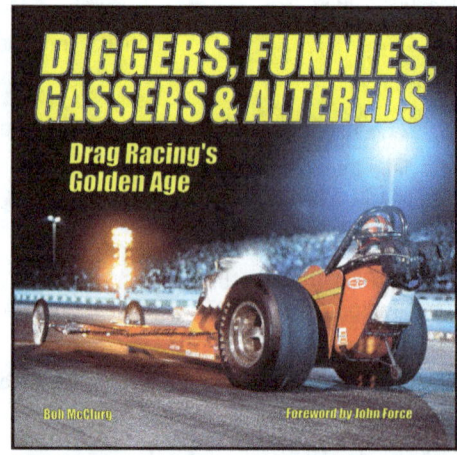

DRAG RACING'S QUARTER-MILE WARRIORS: Then & Now by *Doug Boyce* This book takes a unique look at the most memorable, interesting, and successful cars from the golden age of drag racing, the late 50s through the early 70s. Chronicled are Diggers and Rail dragsters, Funny Cars, wild Altereds, door slammers like Super and Junior Stock cars, early 70s Pro Stock cars, and more. Vintage and modern photography in a unique "then and now" format cover the cars as they first competed, through their evolution (or inactivity) over the years, and how they look today. See cars driven by legends such as Mickey Thompson, Tommy Ivo, Dick Landy, Grumpy Jenkins, Sox & Martin, Don Nicholson, Bob Glidden. Hardbound, 8.5 x 11 inches, 192 pages, 500 color and b/w photos. Item # CT528

LOST DRAG STRIPS: Ghosts of Quarter-Miles Past by *Tommy Lee Byrd* This book takes a look at many of the lost quarter-mile tracks across the country. Some of them are gone completely, paved over to make room for housing developments or strip malls. Others are ghostly remnants of what once was, offering a sad and even eerie subject for the photographer. The images are teamed with vintage shots of drag racing's glory days, sharing what once was one of America's most popular pastimes with the modern reality facing these facilities today. For fans of drag racing's past, it's a sobering and interesting study. Softbound, 8.5 x 11 inches, 160 pages, 315 color and b/w photos. Item # CT514

DIGGERS, FUNNIES, GASSERS & ALTEREDS: Drag Racing's Golden Age by *Bob McClurg* From the 1960s through the 1970s, drag racing grew and changed dramatically, and it all happened in front of Bob McClurg's camera. McClurg is an accomplished magazine writer and photographer, but he's best known for his drag racing images of the period—his lens captured all the action of the Roadsters, Gassers, Altereds, Top Fuel, Funny Cars, Pro Stocks, and even the modern age of nostalgia drag racing. McClurg's best drag racing photos are brought together in this volume—a book that is a necessary addition to any drag racing fan's library. Softbound, 9 x 9 inches, 204 pages, 350 photos. Item # CT521

1001 DRAG RACING FACTS: The Golden Age of Top Fuel, Funny Cars, Door Slammers & More by *Doug Boyce* Spanning the 1950s through the 1970s, this book is packed with well-researched drag racing facts that even some of the most hard-core drag racing fans might be surprised to learn. Covered are all the popular classes of drag racing of the era, including Top Fuelers, Funny Cars, Pro Stocks, and Eliminators including Gassers and Altereds, Stocks, Super Stocks, and more. Softbound, 6 x 9 inches, 416 pages, 125 photos. Item # CT539

Check out our website:

CarTechBooks.com

✓ Find our newest books before anyone else

✓ Get weekly tech tips from our experts

✓ Get your ride or project featured on our homepage!

Exclusive Promotions and Giveaways on Facebook Like us to WIN! Facebook.com/CarTechBooks

www.cartechbooks.com or 1-800-551-4754